THE COLLABO
PLANNE

Practitioners in the n   age

Ben Clifford and Mark Tewdwr-Jones

First published in Great Britain in 2014 by

Policy Press
University of Bristol
6th Floor
Howard House
Queen's Avenue
Clifton
Bristol BS8 1SD
UK
Tel +44 (0)117 331 5020
Fax +44 (0)117 331 5367
e-mail tpp-info@bristol.ac.uk
www.policypress.co.uk

North American office:
Policy Press
c/o The University of Chicago Press
1427 East 60th Street
Chicago, IL 60637, USA
t: +1 773 702 7700
f: +1 773-702-9756
e:sales@press.uchicago.edu
www.press.uchicago.edu

British Library Cataloguing in Publication Data
A catalogue record for this book is available from the British Library.

Library of Congress Cataloging-in-Publication Data
A catalog record for this book has been requested.

ISBN 978 1 44730 510 1 paperback

Cover design by Qube Design Associates, Bristol
Front cover: image kindly supplied by www.alamy.com

Contents

List of figures, tables and boxes

Figures

Tables

Boxes

Abbreviations and acronyms

BERR	Department for Business, Enterprise and Regulatory Reform
BIS	Department for Business, Innovation and Skills (formerly BERR)
BVPI	Best Value performance indicator
CAA	Comprehensive Area Assessment
CBI	Confederation of British Industry
CCT	compulsory competitive tendering
CLG	(Department for) Communities and Local Government (abbreviation used 2007–10 but now referred to as DCLG)
CPA	Comprehensive Performance Assessment
CPRE	Council for the Protection of Rural England
DCLG	Department for Communities and Local Government
DETR	Department of the Environment, Transport and the Regions (former UK government department responsible for planning)
DTI	Department for Trade and Industry
DTLR	Department for Transport, Local Government and the Regions (former UK government department responsible for planning)
DoE	Department of the Environment (former UK government department responsible for planning)
ESDP	European Spatial Development Perspective
ESRC	Economic and Social Research Council
EU	European Union
HPDG	Housing and Planning Delivery Grant
IPC	Infrastructure Planning Commission
LDF	Local Development Framework (development plan produced by English LPAs)
LDP	Local Development Plan (development plan produced by Welsh and Scottish LPAs)
LEP	Local Enterprise Partnership
LPA	Local Planning Authority (unitary, district and National Park authorities)
NHS	National Health Service
NI	National Indicator
NIMBY	not in my back yard
NPF	National Planning Framework (for Scotland)

NPM   New Public Management
NPPF   National Planning Policy Framework (England)
ODPM   Office of the Deputy Prime Minister (UK government
        department responsible for planning in England)
OPSI   Office of Public Sector Information
PCPA   2004 Planning and Compulsory Purchase Act 2004
PDG   Planning Delivery Grant
PINS   Planning Inspectorate (for England and Wales)
PPG   Planning Policy Guidance
PPS   Planning Policy Statement
RSS   Regional Spatial Strategy (for each English region)
RTPI   Royal Town Planning Institute
SCI   Statement of Community Involvement
SEDD   Scottish Executive Development Department
SLBs   street-level bureaucrats
SPiP   Spatial Plans in Practice
TPRA   Third Party Rights of Appeal
WAG   Welsh Assembly Government

Notes on the authors

Ben Clifford is Lecturer in Spatial Planning and Government at the Bartlett School of Planning, University College London. His research focuses on the British planning system, policy, governance and questions of government.

Mark Tewdwr-Jones is Professor of Town Planning at the School of Architecture, Planning and Landscape at Newcastle University. He is an expert in planning, the politics of the city and land use.

Acknowledgements

The empirical research underpinning this book was undertaken as part of a PhD sponsored under the ESRC (Economic and Social Research Council)-ODPM (Office of the Deputy Prime Minister) joint scheme, award number PTA-039-2005-00001, with additional support to fund the in-depth interviews received from the University of London Central Research Fund. All those who completed the survey and agreed to be interviewed are thanked for their invaluable contribution.

We are both extremely grateful for the insight, help and support of David Demeritt, Mike Raco, Kerry Holden, Eamon Mythen, Richard Blyth, Nigel Clifford, Maureen Stagg, Franklin Ginn, James Millington, Kathleen Noreisch, Phil Allmendinger, Yvonne Rydin and The Policy Press's anonymous reviewers at various stages of the original research and subsequent production of this book. Thanks also to Emily Watt, our editor, for her vital support. Final and greatest thanks to Justin and Rob for their enduring support.

Preface

What is it like to be a planner in Britain today? The planning profession has been in existence for almost 100 years, but the role and status of the urban planner has been transformed significantly over that time. Planning remains a 'professional' occupation, an activity of both public and private sectors, a function of the state at several scales of government, and a process through which a balance is sought between short-term needs and long-term trends. It is managed by 'expert' individuals, educated and trained in the so-called art and science of town planning, who provide advice and guidance to elected politicians in the latter's decision-taking obligations. And it necessitates effective communication in dealing with various groups, organisations and interests, and their contestation of choices on future development proposals and the use of land. It is, for the most part, a transparent process, offering communities and citizens an opportunity to become involved in new policy and in decisions affecting the future development and wellbeing of places. Above all, it is an activity that has experienced constant pressure placed on it – from government, politicians, businesses, environmentalists, developers, architects, amenity groups and neighbours. Planners' work has not remained static over the decades, but has ebbed and flowed according to changing professional practice and – more pertinently – changing ideological stances of the state and political preferences of governing parties. What comprises the planner's duties today is far removed from those of the planner in the 1930s, the 1960s, or even the 1980s.

Since the turn of the 21st century, there has been no greater pace of reform to planning in Britain. The New Labour, Coalition and devolved governments have embarked on a continuous cycle of planning reform, intended to make planning more relevant and responsive to the needs of a modern and constantly evolving nation. But planning has also been affected indirectly as a consequence of the processes of devolution, the rolling-back of the welfare state, the rise of neoliberalism, the rolling-out of new public management and its impacts on the public sector, and the enhancement of opportunities for public participation in policy and decision making. Over this time not only has the planning profession been constantly maligned by successive governments and politicians for its failure to deliver change rapidly, it has also continued to work in a somewhat hostile climate during a volatile economic, environmental, social, institutional and professional period. Academic conceptualisation of these changes have sought to keep pace with the political, professional and practical developments over a relatively short period of time, focusing on planning and the changing state, the onset of government and governance, the management, performance and delivery of planning, and the collaborative and communicative potential of new planning arrangements. But what has been missing to date, is the planner's own responses to and perceptions of this maelstrom of change. In fact, the voice of the planner has been curiously absent from both conceptualisations and analyses of planning reform over the last 20 years.

Taking the evolving 21st-century planning reform process across Britain as the context and prompt for discussion, this book aims to tell the story of the components of reform using the direct voices of the planning profession. Anchored around four interrelated issues – system and process reform, management, participation and culture – the book offers a revealing and exceptionally frank account of contemporary planning activities that has not been seen in the literature for some decades. The key question we wish to pose in this analysis is, what has really been the opinion of the planner as the reforms and changes have been experienced? Is there optimism or pessimism in the planning profession towards the purpose and form of change? And have planners accepted the changes with alacrity or with concern? In short, we wanted to explore whether planners have been collaborators or resisters to such ideological ideas as neoliberalism, new public management and democracy.

This is an important story if we are to fully understand planning reform, and indeed the broader issues of how reform of the state is rolled out. We focus on public sector planners because, while there are increasing numbers of private sector planners, it is through these officers that the planning system (which continues to exist in its current form because of statute and government policy guidance in the UK) is enacted. Our arguments are driven by a rich empirical base comprising both survey results and anonymised interview quotations. These data primarily relate to the response and reaction to the New Labour reforms, but through the understanding this gives us about the reaction to, and implementation of, centrally driven change, our arguments remain pertinent under the current UK Coalition government. We argue that the front line or 'coalface' – in the case of planning, local authority professional practitioners – helps shape the contours of modernisation, and that a nuanced, implementation-focused research agenda is vital, rather than simply looking at institutional structures and policy discourses from a state-centred approach. This message also has relevance for how we think about the reform of other public sector activities, beyond planning, and in different contexts internationally.

ONE

Introduction: planning at the coalface in a time of constant change

Planning and ongoing reform

Decades ago, especially in the years after the 1947 Planning Act, people were ambitious about planning. Planning was exciting. It meant New Towns, Garden Cities, clearing slums, creating new communities. It had drive, ambition. It had purpose. But over a period of time, planning became inefficient and ossified. In 1997, we inherited a creaking planning system in need of reform.... Planning has to be more relevant, more interesting, more effective and more efficient. It needs a culture change. It needs to raise its game. (Prescott, 2004)

The planning system helps create sustainable communities by influencing markets to promote more positive outcomes for society. But, over time, the planning system became ossified and inefficient – and so we embarked on a major programme of planning reform. (Prescott, 2006, p 2)

The planning system is vital for a strong economy, for an attractive and sustainable environment, and for a successful democracy. At present, the planning system in England achieves none of these goals. It is broken. (The Conservative Party, 2010, p 1)

We are the party of enterprise. And let me tell you – right now, right here today in Britain 2011, we have got the most almighty job to do. Because for over a decade in this country the enemies of enterprise have had their way.... So I can announce today that we are taking on the enemies of enterprise. The bureaucrats in government departments who concoct those ridiculous rules and regulations that make life impossible, particularly for small firms. The town hall officials who take forever with those planning decisions that can be make or break for a business – and the investment and jobs that go with it. (David Cameron, 2011, speech to the Welsh Conservative Conference)

In the first two quotations, the former Deputy Prime Minister John Prescott raises a number of interesting ideas: that the planning system was an important part of the postwar British welfare state; that the New Labour government in Britain saw this public service as in need of reform when it came to power; and that the Labour administration was determined to reform planning. And yet Prescott also implies that this reform was somehow a simple process, that the planning system had become 'inefficient', 'and so we embarked on a major programme of planning reform.' In fact, as this book will demonstrate, the programme of planning reform that has occurred over the last decade across Great Britain has been far from a simple affair, with local authority planners being tasked with implementing complex and sometimes contradictory reforms. Furthermore, those reforms, particularly those in England, were perceived by some as having mixed success, so much so that prior to the 2010 General Election, the Conservative Party was arguing that planning was 'broken'. Following the election, the UK Coalition government also embarked on a series of further concerted planning reforms which took on a distinctly less pro-planning tone, as the quotation from Prime Minister David Cameron illustrates above. Nevertheless, the Coalition's reform programme is likewise complex and – at times – seemingly contradictory.

This book is about how the reforms to planning and the local state more widely have been received, experienced and understood by professional planners working at the front line of the state, in British local authorities. This is important because the 'planning system' is nothing if not a set of peopled practices, and any accounts of reform need to take account of the groups of people that constitute the system. The book is concerned with planning in Britain, that is, England, Scotland and Wales, since 2000; although we concentrate to a greater extent on reforms under New Labour, and particularly in England, there is also some comparative discussion of events in Scotland and Wales as well as emerging changes under the Coalition government since 2010. This geographical scope is quite deliberate in that there is a common approach to planning and a common professional body for all of Britain.[1] That said, there are differences between England, Scotland and Wales, particularly post-devolution. This, however, makes the inclusion of all territories of interest; planners' reactions to slightly differing reforms within the common British professional framework may expose interesting similarities and differences.

Planning is one of the most high profile activities undertaken by any local authority in Britain.[2] As the system through which development is managed, it is responsible for the shape and appearance of both urban cityscapes and rural landscapes. Planning is conducted by planners, who operate on a professional model – individuals who usually undertake an approved degree course at university and become 'chartered town planners' through membership of the Royal Town Planning Institute (RTPI) following a period of time in practice (Sutcliffe, 1981). Government planning policy sets out the purpose of the planning system. In England, the government's national planning statement, Planning Policy Statement (PPS) 1 of 2005, defined it thus:

> Planning shapes the places where people live and work and the country we live in. Good planning ensures that we get the right development, in the right place and at the right time. It makes a positive difference to people's lives and helps to deliver homes, jobs, and better opportunities for all, whilst protecting and enhancing the natural and historic environment, and conserving the countryside and open spaces that are vital resources for everyone. But poor planning can result in a legacy for current and future generations of run-down town centres, unsafe and dilapidated housing, crime and disorder, and the loss of our finest countryside to development. (ODPM, 2005a, p 9)

The Scottish Executive (2002) and the Welsh Assembly Government (WAG) (2002a) provided similar definitions.

Clearly, planning is an important activity linked to such high profile issues as sustainability, housing provision, environmental protection and urban design. Indeed, over the last decade, governments have come to see planning as a key vehicle for 'delivery', for example, in helping to create 'sustainable communities' (Egan, 2004), and affecting the supply and demand for housing (Barker, 2004). Furthermore, planning has also been subjected to a number of direct legislative and policy reforms in recent years. These include both a concerted programme of 'planning reform' being pushed by central and devolved government in Great Britain – since 2001 in England alone there have been four Acts of Parliament that have enacted legislative reform to planning – and also

3

reforms to the local government and public sector context within which the statutory planning system operates.

Deegan comments that 'the planning system is not about carefully crafted but essentially empty policy statements, but is the means by which society makes hard decisions affecting public resource allocation, and our personal wealth and quality of life' (2002, p 86). It is therefore unsurprising that the British planning system has long been a subject of academic interest. A wealth of scholarship continues to explore planning theory (see, for example, Allmendinger, 2001a, 2002a; Healey, 2007a, 2010; Lord, 2012), and the key components of planning reform in the UK (Davoudi and Strange, 2009; Allmendinger, 2011; Tewdwr-Jones, 2012), through devolution (Haughton et al, 2010), local government public service delivery (Morphet, 2011), citizen involvement and increased public participation (Gallent and Robinson, 2012), national uniformity and the imposition of central policy guidance (Tewdwr-Jones, 2002), measurement and performance targets (Carmona and Sieh, 2004), and the burgeoning environmental and sustainability contexts (Rydin, 2010). Few studies, however, 'have empirically explored how these changes are manifesting themselves … [in] planning practice' (Tewdwr-Jones, 2002, p 3). This is important because the tensions inherent in those reforms and, as we will demonstrate, the continuing discretion of frontline staff, mean that 'policy should be regarded less as the product of policy makers than as the outcome of the activity of frontline organizational actors' (Ellis, 2011, p 222). They are, in essence, the rule intermediaries (Kearl, 1983).

The aim of this book is to understand how ongoing reforms, both of the planning system and of the wider public sector context in which planning is practised, are affecting, and being negotiated into reality by, chartered town planners working in local authorities in Great Britain. This will be done by exploring reaction to both 'top-down' and 'bottom-up' reform streams (Lowndes and Wilson, 2003), corresponding with the key sites of contestation and tension, namely, implementing spatial planning and the reaction to central government targets on the one hand, and the response to attempts to make planning more participatory and customer-focused on the other. A further thread running through these ongoing processes of reform was the desire to change the culture of planning, and this is also addressed later in the book.

Our aim is not to assess the merits of any of this myriad of reform agendas per se, but rather to explore how planners as rule intermediaries on the front line have understood and experienced the reforms. In doing this, our objectives are:

- to examine what local authority planners think about the ongoing programme of planning reform, including the introduction of a spatial planning approach and moves to make planning more participatory
- to investigate reaction to wider public sector reforms such as the increasing use of targets and audit processes and initiatives to promote the 'customer' ideal
- to provide a rigorous empirical evidence base about what planners think of these reform agendas
- to consider the implications arising for how we conceptualise staff working at the front line of the state and for how state modernisation processes are implemented.

We argue that a better understanding of the role and perspective of planners in reaction to planning and public sector reform is vital to fully understanding those reforms. We are in an age of what we may broadly consider neoliberally driven hyper-reform of the public sector and governance context within which the profession and practices of planning are situated, and one might ask to what degree planners and other welfare state professionals are complicit in the implementation of such modernisation of the state. More provocatively, are planners collaborators or resisters to neoliberal political projects?

Planning reform and public service context

When New Labour assumed power in 1997, planning was not immediately a top priority (Anderson and Mann, 1997, in Allmendinger and Tewdwr-Jones, 2000; Allmendinger, 2002b). At first, Labour broadly followed the path set down by the Conservatives in trying to further promote a market-supportive and business-friendly planning system, in keeping with its wider 'discourse on competitiveness' (Allmendinger et al, 2003a). New Labour's agenda for planning was set out in the paper *Modernising planning* (DETR, 1998a), which applied to England and Wales and was soon followed by a similar document for Scotland, *Land use planning under a Scottish Parliament* (Scottish Office, 1999). Both of these emphasised the need for greater speed and efficiency in planning to help economic growth, rather than radical reform overhaul. For instance, the then UK Planning Minister Richard Caborn commented that 'I think the planning process has locked in for far too long, with its procrastination and delays, a considerable amount of potential investment' (1998, quoted in Allmendinger, 2002b, p 368), while the Scottish Office document talked of a need to be more responsive to the needs of industry. The theme of planning being more responsive to business interests has continued to the present day, with government-initiated studies examined by the Barker and Killian Pretty reviews (Barker, 2006; Killian and Pretty, 2008a, 2008b) under Labour, as well as the more recent Conservative and Coalition posturing on the subject (The Conservative Party, 2010; Kirkup, 2012).

The story of planning under New Labour was not, however, simply one of deregulation in order to meet the demands of business. Instead, planning actually underwent something of a renaissance compared to the period before 1997 because of its link to high profile issues such as sustainable development, housing provision, urban design, environmental justice, social justice and economic growth. Planning was clearly expected to help address environmental and social objectives (Scottish Executive, 2002; WAG, 2002a; ODPM, 2005a). In particular, planning became seen as central to the *delivery* of the 'sustainable communities' agenda, which rapidly became a central policy platform in the beginning of this decade (ODPM, 2002; Imrie and Raco, 2003b; Rydin, 2006). The government-appointed Egan review of skills concluded that planners were central to the delivery of these sustainable communities (Egan, 2004), and planning was given a statutory function for the first time explicitly to promote 'sustainable development' (ODPM, 2005a).

Yet linkage to such high profile issues also raised expectations that planning would deliver and deliver quickly. For example, commenting on 'how fundamental the planning profession is to everyday life', Minister for Housing and Planning, Keith Hill, stated that 'the government is committed to a huge programme of housing growth and regeneration and the planning system underpins all of that change' (cited in Winkley, 2004, p 10). At the same time, under their own left-of-centre administrations, the newly devolved governments in Scotland and Wales quickly came to see planning as a route to further the development of their own territorial identities (see below). There was also a growing emphasis on planning 'delivering' at the local level (Baker Associates et al, 2008; see Figure 1.1 for evidence of the prevalence of this 'delivery' discourse).

At the national level, in order to realise these high expectations, central and devolved government engaged in a number of sweeping planning reforms, involving changing legislative and policy contexts across Britain. There were a number of key drivers for change, including the evolution of governance systems from which planning cannot be divorced. This included devolution (Lloyd and Illsley, 1999; Tewdwr-Jones and Allmendinger, 2006), which Marinetto calls 'the most notable

Figure 1.1: Planning's role in delivery

Source: Taken from the professional journal and newsletter, *Planning* (Cowan, 2007b). Reproduced with permission of Rob Cowan.

feature of the Labour government's plan to modernize the constitution' (2001, p 306). Devolution included an increased emphasis on regional governance in England (Marshall, 2004; Glasson and Marshall, 2007), and the establishment of a Greater London Assembly and Mayor (Rydin et al, 2004; Imrie et al, 2009), but it is devolution to Scotland and Wales that is of most relevance here. Tewdwr-Jones suggests that post-devolution 'the potential now exists within each of the four countries of the UK for very different planning systems to be born' (1999, p 420). That said, long before devolution, the Scottish Office in particular, and the Welsh Office to a lesser extent, had considerable separate planning powers to those for England, for example, through the release of distinctive planning policy guidance and in deciding planning appeals. There has also been some debate with regard to the distinctiveness of Scottish planning prior to devolution (see Rowan-Robinson, 1997; Allmendinger, 2001b, 2001c), but the similarities far outweigh any minor technical differences (for example, over neighbour notification).

Nevertheless, 'devolution has naturally led to expectations of legislative and policy divergence' (Allmendinger, 2002c, p 793). Whether these hopes are justified or not has been a matter of some debate. Jeffrey (2004) reports the findings of the Economic and Social Research Council's (ESRC) Devolution and Constitutional Change research programme, which found that devolution had led to both policy divergence *and* convergence. In terms of planning, the general

–
7

trend does not suggest much divergence, and there may even be cycles of divergence followed by re-convergence occurring, with broadly similar reform proposals for England and Scotland (Allmendinger, 2001b, 2001c, 2002b; Hayton, 2002). It is, of course, worth noting that devolution is an ongoing process (Marinetto, 2001), and there could be more divergence in future, particularly as post-devolution politics have matured over 12 years, with changing political parties in power at Cardiff, Edinburgh and London, and an increasing spectre of the possibility of Scottish independence.

Alongside change to the institutional and governance context to planning under New Labour must be added economic and environmental factors, including the rhetoric of sustainable communities and sustainable development, and the growing role of the European Union (EU) in the context of direct impacts on planning. We explore the broader public sector reform context below, and consider the conceptualisation of the overall drivers for change in Chapter Two.

The reform policy has been developed through a number of key publications and pieces of legislation. At the outset of this decade of change, the most important documents in England were the Green Paper, *Planning: Delivering a fundamental change* (DTLR, 2001a), and in Wales, the consultation paper *Planning: Delivering for Wales* (WAG, 2002b). Following consultation and some modifications, a statement was published (ODPM, 2002), and the proposed reforms were enacted as the Planning and Compulsory Purchase Act 2004 (PCPA 2004) (HMSO, 2004a), which applied to England and Wales. In Scotland, the Scottish Executive published a *Review of strategic planning* (2001), and conducted a series of consultations before publishing a White Paper, *Modernising the planning system* (2005). The Planning etc (Scotland) Act 2006 (OPSI, 2006) was then passed by the Scottish Parliament. The main changes resulting from these particular sets of New Labour-initiated planning reform were implemented in England between 2005 and 2008, but implementation is, as of this writing, still ongoing in Scotland and Wales (Scottish Government, 2008a; WAG, 2008a), with the prospect of further reform in the near future.

The Scottish Executive's stated aims in its White Paper were 'to make the planning system fit for purpose ... to make the planning system more efficient ... [and] to make the planning system more inclusive' (2005, p 8), and these themes can be seen in the reforms throughout Great Britain. In terms of policy planning, there have been consistent themes of efforts to make plans simpler, more up-to-date and more flexible (in theory at least). There has also been a rescaling of planning, initially with a greater regional emphasis under Labour

–

in England (Allmendinger et al, 2005; Allmendinger and Haughton, 2007) up to 2010. The reforms relating to development control, the process through which new development and land use change is regulated and managed, were more mixed in scope, but with the agenda concentrating on improving the speed and consistency of decisions. There was a strong emphasis on making planning more participatory, while a process of 'culture change' for the planning profession was also promoted, including a new emphasis on more integrative 'spatial' planning rather than traditional 'land use' planning (Tewdwr-Jones, 2012). Overall, the initial period of reforms have had an impact on what Healey (2006) terms the 'soft infrastructure' of planning practices and the 'hard infrastructure' of planning systems.

Allmendinger et al suggest that we should not conceptualise these changes as part of the usual 'longer-term ebb and flow in development planning' (2003a, p 276) but as substantive changes, including devolution and the growth of a regional agenda, rescaled strategic planning, an increased emphasis on spatial planning, an emphasis on both speed of, and public participation in, planning processes, and changing central control of local government (for example 'Best Value'). Allmendinger et al also suggest that:

> There can be no doubt that the planning and local government changes will be far-reaching, not only for actors outside of planning ... but also for professional planners themselves, who will have to ponder their values, expertise and purpose in adapting to the changes. (2005, p 367)

However, only a few years after this statement was expressed, and even before much of the 2004–05 reforms had been enacted, more planning reform occurred in England. A further planning White Paper, *Planning for a sustainable future* (CLG, 2007a), was released in 2007 to improve procedural issues included in the 2004 Act and also to create a new way of determining development and infrastructure projects of national significance, including new railways, motorways, airport, power stations, reservoirs and power lines. Under the subsequent 2008 Planning Act, the government established an independent Infrastructure Planning Commission (IPC) to take charge of major planning projects that previously had been the subject of long, expensive and adversarial planning inquiries, such as Heathrow Terminal 5. The intention here, as with previous reforms, was to streamline the planning system, and the proposals illustrated the degree to which central government still called the shots on the form of planning existing in the regions and locales of England, but also set out a national case for government on spatial planning matters. Ruth Kelly, then Communities Secretary, referred to the proposals as delivering a planning system fit for the challenges of the 21st century (CLG, 2007a). The reforms generated criticism from environmentalists and community representatives, concerned at the prospect of a 'free for all' on development issues and the state imposing its will over local areas while removing local discretion to determine planning projects. Business leaders, on the other hand, welcomed the proposals that were intended to assist in economic growth and build on Kate Barker's recommendations on planning and the economy of 2006 (Barker, 2006). But Barker was only one influence; other commissioned reports on specific sectoral changes also had an impact on the White Paper, including *The Eddington transport study* (Eddington, 2006), the Stern review on climate change (Stern, 2006) and *The Lyons Inquiry into local government* (Lyons, 2007).

The 2008 Act attempted to strike a balance for future environmental protection, economic growth and sustainable development. Critics remarked that the IPC would ride roughshod over local democratic processes. But individual local authorities have rarely determined such major proposals since they have been 'called in' frequently by the Secretary of State as the potential impacts of such development may be felt beyond the boundaries of one local authority area. The IPC, approved under the Act, was formally established in 2009, but the Conservative Party in Opposition had already announced its intention to abolish the body if it was elected to government (The Conservative Party, 2010).

As the 2004 and 2008 reforms were being rolled out in the mid to late 2000s, with varied degrees of success in terms of speed and delivery, so even further changes were on the horizon politically. After the 2010 General Election and the establishment of the Coalition government, a very different agenda for planning quickly emerged, reflecting the ideological shift between different governments and their policy preferences. In England, the regional level of planning – Regional Spatial Strategies (RSSs) – and other aspects of the institutional framework that had only been inserted after 2004, were abolished, together with the newly introduced national decision-making structure, the IPC, for major development projects. There was no direct replacement for the RSSs, but the IPC's functions were transferred to a revamped Planning Inspectorate agency, which would support decisions on large development projects being taken by the Secretary of State directly in future.

The ethos was now on 'localism' but this was not about simply removing the middle tier of planning between central government and local authorities and focusing attention on Local Development Plans (LDPs) and local authority decision making. The new agenda involved transferring some policy and decision-making powers away from the local authorities directly to local neighbourhoods in a democratic shift. New neighbourhood plans would be established with neighbourhood forums, increased use of referenda to determine projects, and the use of incentives and other fiscal instruments to enable proposals to be realised. This was hailed as a fundamental change to planning (The Conservative Party, 2010), yet another phase of planning's evolving journey, and one still being embarked on.

As planners and elected local politicians started to weigh up the implications of the change, practically and academically, in 2011 the Coalition announced further changes as the localism changes were being debated in Parliament, and these tended to focus less on local democracy and neighbourhoods and more on economic growth and job creation. With the UK still emerging slowly from recession after the global downturn in the latter 2000s, so the government decided that a stimulus was required in the form of planning deregulation. Enterprise Zones returned to the national policy agenda after a 25-year gap (Townsend, 2011), and a policy 'presumption in favour of sustainable development' was announced within a new pro-economic growth National Planning Policy Framework where sustainable development was viewed as job creation and economic growth, a somewhat different interpretation than those of previous governments or even academic ideas about its definition (DCLG, 2012a). Businesses were given powers to prepare their own neighbourhood plans for the first time (as opposed to local authorities and local people), a complete contrast to the 1947 planning system ethos of ensuring democratic accountability through planning decision making. And finally, the government announced the establishment of Local Enterprise Partnerships (LEPs) covering amalgams of local authority areas but of a lesser size and powers than the regional structure they replaced, with the hope that these groupings would support strategic planning (Townsend, 2011; BIS, 2012). In Scotland and Wales, planning processes are being amended with a distinct separation of policies and agendas in those territories and a different ethos towards land use planning to that in England.

The key foci for the planning reform agenda throughout the last 15 years has included the introduction of a broadening out of planning beyond land use planning, calls for more participatory involvement and calls for a culture change in planning. As a system mainly administered by local government, the planning system is also connected to, and impacted by, wider reforms to the public sector and local government, as Allmendinger et al (2005) note. Yet elsewhere, Allmendinger et al highlight that 'development planning is often discussed in isolation from its local government context' (2003a, p 274; see also Campbell and Marshall, 2000; Morphet, 2005, 2011). Where local government has been covered in planning literature, it is often in the context of largely technical articles on the organisation of planning departments (Kitchen, 1999) or reviews of the implications of local government boundary changes (Hayton, 1994). However, 'the enhancement of public sector performance has been a central concern of successive Labour governments since 1997' (Higgins et al, 2004, p 251), and Labour's banner of modernisation included continuing attempts to re-imagine and re-shape the welfare state (Cochrane, 2004). This included a raft of policy and primary and secondary legislation specifically aimed at reforming local government: the 'Local Government Modernisation Agenda' (Cowell and Martin, 2003; Shaw and Lord, 2007).

This agenda had roots in earlier pre-1997 Conservative administrations. Newman et al (2001, p 61) argue that:

> The transformation of local authorities has been central to the political programmes of UK governments over the past two decades. The Labour Government's modernization programme is the latest manifestation of a cross-party agenda to create local authorities which are more dynamic, entrepreneurial, efficient, effective and in touch with their users and citizens.

Such processes can be conceptualised as part of a broader public sector reform agenda seen across the Western world over the last two decades described as 'new public management' (Hood, 1991) or managerialism (Pollitt, 1993) (see also Roper et al, 2005, and Chapter Two, this volume, for further details). Central to this is the idea that 'bureaucratic, unresponsive, one-size-fits-all government cannot last' (Osborne and Gaebler, 1992, p 194). The politics of the New Right (O'Toole, 2004) thus challenged 'the assumptions of Keynesian demand management, of a "universal" Welfare State, and of a "social democratic consensus" which underpinned the "post-war settlement"' (Sanderson, 2001, p 299). Indeed, the New Right looked at the welfare state as under- and poorly managed, and 'professionally dominated and lacking in client involvement' (Ferlie et al, 1996, p 31). Clearly, the planning system was part of that postwar settlement, and the 1947 origins of the statutory system belie its status as a 'welfare state profession'. Box 1.1 summarises the key Conservative reforms of the public sector between 1979 and 1997.

Box 1.1: Key Conservative reforms to the public sector in the UK, 1979–97

i Privatisation

ii Marketisation (including the introduction of quasi-markets)

iii Deregulation

iv Consumerism (including an emphasis on users of public services as customers and on service quality)

v Management decentralisation (including creating agencies semi-independent of central government departments and reducing the role of local government relative to other agencies)

vi Introduction of Private Finance Initiatives (subsequently developed by Labour as Public Private Partnerships)

vii Curtailment of union powers

viii Removal of subsidies

ix An associated focus on value for money, performance indicators and audit

Source: Adapted from Stoker (1997), Goldsmith and Page (1997), Thompson (1992, cited in Barrett, 2004, p 258) and Ferlie et al (1996)

Stoker suggests that as a result of sustained reform of the public sector, by 1997 local government was 'characterized by financial constraint and fiscal stress; a focus on performance and best value; a flagging commitment to the "customer revolution"; and an embryonic vision of a wider role as community governance' (1997, p 226). Many of the reforms pursued by Labour in central and devolved government since 1997 closely followed the earlier Conservative agenda (particularly in England), but many other initiatives were entirely new, or markedly different from what went before: there were continuities and discontinuities (Brooks, 2000; Newman et al, 2001). Differences included an end to compulsory competitive tendering (CCT) in local government, and an increased emphasis on partnership and the framing discourse of 'joined-up government' (Boyne et al, 2001). Nevertheless, New Labour did not reverse the major privatisations, continued to promote central government audit and control and remained enthusiastic towards importing private sector management practice to the public sector (Boyne et al, 2001, p 2).

Significant reforms enacted by New Labour included measures to promote community leadership and innovation in local government and introducing new political structures, targets and monitoring (particularly associated with the Best Value regime). There were also attempts to try to transform local government culture and working practices to promote a customer-centred ethos (Newman et al, 2001; Allmendinger et al, 2003b). With the decline in local authority functions and increasing emphasis on joint working with a myriad of partner organisations from the public, private and voluntary sectors (what Exworthy and Powell [2004] call the 'congested state'), a new 'leadership' role was promoted for local government (Davis and Geddes, 2000). This was encapsulated in the 2001 White Paper *Strong local leadership – Quality public service* (DTLR, 2001b). Local authorities were also tasked to set up Local Strategic Partnerships (England) and Local Economic Forums (Scotland), bringing together public, voluntary and private sector agencies locally. More recently the English Local Strategic Partnerships became closely involved in the Local Development Framework (LDF) process through their role in the production of 'sustainable community strategies' (CLG, 2008b), although their role and influence in planning is waning following the 2011 reforms.

Most recently, the Coalition government has promoted further change to local government in England. There has been an abolition of many central drivers for monitoring performance, most notably the Audit Commission being wound down, among a stated desire to reinvigorate local democracy. As Secretary of State for Communities and Local Government (CLG) Eric Pickles stated, when announcing the abolition of RSSs, 'communities will no longer have to endure the previous government's failed Soviet tractor style top-down planning targets' (quoted in DCLG, 2010). Yet these latest shifts to local governance are occurring in an age of austerity, with 28 per cent cuts in central government grants for local councils in England over a four-year period announced in 2011 (Smulian, 2011a). These cuts are likely to see councils further considering outsourcing and sharing planning services, against a general backdrop of heavy job losses from the public sector (Stewart, 2012), which has led Lowndes and Pratchett to comment that, while there is a strong localist flavour to many current policy developments around local government:

This development may be as much the corollary of savage public spending cuts and the need to externalise responsibility for performance failure as the outcome of a principled commitment to more autonomous local governance. As the impact of the cuts (along with the wider costs of recession) undermine prospects for all but the most affluent communities, it seems probable that localism will leave the great majority of councils 'not waving but drowning'. (2012, p 38)

Looking back throughout these years of vast changes to local governance, a theme of questioning the relationship between central and local government runs throughout all of the reforms. A number of commentators note that, despite the increasingly 'fragmented state' (see Chapter Two, this volume), central government retains extremely close control over local government, particularly through its control on resources, funding and the ability to pass legislation (Davies, 1998; Jackson, 2001; Green, 2003; Rydin, 2007). Indeed, Freeden (1999) highlighted the 'centralising tendencies of New Labour' despite talk of greater local devolution and 'new localism' (Preston, 2006), a phrase that pre-dated the Coalition government's use of the phrase to label the 2011 reforms. Crucially, many of these reforms of local government were top-down and there are some claims that they have been imposed against the wishes of some of those having to implement them (Ferlie et al, 1996; Goldsmith and Page, 1997; Kirkpatrick and Ackroyd, 2003). Even the 2011 localism push was, in effect, a centrally initiated and led reform. There is a danger, however, in being overly deterministic in talk of 'central imposition', given the crucial line of 'frontline' staff in actually realising the reforms (Gaster and Rutqvist, 2000).

Despite the vastly decreased emphasis on audit and targets under the Coalition government, looking back across the last 15 years, the most important agendas for local government services such as planning include, first, an explosion in the number of targets for services and the auditing of performance against those, and second, a push to make public services more responsive to their 'customers' (Sanderson, 2001). Indeed, it is also noteworthy that despite the abolition of the majority of national performance indicators for local government, the speed of planning application processing continues to be monitored and a cause for government concern, with talk of Department for Communities and Local Government (DCLG)-imposed sanctions for poor performance (Smulian, 2011b).

Taken together, this range of planning-specific and broader local governance reforms has had multiple, complex implications for the planning system. The key changes fall into four broad categories: reforms to planning processes and systems; reforms to local government management; reforms of trying to make the system more participatory and responsive to its customers; and attempts to try and change the culture of the planning profession. We now explore the major modernisation impulses associated with each in turn.

Process: implementing spatial planning

Central to the changes to planning processes have been attempts to introduce a 'spatial planning' approach to British planning practice. Nadin (2007) and Tewdwr-Jones (2012) discuss the germination of the spatial planning approach in the UK. In less than 10 years this became the organising discourse framing planning in Britain, a new 'planning orthodoxy' (Vigar, 2009) or 'zeitgeist' (Durning et al, 2010). Legislation replaced traditional county land use Structure Plans and district Local Plans (and Unitary Development Plans) with RSSs (now repealed) and LDFs in England, the latter being the focus for local authority planning. In Greater London, the Mayor's Spatial Development Strategy (commonly referred to as the 'London Plan') was created and has become a high-profile document associated with each of the newly elected London Mayors. In Scotland and Wales, spatial planning has been thus far institutionalised more at the national rather than local level, with the adoption of *The Wales spatial plan* (WAG, 2004; updated by WAG, 2008b) and the *National planning framework for Scotland* (Scottish Executive, 2004a – a third version is due to be published after 2012; Scottish Government, 2008b; see also Lloyd and Peel, 2005, 2007). Further changes have, however, seen Local Plans in both territories become LDPs, with a greater emphasis on evidence, infrastructure and delivery. There is currently no English or indeed UK national spatial strategy (Wong, 2002).

According to the government in 2005, spatial planning '... goes beyond traditional land-use planning by bringing together and integrating policies for the development and use of land with other policies and programmes which influence the nature of places and how they function' (ODPM, 2005c, para 1.8). Box 1.2 illustrates the definition of spatial planning given in PPS 12, the document setting out government policy (at the time) for the production of LDFs (CLG, 2008a). That said, the definition on the concept is contested and continues to evolve (Haughton et al, 2010), with some arguing that spatial planning has been scrapped under the Coalition government, although the critics of this view point out it is dependent on whether one takes a narrow or broad view of the phrase (Tewdwr-Jones, 2012), and local planning policy processes remain different in character today from those in place before 2004. Shaw and Lord (2007) explain

Box 1.2: Defining spatial planning

The government's *Planning Policy Statement 12* of 2008 explained the concept of spatial planning as rolled out into the English planning system in the following way:

'Spatial planning is a process of place shaping and delivery. It aims to:

- produce a vision for the future of places that responds to the local challenges and opportunities, and is based on evidence, a sense of local distinctiveness and community derived objectives, within the overall framework of national policy and regional strategies;

- translate this vision into a set of priorities, programmes, policies, and land allocations together with the public sector resources to deliver them;

- create a framework for private investment and regeneration that promotes economic, environmental and social well being for the area;

- coordinate and deliver the public sector components of this vision with other agencies and processes [eg LAAs];

- create a positive framework for action on climate change; and

- contribute to the achievement of Sustainable Development.' (CLG, 2008a, p 4)

Key to a spatial planning approach is an idea of focusing on the outcomes sought for the community and ensuring more effective cross-working with a variety of stakeholders and agencies that help to shape local areas and local services.

that spatial planning is intended to take a more proactive role by coordinating increasingly diverse and fragmented agents of the state and thereby to be faster, more efficient and more economically sensitive than previous planning work, while Inch argues that:

> The concept of spatial planning, drawing on wider European thought, was an attempt to reinvent planning as a flexible tool for strategic place shaping, able to proactively deliver sustainable development in the interests of local communities through partnership working across government, and with actors in both the private and voluntary sectors. (2009, p 90)

There is certainly a growing awareness of 'spatial' considerations of policy across the public sector (Harris and Hooper, 2004) and which continues to be present. Nadin (2007) sees spatial planning as a new approach that is more embedded in the apparatus of governance and through which planning will need to respond to a wider range of interests than just the public sector agenda. Healey, however, is concerned that 'the new spatial planning agenda assumes a governance landscape that does not yet exist in the UK' (2006, quoted in Vigar, 2009, p 1586), and Inch argues that in the UK context, the term remains ambiguous and difficult to define: 'It can perhaps be best understood as a rhetorical construction of change' (2010, p 262).

Although heralded as a new approach, spatial planning draws on traditions within the UK. Abercrombie's plan for postwar London was essentially a spatial planning document, and planning in the 1950s was associated with industrial location and New Town policies in a spatial manner (Scott, 1997). It is interesting to speculate about the origins of the contemporary drive towards spatial planning in Britain. There appears to be a European context to this, following the production of the European Spatial Development Perspective (ESDP), the European focus on sub-national planning and the European origin of most British environmental legislation (European Commission, 1999; Tewdwr-Jones et al, 2000; Allmendinger, 2001c; Tewdwr-Jones, 2001; Tewdwr-Jones and Williams, 2001; Faludi and Waterhout, 2002; Allmendinger et al, 2003a; Counsell et al, 2003). The Labour government certainly made an early commitment to integrate British and European planning more closely (DETR, 1998a).

There may be further research to be done drawing out the spread of the spatial planning discourse around the British Isles and the involvement of key figures from the civil service, professional bodies and academia in that process. For now, however, it is sufficient to note that there have been major reforms involving direct change to the planning policy process across Great Britain associated with the idea of spatial planning, even though it is acknowledged that it remains a contested phrase, conceptually and practically. Academic study to date has tended, however, to focus much more on what spatial planning is, on defining the idea and describing the structures rather than on considering how it is being realised, as Shaw and Lord (2007) note. Work on English LDFs has been under way since 2005 (ODPM, 2005c) but, despite a government expectation that all authorities would have adopted Core Strategies (the key LDF document) within three years, in fact only 22 out of 396 Local Planning Authorities (LPAs) had them in place by March 2008 (Killian and Pretty, 2008a). Clearly there have been major issues surrounding the implementation of this key area of planning policy, so much so that changes to the LDF system were proposed as a small part of the 2007 White Paper (CLG, 2007a), and amended regulations and policy were introduced in the summer of 2008 (Baker Associates et al, 2008; CLG, 2008a; HMSO, 2008). There has been some suggestion that this slow progress is down to a lack of skills on the part of frontline planners (Baker Associates et al, 2008; Vigar, 2009). Inch, however, argues it may not just be down to 'the failure of professionals to understand and commit to change', but 'the product of complex mediations between the hybrid aspirations of spatial planning, personal and professional values, the power of the statutory planning system, and the local governance contexts in which new practices are being uncertainly negotiated' (2010, p 372). Examination of the views of local authority planners is thus essential to fully understanding how spatial planning is working in practice, and to highlighting any important lessons concerning the roll-out of modernisation agendas.

Management: the efficiency agenda, audits and targets

The local government context within which planning sits has been transformed through the rise of managerialism over the past two decades (Clarke and Newman, 1997; Campbell and Marshall, 2000), with a common conception of local government as inefficient, bureaucratic and unaccountable and thus in need of reform (Campbell and Marshall, 1998). An overarching theme of New Labour's public sector reforms was the growth of targets and audit processes, what Hood (2007) terms 'management by numbers'. Power has termed the growth of such audit processes an 'audit explosion' leading to the rise of an 'audit society' obsessed with 'rituals of verification' (Power, 1999). Power contends that the rise of audit 'refers to a deeper set of issues about the organization of trust in developed societies and the related institutionalization of checking mechanisms' (2002, p xvi). Indeed, this agenda can be understood through a critique of the public sector professional bureaucracy as incapable of guaranteeing standards and efficiency in the public sector (Sanderson, 2001).

The impact of this growth of audit was particularly felt at the local government level in the UK, with Rashman and Radnor (2005) talking of an 'army of auditors' descending on local authorities. The dominant theme was top-down control through centrally imposed targets, particularly through the Best Value regime that was central to the New Labour agenda for modernising local government (Ball et al, 2002; Allmendinger et al, 2003a). Best Value was introduced in England and Wales through White Papers (DETR, 1998b; Welsh Office, 1998), which were followed by the Local Government Act 1999. The Act defined Best Value as 'the duty upon Best Value authorities to make arrangements to secure continuous improvement in the way in which they exercise functions, having regard to a combination of economy, efficiency and effectiveness' (DETR, 1999, quoted in Rashman and Radnor, 2005, p 19). In Scotland, Best Value was made a statutory obligation through the Local Government in Scotland Act 2003 (Best Value Task Force, 1999), the Scottish Executive commenting that 'the objective of Best Value is to ensure that management and business practices in local government deliver better and more responsive public services' (2004c, p 1). Best Value replaced the widely disliked (among local government officers) CCT (Rashman and Radnor, 2005) and was more focused on quality as well as economy, and on the expectations of users (Boyne et al, 2001).

The implications of this audit explosion were manifold and significant in transforming local government, for example, through internal performance indicators replacing traditional hierarchical ways of managing (Boyne et al, 2002a). There was concern, however, that under Best Value there was far too much emphasis on 'hard aspects' – performance indicators – and not enough on the 'soft aspects' supposed to accompany these, such as learning, development and improvement, and that the focus had tended to be on process rather than outcomes (Boyne et al, 2002a; Higgins et al, 2004; Rashman and Radnor, 2005). The increased use of performance targets led to growing concern about unintended consequences, particularly on aspects of services that were not measured, and about how the focus had become conformance with targets rather than real improvement in services (Sanderson, 2001; Rashman and Radnor, 2005; Boyne and Chen, 2006; Hood, 2007). Finally, there was also concern that Best Value was poorly implemented, central government expecting too much change too quickly (Ball et al, 2002; Boyne et al, 2002a).

Within this Best Value agenda, there was a particular push for improved speed and efficiency of planning services (Hull, 2000). Best Value targets for planning directly became part of the planning modernisation agenda (Thomas and Lo Piccolo, 2000). Targets in planning long predate Best Value, with the 8- and 13-week development control targets emerging as long ago as 1975 at the Department of the Environment (Carmona and Sieh, 2005), and during the 1980s quarterly performance league tables were produced showing the speed with which LPAs were processing planning applications (Carmona and Sieh, 2005). Best Value made planning performance measurement more sophisticated, however, with the addition of new indicators and a link between planning performance and the overall performance of local authorities against National Indicators (NIs) (Carmona and Sieh, 2004). In England, Best Value saw a wide range of targets for planning. The Office of the Deputy Prime Minister's (ODPM) 2005 list of Best Value performance indicators (BVPIs) for planning is indicated in Table 1.1, below. A notable development was the linkage in 2001 of the Planning Delivery Grant (PDG) – a significant fund of money given to LPAs to improve their planning services – to performance against the targets, most particularly speed of processing planning applications (ODPM, 2006). There has been some criticism of these targets within the planning literature, most especially of the sometimes arbitrary time-related targets: 'Ministers' obsession with speed as the prime test of the efficiency of the planning system continues to be depressing' (Gwilliam, 2002, p v). As well as the targets, planning was also monitored as part of the wider Comprehensive Performance Assessments (CPAs) of local authorities conducted by the Audit Commission (see, for example, Audit Commission, 2005a). The issues dealt with by these inspections are shown in Table 1.2. Best Value targets first became part of the new system of CPA (ODPM, 2002, quoted in Allmendinger et al, 2003b). This included an overall performance indicator for each local authority based on performance against each individual target as well as Audit Commission inspections of services. This was then replaced by a process called Comprehensive Area Assessment (CAA), which includes a slimmed-down list of NIs for use in England (CLG, 2008c).

Table 1.1: Best Value planning performance indicators for 2005/06

Indicator	Measure
BV106	Percentage of new homes built on previously developed land
BV109a	Percentage of major applications determined within 13 weeks
BV109b	Percentage of minor applications determined within 8 weeks
BV109c	Percentage of other applications determined within 8 weeks
BV179	Percentage of standard searches carried out in 10 working days
BV200a	Did the Local Planning Authority submit the Local Development Scheme (LDS) by 28 March 2005 and thereafter maintain a three-year rolling programme?
BV200b	Has the Local Planning Authority met the milestones that the current Local Development Scheme (LDS) sets out?
BV200c	Did the Local Planning Authority publish an annual report by 31 December of each year?
BV204	The number of planning appeal decisions allowed against the authority's decision to refuse on planning applications, as a percentage of the total number of planning appeals against refusals of planning applications
BV205	The local authority's score against a 'quality of planning services' checklist

Source: ODPM (2005b)

Table 1.2: Audit Commission 'Key lines of enquiry' for planning service inspections

Judgement	Question
How good is the service?	1. What has the service aimed to achieve?
	2. Is the service meeting the needs of the community and/or users?
	3. Is the service delivering value for money?
Prospects for improvement	4. What is the service track record in delivering improvement?
	5. How well does the service manage performance?
	6. Does the service have the capacity to improve?

Source: Audit Commission (2005b)

There were concerns about this new approach, since for planning the only indicator was speed of processing planning applications (NI 157) (Killian and Pretty, 2008a, 2008b).

In Scotland, there has been less focus on targets as part of Best Value (Allmendinger et al, 2005), and the monitoring of local government services by Audit Scotland included just two BVPIs for planning, as illustrated in Table 1.3 (below). However, the Scottish Executive's Development Department (SEDD) has a specific Planning Audit Unit that carries out detailed inspections of each LPA in Scotland on a rolling basis (see, for example, City of Edinburgh, 2005). The factors considered as part of these inspections are listed in Box 1.3 (below). Finally, this Planning Audit Unit also published an annual report on LPA performance, including the average age of development plans (with a target for 100 per cent being five years old or less) and the total number of planning applications decided within two months (with a target of 80 per cent). In the foreword to the report, Malcolm Chisholm, then the minister responsible for planning in Scotland, comments that 'The figures in this show very clearly that there is considerable scope to improve the efficiency of the planning system in Scotland' (SEDD, 2005, p 2).

Finally, this explosion monitoring and audit can also be seen in Wales. Best Value became part of a wider 'Wales Programme for Improvement', which placed more emphasis on self-assessment by authorities (WAG, 2005b). In terms of the Best Value/Wales Programme for Improvement monitoring, planning was one of a number of local authority functions

Table 1.3: Best Value planning performance indicators for 2004/05

Indicator	Measure
52	Percentage of householder applications dealt with within 2 months
53	Percentage of all applications dealt with within 2 months

Source: Audit Scotland (2005)

Box 1.3: Scottish Planning Audit Unit's key lines of inquiry for inspections of LPAs

Factors considered in Scottish Planning Audit Reviews
- Culture and ethos of the service
- Staff resources
- Customer care
- Process
- Delegated powers

Source: City of Edinburgh (2005)

monitored, covering Unitary Development Plan progress, aspects of development control and the quality of customer service (WAG, 2002a). Furthermore, planning has also been monitored specifically by WAG, with use of the performance targets for planning applications at 8 and 13 weeks (WAG, 2002b).

These 8- and 13-week targets for planning application processing seem remarkably resilient. The Coalition government has quickly moved away from heavy auditing of local government and reduced targets drastically, but the speed of planning application determination remains a measure on the new 'single data list' in England (DCLG, 2011a), and continues to be measured and reported on in Scotland and Wales (Scottish Government 2011; Welsh Government, 2011).

It is clear, therefore, that planning has been enveloped in a cloak of audit throughout Great Britain, and that a key measure for local planning authorities remains the speed with which they determine planning applications. These targets are not without their critics. For instance, the Egan review commented:

> Current processing targets do not work – they are not about delivering quality decisions or development, and we heard numerous complaints that they focus too much on numbers and box ticking, and can distort decision making. (Egan, 2004, p 46)

Given the concern about unintended consequences of targets, a host of issues are raised by the strong emphasis placed on these targets, particularly the emphasis across Great Britain on planning application processing speed. Audit, as Power notes, 'is not merely neutral verification but an agent of change' (Power, 1999, p 115).

Participation: planners and their customers

As Hull (2000) notes, New Labour came to power in 1997 with a specific manifesto to 'modernise' the welfare state, including strengthening citizen participation. This became a key agenda across all policy areas, particularly local government functions: the White Paper *Modern local government: In touch with the people* stated that 'the Government wishes to see consultation and participation embedded into the culture of all councils' (DETR, 1998b, quoted in Lowndes et al, 2001a, p 205). This included planning. Despite the long history of 'public participation' in planning (for example, the Skeffington Report of 1969), attempts to make planning even more participatory have been a pressing concern for central and devolved government alike. Participation is often seen as a way to restore declining trust in local government (Bedford et al, 2002), as well as a key part of sustainability (Myers and Macnaghten, 1998), although this link is often made unthinkingly (Portney, 2003).

There appears to have been an emphasis on both increasing the amount of public participation and on introducing new types of participation. The planning Green Paper (DTLR, 2001a) set out a number of initiatives aimed at improving public participation in planning, most particularly the requirement for LDFs to include a Statement of Community Involvement (SCI) setting out how the public had been involved in the preparation of the plan (see Baker et al, 2007). There has also been good practice guidance aimed at improving participation in planning (ODPM, 2004a; Scottish Executive, 2007). In the Green Paper, the rhetoric was certainly rich, with one paragraph commenting that:

> People can be dramatically affected by the quality of their environment and they care deeply about new development.... That is why we need a planning system that fully engages people in shaping the future of their communities. (DTLR, 2001a, p 1)

It is worth noting, however, that, despite such rhetoric, the general thrust of the Green Paper and subsequent ministerial statements seemed to be more aimed at efficiency than participation. Indeed, Barnes et al (2007) suggest that across government, neoliberal reforms mean that there is in effect more participation on less, as participation increases but the public sphere shrinks. This contradiction continues under the Coalition government, who have focused much more attention around neighbourhood and community participation in planning. This has included transferring some planning powers from the LPA directly to citizens through Neighbourhood Forums, that are empowered to draw up Neighbourhood Plans that become part of the statutory development plan. The intention of this reform is to bring more people into the planning system by giving neighbourhoods a direct say over development proposals, but there are limitations on these neighbourhood plans, which have led Holman and Rydin to suggest that 'currently the rhetoric of localism is in danger of delivering only failed promises and thwarted desires for local communities' (2012: forthcoming, p 15).

The issue of so-called Third Party Rights of Appeal (TPRA) is noteworthy in the participation context.[3] No real consideration was given to allowing TPRA in England and Wales, with the Green Paper rejecting the idea because it could add to the costs and uncertainties of planning (DTLR, 2001a). In Scotland, however, some consideration was given to introducing them, and an extensive consultation was launched (Scottish Executive, 2004b). This may be linked to both political and cultural factors (for example, the fact that Labour was then in a coalition in Scotland with the Liberal Democrats as well as the desire to appear distinctive from Westminster) and, perhaps, to the institutional setting of planning being dealt with by the Communities Minister of the then Executive. But when the White Paper was published, it concluded that 'we are seeking to restore fairness and balance to the system ... we are not satisfied that these objectives would be best achieved by introducing a third party right of appeal' (Scottish Executive, 2005, p 45). As with the English and Welsh reforms, there were a number of small-scale technical proposals to increase participation opportunities, for example, over notifying neighbours of proposed developments, but nothing radical. Again the general tone seems to be one of promoting efficiency of the planning system over all other factors. Since 2011, the Coalition government in the UK has also not embarked on the idea of TPRA (despite proposing it in *Open source planning*; see The Conservative Party, 2010).

During the Scottish Executive consultation on TPRA, some 56 per cent of individual planning professionals and 79 per cent of planning authorities that responded opposed TPRA. In contrast, 99 per cent of individual members of the public and 94 per cent of environmental and heritage groups supported TPRA (Scottish Executive, 2004b). Ellis explains professional resistance by noting that:

> The creation of third party rights can be portrayed as a final admission of the failure of the system, both democratically

and in terms of the professional aspirations of planning officers. (2000, pp 212-13; see also Ellis, 2002, 2004)

Thus, the rise of public participation may be linked to the issue of a long-standing decline in the public's trust of professionals and elected members to represent public interests (Townsend, 2002), and some concern about corruption in the planning system (Manns and Wood, 2001).[4] It is unsurprising that there might thus be some concern within the planning profession about participation, which can be seen as threatening to 'de-skill' planning and undermine practitioners' autonomy (Tewdwr-Jones and Allmendinger, 1998; Davies, 2001; Albrechts, 2002; Barnes et al, 2003). This makes a full understanding of professional reaction to this important aspect of planning (and public sector) reform of the utmost import.

Alongside these moves to make planning more participatory, there has been the emergence of the 'customer' concept, which is central to new public management (Rosenthal and Peccei, 2007). This similarly questions whom planning is for, and how it serves its users. Orientation toward the customer has been one of the 'strong themes' of public service management since the early 1980s (Stoker, 1997) and is closely linked to ideas of consumerism and discourses of access, choice, information, redress and representation (Clarke and Newman, 1997). Indeed, the reorienting of public services towards their 'customers' was a key theme of the Best Value programme under New Labour (Boyne et al, 2002a).

Yet the mobilisation of the customer discourse in the public sector raises a host of issues. Stoker expressed some concern that change towards a customer focus was only surface deep in local authorities, and highlighted 'the ambiguity of using the language of the customer in public services ... the public is both a citizen and a customer with respect to public services' (1997, p 230). Goldsmith and Page (1997), meanwhile, expressed concern that the 'customer ideal' might threaten the 'public sector ethos', while Rosenthal and Peccei (2007) questioned the appropriateness of the customer concept to the public sector, particularly as the 'customer' often had no choice: you cannot shop around for an LPA to process your planning application. The very notion of a 'customer' is thus a contested concept.

In planning, there is further complexity surrounding just who the customer is (Allmendinger et al, 2003b). Kitchen (1997) offers a list of 10 broad 'customer clusters' for local authority planning services (see Chapter Six, this volume). Back in 1981, Underwood asked development control planning staff who they conceptualised as their client:

> In the main the client was broadly defined as 'the community', 'society', 'the public interest'. Few officers mentioned specific groups or interests.... It is very clear that development control is regarded as a public service. (1981, p 156)

Indeed, according to Underwood, the 'customer' of planning is the whole of society with planning regulating the use of land in the interests of the public at large.

Nevertheless, the rhetoric of the 'customer' can now be seen throughout planning, with audit inspections of LPAs routinely talking about planning authorities providing 'a good range of guidance for customers' (Audit Commission, 2005a, p 4) and 'customer care' (City of Edinburgh, 2005). This process has been occurring for several years, with Allmendinger et al (2003b) outlining how, from 1993, the government introduced Planning Charters. With increased impetus of Best Value, planning is apparently now a 'service' with 'customers' whose views can be measured during audit inspections:

> The survey carried out in November 2003 to measure customer satisfaction in connection with BVPI 111 shows below average (69 per cent) satisfaction with the planning service.... These surveys provide a valuable insight into public perceptions of the service and the need for the service to market itself more effectively. (Audit Commission, 2005a, p 18)

Du Gay and Salaman (1992) argued that an emphasis on 'customers' had profound implications for the working practices and identities of public sector employees. Additionally, Rosenthal and Peccei highlight the importance of a context-specific understanding of deployment of consumer discourses:

> Despite the prevalence of interventions designed to instil customer-oriented behaviours and attitudes among front-line service workers, little is known about their impact on employees. (2006a, p 580)

This is apparently the case across the public sector, but appears to be a pressing concern in planning given the complexity of defining its customer.

Culture: the planning 'ethos'?

Underpinning much of this programme of planning reform has been a desire for a so-called 'culture change' in planning (Inch, 2010). The Egan review commented that:

> We believe that the opportunities presented by the proposed planning reforms will only be realised if there is a change in the way that the process of dealing with planning applications is managed, and in the culture and attitudes of organisations, professions and individuals involved, including developers. (Egan, 2004, p 40)

The need for such a 'culture change' in planning has been promoted as part of the planning reform process across Great Britain. Government planning policy commented that 'good planning is a positive and proactive process' (ODPM, 2005a, p 9), and the specific culture change pursued by government focused particularly on the education and training of the planning profession, as well as its morale. Similarly, the Scottish Executive commented that 'the planning system should be responsive to social and economic changes.... This requires a consistent approach that is inclusive rather than exclusive; that anticipates rather than reacts; and that is consistent rather than arbitrary' (Scottish Executive, 2002, p 29). More explicitly, Carwyn Jones, the then Minister for Planning in Wales, commented that there was need for 'embedding a cultural change in the way we deliver the planning service' (WAG, 2005a, p 1).

In general, two common strands can be seen in this culture change agenda (Hayton, 2002). The first is the idea that planning should be more inclusive, engaging with stakeholders, and more proactive than reactionary. The term 'development control' has been replaced with 'development management' in all three British planning regimes.[5] Box 1.4 contains a recent definition of the idea of development management. The key concern here is that planners need to adapt new ways of working – to re-skill – in line with the evolving planning reform agenda. This is an ongoing concern (see, for example, Baker Associates et al, 2008). Figure 1.2 (below) is suggestive of how the concept is being received by some within the profession.

Box 1.4: Defining development management

A recent guidance document from the Planning Advisory Service explains development management in the following way:

'Development management is not just a new name for development control, although the familiar development control activities will still remain part of the suite of development management functions. Five principles have been identified that characterise the role of development management as compared to development control:

i   development management is an integral part of the spatial planning process; it puts spatial development plans into action;

ii   development management is the end to end management of the delivery chain for sustainable development;

iii   the development management approach signals a culture change, underlining the role of the local authority as a place shaper in partnership with others;

iv   the processes for considering proposals need to be proportionate and appropriate to the impact of the individual development;

v   the development management approach will necessitate changes in the structure and allocation of resources within local planning authorities.' (PAS, 2008, pp 5-6)

Development management is about putting spatial development plans into practice, and about authorities actively trying to promote sustainable development and deliver the vision in their plans. A development management approach needs a change in culture, away from reactive control of development to a more positive and proactive role for planning.

The second strand has been promoting the idea that planning needs to be more economically responsive and effective. There has been a particular focus on the speed of the system and its efficiency (Hull, 2000). This concern has been most acute in England, with two Treasury-commissioned reports by Bank of England economist Kate Barker (Barker, 2004, 2006) highlighting the impact of the planning system on the economy and housing supply. In the 2004 report, Barker made a central recommendation, that 'planning should take more account of, and use market information' (2004, p 6). The Killian

Figure 1.2: Linking development management with target culture

Pretty review (Killian and Pretty 2008a, 2008b), commissioned jointly by CLG and the Department for Business, Enterprise and Regulatory Reform (BERR), raised further concerns about the 'regulatory burdens' imposed by planners on business. There certainly seems to have been a drive towards making planning more market-supportive, with heavy campaigning by the Confederation of British Industry (CBI), which sees itself as a driving force behind planning reform (CBI, 2005). Allmendinger (2001c, 2002b) notes that both the Department of the Environment, Transport and the Regions (DETR) (1998a) and the Scottish Office (1999) drew on the Department for Trade and Industry (DTI) competitiveness White Paper (DTI, 1998) concerning the delays and costs of the planning system on economic growth. There has also been strong criticism of planning by business leaders and housing developers in the press (Clifford, 2006). This has become an issue of even greater importance under the Coalition government (Donnelly, 2011a).

Although specific to planning, the attempts to change the way planners work and interact with users of the planning service are similar to initiatives aiming to change the culture of other public sector staff (Gillman, 2008). In this context, Rashman and Radnor (2005) note the failure of central government to so far develop a workable method of implementing culture change among local authority staff (with too much emphasis on performance targets instead), while Thomas and Lo Piccolo (2000) suggest that there have been many attempts to change the culture of British local government post war, but that these faced a set-back as local authority staff in the 1980s became adversarial, often fighting for their very existence during a time of public sector cuts. Since then, local government has seen a growth of managerialism (as noted by Sanderson, 2001), yet some authors argue that a 'traditional hierarchy and an entrenched culture' has continued in many public sector organisations (McHugh et al, 2001, p 41).

Despite the importance attached to it, Goldsmith and Page argue that 'it is extraordinarily difficult to assess the significance of a "culture" and the lack of correspondence between expressed attitudes and actual behaviours makes questionable the impact of "culture" beyond paying lip-service to norms' (1997, p 161), and Ferlie et al (1996) find the idea of culture change 'ambiguous and loose'. Similarly, Newman notes that culture change is a complex matter: 'Change in the UK civil service is multi-faceted, with different kinds of initiative interacting with each other' (2001, p 94). There has also been concern in some of the literature that culture change and public sector reform could threaten the so-called 'public sector ethos' of public servants (Goldsmith and Page, 1997). This is clearly an area requiring further empirical investigation.

Understanding change through the 'lens of planners'

We have seen that there has been a concerted effort of planning reform pursued by New Labour, particularly since the publication of the Green Paper in England in 2001, and by the Coalition government since 2010, with programmes of reform also pursued by the devolved administrations in Scotland and Wales. Such has been the pace and extent of change, it feels as though planning reform is a continual process, rather than an end objective. Alongside the changes within the planning system, there has been a wide-ranging public sector reform agenda having a heavy impact on the local government context within which planning sits. A great deal of academic literature assesses these reforms, but by far the majority of this (particularly in the planning sphere) is focused on analysing central government policy and on the structures of the planning system rather than what we might term the 'peopled practices' of planning and the state (Peck, 2004). This accords with a wider trend for frontline workers to be vilified and silenced (Jones, 2001). Pratchett and Wingfield complain that:

> Little attention has been paid to the effects of recent changes on the perceptions and values of local government employees. Yet they were the target (and often victims) of

---

31

many of the changes and their complicity was essential for their implementation. (1996, p 639)

There are a number of rationales to explain why the perspective from frontline planners on planning and public sector reforms is so important.

First, there are some striking empirical gaps within the literature about each individual reform strand, much of which tends towards more theoretical than practice-based discussion. Thus Rosenthal and Peccei comment that, 'there is a dearth of empirical research providing focused and detailed analyses of how "the customer" is being enacted/ represented in particular sites within the new public management' (2007, p 210). Similarly, Hull (2000) highlights a greater need for an empirical understanding of how planners, as actors, are responding to the participation agenda and push to 'strengthen democracy', given the simultaneous demand for planners to improve the efficiency of local government and the speed of planning processes.

This highlights a second vital issue, which is the fact that there are tensions between the different strands of planning and public sector reform (Inch, 2010; Allmendinger, 2011). A good example is the participation agenda. At the same time as promoting greater participation in planning, there has also been a focus on speeding up the planning system. Since, on the one hand, public participation exercises take time and resources and, on the other hand, the speed and efficiency of the planning are increasingly of concern to, and monitored by, government, there is thus a major tension running right to the heart of planning reform in Britain. Hull asks 'how will the tension between more efficient government and an active role for citizens be played out in the planning arena?' (2000, p 774; see also Manns and Wood, 2001; Haughton and Counsell, 2002; Warburton, 2002). These tensions appear to be even starker since 2010.

This particular conflict is far from unique in the modernisation agenda. Discourses of reform can frequently be contradictory and tension-ridden (Proudfoot and McCann, 2008). Indeed, this can be seen as indicative of a wider tension between social democratic and neoliberal ideals that lay at the heart of Labour's 'third way' (Lloyd and Illsley, 2001). Clarke and Newman highlight further potential conflicts:

Doing more for less in pursuit of the holy grail of efficiency; trying to be 'strategic' while juggling an ever increasing number of injunctions and restrictions from central government; managing the problems arising from overlapping, fast changing and often contradictory policy agendas; and struggling to balance all this with living a life beyond the workplace. (1997, p x)

Given these tensions, it is vitally important to see how the interplay of agendas works in practice by considering the views of frontline staff who can be both constrained by some and empowered by other elements of the reforms (Rosenthal and Peccei, 2006a). Furthermore, the full implications of such tensions might be missed by research focusing solely on one particular reform strand, such as participation. There is, instead, a need for broader analysis considering how planners are reacting to the full reform agenda, including the often insufficiently studied local government modernisation processes.

A third consideration is that context matters. Painter highlights the fact that through broad public sector reforms, a widely criticised one-size-fits-all Fordist approach is being replaced by another one-size-fits-all approach that offers similar prescriptions based on 'flawed theories of organizational change management' that pay insufficient regard to distinctive institutional contexts (Painter, 2005, p 307; see also Painter, 2004). In practice, policies can 'play themselves out in different ways in different places at different times' (Campbell, 2002, p 274). Clarke and Newman suggest that the consequences of reform, for particular organisations, groups and individuals cannot simply be read off from these general trends, which they call the danger of 'determinism' in accounts of state restructuring:

> The primary danger of determinism is that of seeing change as the inevitable product of economic and political forces. The process of constructing managerial regimes has been contested, and the dynamics of change are partly conditioned by the different power bases of professions and unions across different sectors. (1997, p 83)

In other words, to fully understand planning reform, we need to look not at the general trends but at the actual resultant practice. Similarly, there is insufficient consideration of the planning context for broader public sector reforms; the planning academy has tended to focus on direct planning reform and scholars of public sector reform generally have tended to overlook the local government and planning nexus.

Finally, the view from the front line is essential because policies are shaped and made and re-made from formulation to implementation, as people negotiate, modify and act to protect or pursue their interests and values (Hill, 1981; Barrett, 2004). As Barrett suggests, 'policy may thus be regarded as both a statement of intent by those seeking to change or control behaviour, and a negotiated output emerging from the implementation process' (2004, p 253). There is a widespread literature on implementation (for a good overview, see Jordan, 1995), yet little attention has been placed on the local implementation of planning reform. We can, arguably, conceptualise local authority planners as 'street-level bureaucrats' (SLBs) (after Lipsky, 1980; see Chapter Two, this volume) with a vital role in the implementation of public policy. Rosenthal and Peccei give an example from a study of the mobilisation of customer ideals:

> The JobCentre Plus project, like all strategies and tactics of organisation reformers, is interpreted and rendered into a negotiated reality by the 'street level bureaucrats' (Lipsky, 1980) charged with its delivery. (2006a, p 665)

It is because the public's experience of any new policy will be the actions of these SLBs that their perspective is of the utmost importance:

> Whatever is done at the front line affects citizens' perceptions of the whole organisation, while the whole organisation depends on the front line to deliver its policies and services efficiently, effectively and to a decent quality. In democratic organisations, the front line is both a key element in bureaucratic and managerial effectiveness *and*, formally or informally, a channel for local democratic practice. (Gaster and Rutqvist, 2000, p 53; original emphasis)

Planning reform has been an important policy agenda for central and devolved government in Great Britain in recent years, to the point that over £600 million was allocated in England on the PDG between 2001 and 2006 (Shaw and Lord, 2007). This is a considerable investment. But to fully understand this policy agenda and to understand the emerging planning system (a 'structure-in-progress') (Jensen and Leijon, 1996, quoted in Hull, 2000), there is clearly a need to consider the interaction of the planning-specific and wider public sector reform agendas. More importantly, there is a clear need to move beyond over-arching narratives of 'the state' and 'citizens' and to consider the perspectives of the people who comprise the state, fully recognising the differentiation between central and local state, between policy makers and frontline professionals involved in the implementation of policy, and accounting for the dialectic between structure and agency in the process of change. As Proudfoot and McCann argue: 'the state – as a sociospatially embedded set of institutions, individuals and practices – also requires *explanation*. This can be achieved in part by examining the practices of street-level bureaucrats' (2008, p 350; original emphasis). It is here that this book, which focuses on what we term 'planning at the coalface', is located.

A note on the research

The key arguments made in this book are grounded in data from a large-scale empirical research project that examined the relationship between frontline planners and reform under New Labour between 2004 and 2008. Data was collected using a mixed-methods iterative approach. The first stage was 17 exploratory interviews with heads of planning from a cross-section of local authorities (a mixture of type, size and location) conducted in late 2005. These were recorded, transcribed and coded. For anonymity, interviewees were referred to a pseudonym appropriate to their sex and ethnicity. These exploratory interviews allowed key themes to be identified, which were then taken forward through the second stage, a six-page questionnaire, including a series of Likert agreements. These asked respondents how much they agreed or disagreed with a series of both positive and negative statements referring to the planning reforms that had been used by interviewees during initial interviews. The survey was posted to a random sample of 1,987 local authority planners selected from the RTPI membership list in summer 2006 (meaning all respondents were practising professional planners). A 31 per cent response rate yielded 612 questionnaires returned, which were then analysed using the computer program SPSS. Survey respondents were asked to volunteer for in-depth interviews, and a further 53 in-depth interviews were conducted with planners nationally during 2007–08, representing a mix of experience and managerial responsibility. These interviews were analysed in the same way as the exploratory interviews. Data from the various stages was triangulated and presents a rich picture of how frontline planners respond to change.

Structure of the book

In this chapter, we have shown that there is an ongoing programme of planning reform being pursued by central and devolved government in Great Britain. A particular drive for reform was promoted by New Labour, but has since continued under different political leadership, including the UK Coalition government. This has interacted in important ways with a wider agenda to modernise local government and the public services. In Chapter Two, we explore how we can conceptualise planning reform and the nature of broad changes from government to governance. Contextualising planning reform as part of a broader frame of public sector modernisation, the way this can be understood through the lenses of governance, neoliberalism, New Labour's third way, and localism are all explored. The role of planners in the reform processes is considered in Chapter Three by outlining how they can be understood as professionals, as subjects of neoliberalism and as frontline SLBs. We conclude by a brief exploration of 'sociological institutionalism', which draws on Giddens' structuration theory, and suggest this offers a useful research framework.

In Chapter Four, we consider reaction to the spatial planning agenda, primarily within planning policy. As with Chapters Five, Six and Seven, we start by considering the New Labour approach as providing the context for where we have come from, then present detailed empirical material helping us better understand how planners reacted to the Labour policies and how this helps us conceptualise the role of the planner, before discussing the emerging contemporary policy context and concluding with how the reaction to the previous government's reform agenda helps us consider the implications for the current agenda. Chapter Five explores how local authority planners responded to the Labour government's performance management agenda for planning, particularly the targets for speed of the development control function. We find that the performance agenda has had a massive impact on the professional life of planners at the coalface. In common with other public sector professions, a range of negative consequences were associated with the targets, including concerns about a focus on process over outcome and a range of unintended consequences. Chapter Six considers how planners are reacting to the emphasis on public participation and the rise of a 'consumerist' approach in the planning reform agenda. This leads to discussion of the tensions between the participation and other planning reform agenda, of the arguments planners find in favour of participation and of the many difficulties it presents for local authority planners in practice. In Chapter Seven, we examine how planners continue to make appeals to the 'greater good', drawing on conceptions of planning serving society, and seem more motivated by technical achievements and ideals of serving society and the environment than by providing a high quality service. This understanding of planning identity is then used to consider collaborative planning, and the motivation to act and collaborate within new forms of planning.

The concluding chapter considers the cross-cutting themes emerging from the range of empirical data presented in earlier chapters about planning reform under New Labour, and takes this forward to look at the Coalition government reforms. We consider what 'planning at the coalface' can tell us about the implementation of modernisation agendas, about power and agency, and about planning as a profession.

TWO

Conceptualising governance and planning reform

The age of continual reform

We saw in Chapter One that both the planning system and the wider public sector context in which British planning is situated have been the objects of concerted reform over the last 15 years in central and devolved government in Great Britain. Hull sums up the reforms thus:

> Public service provision has been slowly re-configured since the early 1980s by the introduction of 'market' measures of efficiency. So far, the 'hard' infrastructure of the planning system has remained relatively unscathed from the privatisation of services and State assets…. The main changes have been to the 'soft' infrastructure of the planning system; the values, norms and standards. There have been ministerial statements and calls from business interests for a more transparent and efficient planning system, to help create policy certainty and to more effectively support the development industry. (2000, p 772)

This largely summarises the situation up to the present day, and there has been no slowdown in reform to planning with changes in power in devolved administrations and the election of the UK Coalition government in May 2010.

In this chapter, we provide, briefly, the contextual frame for understanding what is driving these planning reforms, before turning in Chapter Three to consider the lenses we can use to consider the role of planners.

Understanding reform

The reform processes which have been affecting planning over recent years can be understood through a number of connected theoretical approaches, including neoliberalism and managerialism generally, the so-called 'third way' associated with New Labour and the emerging 'localism' associated with the Coalition government. These approaches vary between the normative and the more analytical in terms of both stated aim and common usage. In this section we briefly explore each of these approaches in turn before considering, in the following section, the broad frame of governance.

Neoliberalism

An increasingly common approach to understanding the modernisation of the state within human geography and cognate disciplines has been through the lens of 'neoliberalism'. Neoliberalism grew out of a critique of the welfare state, which began to be understood 'as a uniform provision that is bureaucratic, hierarchical, sometimes coercive and oppressive, and often unresponsive to the needs and differences of individuals and communities' (Dean, 1999, p 153). Under the neoliberal logic, the past 20 years of 'entrepreneurial governance' (du Gay, 2000) has been about wrestling power and legitimacy from bloated, wasteful, unresponsive government bureaucracies and restoring it to 'citizen-consumers' (Rosenthal and Peccei, 2007). It is argued that the period since the mid-1970s have represented a new era of institutional regulatory fixes, at different spatial scales, involving new modes of governance and regulation (Raco, 2005).

The linchpin of neoliberal ideology is the belief that open, unregulated markets free from state interference will provide the optimal mechanism for economic development. Moody has described neoliberalism concisely as:

> A mixture of neoclassical economic fundamentalism, market regulation in place of state guidance, economic redistribution in favor [sic] of capital (known as supply-side economics), moral authoritarianism with an idealized family at its center [sic], international free trade principles (sometimes inconsistently applied), and a thorough intolerance of trade unionism. (1997, quoted in Brenner and Theodore, 2002, p 352)

Within a 'neoliberal regime' (Jessop, 2002), there is economic liberalisation and a rolling back of the state, a favouring of free markets and strong individual property rights, individualism, privatisation, competition, deregulation and a desire for 'efficiency' above all else (Clarke, 2004; Harvey, 2007). These ideas have travelled with remarkable ease, and have been characterised by a tendency for governments globally to copy reforms with little reference to the social and political climate in which they were developed or were to be implemented. Several New Labour policies 'bear testimony to the longevity and de-contextualized global reach of neoliberal thinking' (Bondi and Laurie, 2005, p 2). Harvey conceptualises neoliberalism as a distinct class project and highlights how the economic configuration of globalisation requires the state to create and preserve appropriate institutional frameworks for neoliberalism to thrive (Harvey, 2005, 2007). Indeed, an overarching theme is the rescaling of state activity to support economic growth (Brenner and Theodore, 2002), and a dominant emphasis within public policy on growth and competitiveness (Raco, 2005).

Peck and Tickell (2002) define distinct phases within the neoliberal project over the past 20 years (see also Jessop, 2002). The first shift saw 'proto-' neoliberalism replaced by 'roll-back' neoliberalism, during which abstract free market economic theory was operationalised through strategies of deregulation, privatisation and commodification of the state. This period was marked by a savage critique of the capacities and practices of postwar state management. The second shift saw 'roll-back' become 'roll-out' neoliberalism, signalled by a proliferation of regulatory systems through which quasi-market mechanisms extended into an ever-widening range of activities. This shift was driven by the increasing negative externalities of 'roll-back' neoliberalism, and hence involved less visible processes of consolidating neoliberal state forms and modes of governance, but still with the overarching theme of subordinating political and cultural forces to the broader requirements of capital accumulation (Raco, 2005). Larner and Le Heron (2005) highlight how different phases can be seen in the neoliberalising project, and link these with distinctive 'imaginaries'. As Allmendinger notes, such variance in neoliberal solutions and practices 'focuses attention on the ways in which the state, at all levels, creates and destroys modes of governance in the impatient search for new, more efficient and more effective mechanisms that overcome the contradictions and crises of liberalise and globalisation' (2011, p 157).

Neoliberalism embodies a commitment to forms of intervention and control which are more indirect and distant, seeking to act on and through the interests and motivations of subjects and organisations (Rose and Miller, 1992), and even their identities (Larner and Le Heron, 2002). There is a marked distrust of professionals for securing value for money in public services and thus a central place for audit processes in the neoliberal state (Power, 1999; Sanderson, 2001). A common approach to understanding neoliberalism has been to draw on a neo-Foucauldian governmentality framework (see Barry et al, 1993; Clayton, 2000; Larner, 2000). In this perspective, targets, for example, can be understood as a technology of government. The conduct of government becomes one of using knowledge to render domains governable and then controlling those objects of government at a distance through networks and through the use of governmental technologies, which in turn recast subjectivities (Rydin, 2007).

This apparent recasting of subjectivities is a common feature in studies exploring neoliberal state reforms, and we explore this further in Chapter Three. For now, it is important to highlight that there is a tendency in some studies to see neoliberalism as a unified, coherent project enabling comprehensive 'conduct of conduct'. In fact, neoliberalism is ridden with tensions and contradictions and is less a coherently bounded end state and more a process in action: 'neoliberalisation' (Brenner and Theodore, 2002; Wilson, 2004; see Harvey, 2007, for an exploration of some of the contradictions). Larner (2003) warns against monolithic accounts of the 'neoliberal project', highlighting how there are multiple forms of political strategies and techniques associated with neoliberalism and profound experimentations rather than the rolling out of a coherent programme. Furthermore, as Brenner and Theodore highlight:

> Neoliberal doctrine is premised upon a 'one size fits all' model of policy implementation that assumes that identical results will follow the imposition of market-oriented reforms, rather than recognizing the extraordinary variations that arise as neoliberal reform initiatives are imposed within contextually specific institutional landscapes and policy environments. (2002, p 353)

Brenner and Theodore call attention to the need to explore the plurality of spaces formed by neoliberal reform, what they term the geographies of 'actual existing neoliberalism'. They add that:

> ... we emphasize the contextual *embeddedness* of neoliberal restructuring projects insofar as they have been produced within national, regional, and local contexts defined by the legacies of inherited institutional frameworks, policy regimes, regulatory practices, and political struggles. (2002, p 351; original emphasis)

Neoliberalism will often unfold in pragmatic and variable manners as it interacts with existing institutional arrangements and 'conceptions of neoliberalism must be more attentive to historical contingency, geographical specificity and political complexity' (Larner and Le Heron, 2005, p 845). In seeking to understand how planners respond to reform agendas, this book offers a professionally specific context to highlight the embeddedness of such modernisation processes.

There is some debate surrounding the extent to which New Labour's agenda after 1997 was neoliberal given that there were both continuities and discontinuities with the previous – and undoubtedly neoliberal – 1979–97 Conservative government's approach (Clarke, 2004; Davies, 2008). Newman (2005) argues that New Labour softened competition and introduced a new emphasis on joined-up government and participation, with a focus on institutional renewal, democracy and citizenship which were quite distinct from, and indeed somewhat a reaction against, the narrow agenda of the Conservatives, even if targets, efficiency savings and so on were pursued with even more vigour that they had been previously (Newman, 2005). In this sense, Newman does not see the Labour agenda as neoliberal, but a more common view sees New Labour as continuing the neoliberal agenda, albeit in a new form (Clarke, 2004). Thus the participation agenda Newman suggests is a break from neoliberalism can actually be understood through the neoliberal agenda of making citizens subjects in their own governance, free agents and 'active citizens' consuming services (Dean, 1999; Rose, 1996, quoted in Raco and Flint, 2001; Campbell and Marshall, 2000; Raco, 2000). There was much criticism of Labour's uncritical relationship to business (Cutler and Waine, 2000), particularly in the way that as a result of business lobbying there has been an obsession with speeding up the planning process almost above all other objectives (Carmona and Sieh, 2004). Allmendinger (2011) argues that the underlying approach of New Labour and the inherent contradictions and tensions present in their policy approaches can indeed be understood through a focus on neoliberalism, and that the post-2010 UK Coalition government seems to signify a shift away from New Labour's 'rolled-out' neoliberalism towards a more 'rolled-back' neoliberalism. Kerr et al (2011) similarly suggest the actions of the current Coalition government can be understood through a neoliberal governmentality perspective.

Some distinctly neoliberal rhetoric can clearly be seen in the planning reform context. Although planning has largely escaped marketisation, with very few authorities having contracted out their planning services, and planning remaining a prescribed local authority function, the Audit Commission has tried to promote private sector operation of local authority planning services as if it were the only alternative to improving planning services (Audit Commission, 2006a, 2006b), the *pensée unique*. Allmendinger (2011, p 157) argues that spatial planning 'can be seen as a form of neoliberal spatial governance providing the necessary strategies and institutional fixes in order to legitimise and facilitate growth.' Therefore, while Foster and Hoggett (1999) suggest that restructuring in the public sector is complex and cannot simply be understood as the result of a coherent and consistent neoliberal restructuring strategy, there is evidence of a deeper neoliberal hegemony. Approaches starting from a questioning of this hegemony thus remain a strong analytical addition to our understanding of the ongoing process of state modernisation in Britain.

New public management

Closely associated with neoliberal doctrine has been the idea of new public management (NPM), the former concept dominating geographical approaches to the ongoing modernisation of the state and the latter more common among policy, administration and management scholars. Clarke (2004) terms them 'linked discourses', but notes new public management is not simply reducible to neoliberalism. Indeed, a key difference is that studies that talk about 'neoliberalism' often use the concept analytically to understand contemporary state modernisation, whereas new public management, while offering some analytic power, also has strong normative associations.

New public management, first named by Hood (1991), is concerned with 'doctrines of public accountability and organizational best practice' (Hood, 1995, p 93), and can be understood as an attempt to conceptualise the agenda arising from the New Right in the 1980s (Broadbent and Laughlin, 1997; Barrett, 2004). It was, and is, 'a new discourse and guiding principle for the institutional form and structure of modern welfare states' (Hansen, 2001, p 105), with a principal aim 'to "get more for less" from public services' (Kitchener et al, 2000, p 216). Although new public management is a contested and complex group of overlapping ideas (Ferlie et al, 1996; Power, 1999; Maesschalck, 2004), it is now seen as the prevailing model for public sector reform (Rosenthal and Peccei, 2006a).

At its most basic, it is often defined in terms of the importation of private sector management concepts and ideas into the public sector (Osborne and Gaebler, 1992). This can be seen in terms of an ideal of replacing the supposed inefficiency of hierarchical bureaucracy with the presumed efficiency of markets, acting as a drive for the contracting out of public functions to the private sector and applying market principles to those services remaining within the public sector (Power, 1999; Sanderson, 2001). The result is a highly normative corporate archetype of public sector organisation quite distinct from the traditional public administration models of bureaucracy and a stated desire for a shift in power from bureaucracies to their sovereign 'customers' (Kirkpatrick and Ackroyd, 2003; Rosenthal and Peccei, 2006a). Alongside this, new public management emphasises apparently lean and purposeful administrative structures (Hood, 1991), and has resulted in 'new wave management' theory which has permeated public sector thinking (Brereton and Temple, 1999). Hood (1991) sets out the doctrinal components of new public management (see Table 2.1), and Osborne and Gaebler (1992) offer 10 'essential principles' of what they term 'entrepreneurial governance' (see Box 2.1).

Sanderson (2001) suggests three key themes of new public management: 'marketisation', 'consumerism' and 'managerialism'.

Table 2.1: The doctrinal components of new public management

* Explicit formal measure standards and measures of performance success
* Accountability means clearly stated aims; efficiency needs hard looks at goals
* Qualitative and implicit standards and norms
* Erosion of self-management by professionals
* Performance indicators and audit

Source: Hood (1991, in Hood, 1995, p 96)

Box 2.1: Principles of 'entrepreneurial governance'

Ten 'essential principles' of entrepreneurial governance

1. Competition between service providers
2. Empowering citizens through pushing control out of bureaucracies and into communities
3. Performance measured on outputs, rather than inputs
4. Organisations and people driven by missions and visions, not by rules and regulations
5. Redefining clients as customers
6. Preventing problems before they emerge rather than simply treating them once they have arisen
7. Earning money, not just spending it
8. Decentralising authority and encouraging participative management
9. Using market-type mechanisms rather than bureaucratic techniques
10. Catalysing partnership between public, private and voluntary sectors

Source: Osborne and Gaebler (1992, pp 19-20)

'Marketisation' involves the creation of market and quasi-market mechanisms, separating purchasing and providing functions and linking them via contracts. This is associated with processes of contracting out, public–private partnerships and competitive tendering (Power, 1999; Sanderson, 2001; Hansen, 2001; McHugh et al, 2001; Maesschalck, 2004). 'Consumerism' is concerned with making public services more responsive to users and 'customers', and has involved efforts 'to provide users of services with more choice and more influence about policies and services as a spur to improved quality and value for money' (Sanderson, 2001, p 299). The aim is a public service ethos focused on outputs, and seeing the public as consumers rather than clients (Brereton and Temple, 1999). While the centrality of the customer ideal to new public management is clear, the nature, appropriateness and implications of its use in the public sector are less so, particularly given customer orientation is often seen in terms of providing 'choice' (Lane, 1997; Rosenthal and Peccei, 2007).

'Managerialism' appears to be the element that was most stressed by Labour while in power (the Conservatives under Thatcher and Major pushing marketisation more), and hence has become a particular focus for recent academic analysis. Managerialism includes business-like management techniques and administrative systems, with the devolution of management responsibilities (Hansen, 2001; Sanderson, 2001). Alongside this are ideas such as performance-related pay and appraisal (Sanderson, 2001). Finally, and attracting most attention, there is the setting of service standards and the development of audit systems, particularly performance-related targets, to assess performance against those standards (McHugh et al, 2001). This is based on an ideal of increasing accountability to citizens about the quality of service (Ferlie et al, 1996; Power, 1999). There was an 'audit explosion' (after Power, 1999) under New Labour with a growing emphasis on its use for control and rationalising public services (Boyne et al, 2002a; Carmona and Sieh, 2004; see Chapter Five, this volume). Overall, the aim of is to drive out perceived inefficiency in the public sector (Davies and Thomas, 2003).

Broadbent et al (1996) talk of the rise of managerialism meaning that there has been a move in local authorities away from a 'civic culture' towards more of a 'business culture', with an explicit attempt to replace planning and professionalism with the market and managerial control as the 'rationality' for organising public services (Sanderson, 2001). Indeed, Obsorne and Gaebler (1992) specifically call for a culture change so that the public sector is less 'bureaucratic' and more 'entrepreneurial'. Clarke and Newman talk of the 'managerial state' as an emergent political settlement, and locate managerialism as a cultural formation with distinctive ideologies and practices:

> Managerialism, we argue, is shaping the making of the British state – its institutions and practices as well as its culture and ideology. (1997, p ix)

Box 2.2 illustrates the dualisms used to legitimate managerialism.

New public management has both its advocates and critics. For many advocates, the failings of the unreformed public sector are argument enough for the importance of new public management reforms (see, for example, Kitchener et al, 2000). Such work highlights the tendency for the old-style public sector, formed around a bureau-professional model, to be self-serving, indifferent to difference and inefficient. Others promote it on the basis of the strength of the private sector model it promotes (see, for example, Hood, 1995). Combined, such work suggests that introducing consumer and market discipline where possible, or targets and tighter managerial control where not, will result in services which serve the public better, and it is here that new public management can often be seen in usage as a normative concept.

Box 2.2: Dualisms used to legitimate managerialism

Legitimating managerialism

BUREAUCRACY IS:	MANAGEMENT IS:
rule bound	innovative
inward looking	externally oriented
compliance centred	performance oriented
ossified	dynamic

PROFESSIONALISM IS:	MANAGEMENT IS:
paternalist	customer centred
mystique ridden	transparent
standard oriented	results oriented
self-regulating	market tested

POLITICIANS ARE:	MANAGERS ARE:
dogmatic	pragmatic
interfering	enabling
unstable	strategic

Source: Clarke and Newman (1997, p 50)

Critics point to the lack of evidence base for the proposed management styles actually being better for public services and the tendency for one-size-fits-all approaches ignorant of context (Power, 1999). There has been 'surprisingly little' evidence to demonstrate that extending market forces has either improved the standard of services or reduced inefficiency in the public sector (Boyne et al, 2001, p 3). This links to a concern about whether old-style public services were as inefficient as is implied:

> Like all good discourses, the new managerialism announced the conditions of its own necessity – elaborating a tale of the failings of the old management and its dire consequences. (Clarke and Newman, 1997, p 35; see also Denhart and Denhart, 2000)

A wider critique is whether the private sector model is appropriate to the public sector, with some authors promoting the difference between the sectors: 'There is a strong sense of vocation, reinforced by the presence of strong self-regulating professions with their own ethical codes of practice amongst public sector employees, a key difference from the private sector' (Ferlie et al, 1996, p 21). This critique is made most cogently by du Gay, in his book, *In praise of bureaucracy* (2000). Similarly, there is some concern that new public management techniques may lead to a decline in ethical behaviour by threatening the traditional public service ethos (Hebson et al, 2003; Maesschalck, 2004).

Concern has also been expressed at the overly top-down manner in which many new public management reforms have been implemented (particularly performance orientation) (Sanderson, 2001), with 'a certain kind of colonization as an explicit goal. The intention is not only to remedy weaknesses in financial control practices but also to challenge the organizational power and discretion of relatively autonomous groups' (Power, 1999, p 97). Power says 'NPM is problematic because it puts itself as doctrine beyond question' (1999, p 93), and du Gay (1996) refers to as it an explicit 'identity project' and a 'cultural crusade'. The implications of this are considered throughout this book, but particularly with respect to the ethos of planning in Chapter Seven.

Whatever its pros and cons, clearly new public management doctrine has, and continues to play, an important role in the reformation of the British public sector. As Ferlie et al comment:

> New Public Management style reforms, taken as a whole, represent a major attempt to restructure the public services,

changing the nature of their organization and management. These reform programmes contain multiple strands with effects at system, group and individual role levels alike. (1996, p 224)

The multiple and strong impacts of new public management on the British public sector mean it is important to try to evaluate it. However, a number of authors suggest new public management reforms have still not been fully and properly examined (Broadband and Laughlin, 1997; Jackson, 2001), and believe in the need for a more reflective reform process (Stoker, 1997). One interesting example of just such an examination is Davies and Thomas (2003), who examine the impact of new public management on the UK police service. Similar work concerning new public management and local authority planning services appears to be lacking to date.

New Labour's third way

The most explicitly normative of the various frames which seem most helpful for understanding the ongoing planning and public sector reforms in Britain is the 'third way'. This was the stated ideology of New Labour, supposedly guiding its approach to public sector modernisation. The 'third way' is most closely associated with the work of academic Tony Giddens, and sought to find a new approach to government located between the New Right ('pure neoliberalism') and the Old Left ('social democracy') (Giddens, 1998). The concept has had a geographically differentiated uptake, being reframed by different political parties globally, but it can be understood in the UK context:

As an attempt to retain the economic gains of Thatcherism, while invoking a set of moral and civic values through which Labour sought to reshape civil society. A new emphasis on issues of citizenship, democratic renewal and social inclusion appeared alongside a continued emphasis on economy and efficiency. (Newman, 2005, p 2)

The defining concepts on the third way, according to Giddens, are illustrated by Table 2.2. It has been argued that the third way is a distinctive philosophy with a relationship to neoliberalism, socialism and social democracy (Le Grand, 1998). Freeden (1999) places the third way between the three great Western ideological traditions of

Table 2.2: The 'Third Way' framework

Social Democracy (Old Left)	Neoliberalism (New Right)	Third Way (Centre-Left)
Class politics of the Left	Class politics of the Right	Modernising movement of the Centre
Old mixed economy	Market fundamentalism	New mixed economy
Corporatism: state dominates over civil society	Minimal state	New democratic state
Internationalism	Conservative nation	Cosmopolitan nation
Strong welfare state	Welfare safety net	Social investment state

Source: Giddens (1998)

liberalism, conservatism and socialism but notes that it is not equidistant between them all.

In contrast to Giddens, a number of authors see the elements of the third way as inherently incompatible, both theoretically and practically. Indeed, in implementing reform, a number of policy, value and cultural tensions have become apparent (Painter, 2005), for example, between devolution and centralisation agendas (Brooks, 2000; Newman, 2005). Such tensions are seen by many as the inevitable product of the third way approach, which fundamentally tries to combine incompatible elements (Freeden, 1999; Cutler and Waine, 2000; Driver and Martell, 2000; Painter, 2005). Indeed, this reflects a wider critique that there is no such thing as the 'third way' at all, but that it is, instead, simply a mask for further 'neoliberal' reforms. Leadbeater (1998, quoted in Allmendinger and Tewdwr-Jones, 2000, p 1385) highlights that the third way can be mocked 'as the ideological equivalent of a society-wider group hug'. It thus offers little analytical strength in furthering our understanding of the deeper impulses behind planning and public sector reform.

Finlayson (2009) argues that rather than trying to fit New Labour into a particular ideological category, we should instead examine the rationality of the administration – more *how* it thought rather than *what* it thought. Hay (1999, quoted in Allmendinger, 2011) suggests that New Labour was heavily influenced by globalisation and ideas about it, and Finlayson (2009, p 11) argues that there was a 'particular rationality and strategy of governance concerned to engender and enable the kinds of people believed to be best able to act in the "knowledge economy"' and that modernisation became the goal itself for the government. Finlayson adds that 'change has consistently been central to the way New Labour understands the problems it faces and it had also consistently sought to address them by trying to adapt values, institutions and individuals to it' (2009, p 16).

The approach adopted to public sector reform by Labour in power saw a strong drive for the modernisation of the state (Roper et al, 2005). Freeden (1999) terms this an 'obsessive focus' on modernising, on change and renewal, while Jones (2001) talks about a 'flood' of policy initiatives. The central themes of the New Labour approach appear to be those of managerialism, partnership, performance and participation (Cutler and Waine, 2000; Newman, 2005). There was a particular focus on efficiency, but some concern with quality as well (Cutler and Waine, 2000; Painter, 2005). New Labour seemed to view the public sector as a 'one-size-fits-all' body trapped in 1945 in desperate need of reform (Blair, 2002, quoted in Davies, 2008). A particular feature of Labour in power was its top-down approach to such reform (Painter, 2005), so much so that former Prime Minister Tony Blair was talking in 1999 about the 'scars on his back' due to a perceived unwillingness of public sector employees to innovate rather than accept reforms (Newman, 2005), while in 2005 he was announcing that change can either overwhelm or improve us, but *cannot be avoided* (Finlayson, 2009). Whatever the realities of New Labour's ideology, and despite the fact that the third way is not a particularly powerful concept in helping to explain and understand planners and planning reform, the rationality of New Labour as focused on modernisation is an important point in the story.

The Coalition's localism push

As discussed in Chapter One, the formation in the UK of the Coalition government in May 2010 led to further rapid reform of the planning system in England. Although still a relatively new government, clear trends are visible in the changes promoted by this administration at an early stage and, at the heart of them, there is a reinvention of a distinct Conservative view of civil society at work and a distrust of the role of the central state, linked to the work of philosopher Michael Oakeshott (Hickson, 2011).

Looking particularly at David Cameron, Kerr et al argue that they view 'Cameronism as: a continuation of Thatcherism; a development in the unfolding forms of neo-liberal governmentality, linked to the process of depoliticisation; and as a movement towards the cartelisation of political parties' (2011, p 193). According to Hickson, a key strand in the ideology of the current government has been the 'civic conservatism' of David Willetts, which argues strongly in favour of free markets, to deliver freedom and prosperity, but also (and in contrast with Thatcherism) strongly in favour of community to sustain values. The institutions of civil society are seen as important to Cameron's Conservatives, and New Labour is seen as having been too reliant on the state to achieve its objectives. In this, there are similarities with the ideology of the Liberal Democrats as seen in the 2004 *Orange Book* (Marshall and Laws, 2004) which, combined, leads to the Coalition government being characterised by a desire for a 'non-state, or even anti-state, form of collectivism' (Hickson, 2011, p 9), seeking to reinvent civil society as 'the big society'. This clear objective can be seen in a range of policy areas where there is a desire to replace the central state – which is seen as crowding out civil society – with local and voluntary activity in an attempt to reassert social responsibility. Neighbourhood planning can clearly be seen as an example of this. Indeed, Lowndes and Pratchett (2011, p 32) highlight that, in contrast to New Labour, who seemed to believe 'a vibrant civil society tends to go hand in hand with a vigorous local council', the Coalition government seem to believe that there is a 'zero-sum concept of the relationship between civil society and the state, whereby more "society" involvement equates to less "state" activity'.

This push for 'big society' has been particularly associated with a politics of 'localism'. Although the anti-state approach that appears to be pursued by the Coalition government is clearly distinctive from that of their New Labour predecessors, there are policy continuities with regard to localism, which began to emerge towards the end of the Labour administration, albeit with some authors questioning the depth of commitment from a government widely seen as wedded to central state paternalism. The 'new localism' is a 'strategy aimed at devolving power and resources away from central control towards front-line managers, local democratic structures and local consumers and communities, within an agreed framework of national minimum standards and policy priorities' (Stoker, 2004, p 117).

Stoker (2004, p 118) argues that it is at the local level that 'the complexity of what the modern state is trying to achieve, the need for a more engaging form of politics and a recognition of the importance of issues of empathy and feelings of involvement to enable political mobilisation … can best be met', and suggests localism can help build social capital and capacity for local solutions to the complex problems of government. He dismisses arguments that localism can lead to parochial narrow-minded individuals dominating situations and that inequality requires national intervention, suggesting it is a valuable part of multi-level governance (cf Walker, 2002, quoted in Pratchett, 2004).

There are very real concerns about localism, however. Lane and Corbett (2005) talk about the 'tyranny of localism', arguing that the decentralisation of governance can result in the marginalisation of minorities. Thus, while community-based planning is widely advocated as a more democratic process, sensitive to local circumstances and able to use local knowledge to minimise social impacts and unintended consequences of plans, power relations at the local level are magnified and become a key determinant. There is often an assumption 'either that "community" is a distinct, relatively homogenous, spatially fixed social group which is characterised by consensus and solidarity or that the process of facilitating the participation of local actors and developing a "community" position is a democratic process and free of the exercise of power' (2005, p 144).

As 'community' is often multidimensional, both in terms of meaning and scale, then participation and consensus must be constructed and in doing so equity problems can occur. Lane and Corbett (2005) cite McConnell (1966), who argues the localism can buttress local elites, enforce conformity and eliminate difference in the political process, actually increasing inequality. This is in contrast to centralised bureaucracy, Ehrenberg (1999) argues, where the very impersonality can actually ensure procedural fairness. As Harvey (1997, quoted in Lane and Corbett, 2005, p 154) notes, community has 'ever been one of the key sites of social control as surveillance, bordering on overt social repression', and localism can actually hinder, rather than promote, democracy.

Whatever the arguments surrounding localism – and it is notable that Stoker himself has recently suggested that under the Coalition government 'we are being offered an anti-state vision of localism, a particular ideological brand rather than an expression of a consensual commitment to decentralisation' (2011, quoted in Lowndes and Pratchett, 2011, p 32), and has also argued that localism is now being used as a cloak for cuts and attacks on the welfare state (Taylor-Gooby and Stoker, 2011) – there is no doubt that a distinct anti-state ideology characterises the current UK Coalition government, and that localism is an important idea for understanding the current direction for planning reform in England (although the implementation of neighbourhood planning in England is also influencing policy in the devolved nations).

Government, governance and planning

A quite different approach is that of 'governance'. The concept of 'governance' now dominates policy and administrative debates (Newman, 2001). Newman outlines the concept as:

> At its simplest, governance refers to ways of governing, whether of organisations, social systems of the state itself.... Much of the literature argues that the governance of modern states is characterised by the increasing importance of networks in both the shaping and delivery of public policy. They represent a shift from the traditional forms of governance through state hierarchies and neoliberal focus on markets as a form of self-regulating governance. (Newman, 2005, p 4; see also Painter, 2000)

While it can simply be a way of describing a system of government, 'governance' is usually used to signify a 'a change in the meaning of government, referring to new processes of governing; or a changed condition of ordered rule; or the new method by which society is governed' (Rhodes, 1996, quoted in Stoker, 1998, p 17; see also Rhodes, 1997).

The term is now a defining (and somewhat over-used) narrative, yet *also* an analytical concept questioning forms of power and authority (Newman, 2005). Stoker (1998) offers five propositions central to thinking about governance (see Box 2.3), while Newman (2005) suggests that governance theory contains three key strands: first, the idea that global political and economic shifts, broadly termed globalisation, alongside an ideological climate hostile to 'big government' has 'hollowed out' the state. The second strand seeks to understand how economic activity is coordinated in contemporary Western society through markets and networks, and how privatisation and the decline of a traditional hierarchical bureaucracy means the state must develop new forms of control such as contracts, targets and service standards. The third strand focuses on social changes, and how in increasingly complex and fragmented societies the state must respond to diversity through a fragmented public realm with knowledge residing in multiple agencies.

Central to the concept of governance is the idea of the diminishing capacity and 'hollowing out' of the state (Rhodes, 1997), with an emphasis on partnerships and the use of strategies to influence the actions of other actors (Newman, 2005; Kelly, 2006). There is, however, some debate about the decline of state power given that while power

Box 2.3: Understanding governance

Stoker offers five propositions and associated dilemmas central to thinking about governance:

1. 'Governance refers to a set of institutions and actors ... drawn from but also beyond government', which can be associated with the tension between the complex reality of decision-making and the usual justifications of government

2. 'Governance identifies the blurring of boundaries and responsibilities for tackling social and economic issues', yet this blurring can lead to a 'responsibility deficit'

3. 'Governance identifies the power dependence involved in the relationships between institutions', which can then give rise to problems associated with unintended consequences

4. 'Governance is about autonomous self-governing networks of actors', but this can lead to democratic accountability deficits

5. 'Governance recognizes the capacity to get things done which does not rest on the power of government to command', but however flexible a government, governance failure may still occur.

Source: Stoker (1998, p 18)

appears to have moved 'upwards, downwards and sideways', and the role of non-state actors has increased (Held, 1995; Rhodes, 1997; Jessop, 2000; Painter, 2000), the state retains regulatory, legislative and taxation monopolies, and national politics and state traditions remain strong (Jessop, 1998; Pierre, 1999; Hull, 2000). Hirst (2000) sees governance as a reconfiguration rather than decline in state power so that 'govern*ance* still operates in the shadow of govern*ment*' (MacLeod and Goodwin, 1999, p 522; original emphasis).

For local government, there has been a re-shaping away from a direct service delivery role to a broader steering and coordination role (Painter and Goodwin, 1995; Newman, 2005). This shift has seen increasing central control of finances, privatisation and commodification of some services and the loss of local autonomy over others, and the expansion of unelected local and regional agencies, as well as a rise in the linkages between the public, private and voluntary sectors locally (Hay and

Jessop, 1995; Goodwin and Painter, 1996). There have been concerns about the democratic accountability of these new structures (Hay, 1995).

This steering role for local government is one way in which elements of planning reform can be understood. For example, Gallent et al (2008) and Tewdwr-Jones (2012) see the rise of spatial planning as intimately linked to the rise of new governance, so that the spatial planning system becomes important as a route to try and coordinate the spatial impacts of the diverse organisations involved with local and regional governance. Interestingly, a concern within the Killian Pretty review (Killian and Pretty, 2008a, 2008b) was that various government departments were increasingly seeing the planning system as a route to delivering their agendas and objectives.[1] This can clearly be linked to the fact that planning has remained in public sector hands, so becomes a route to implement policy in an increasingly fragmented state.[2] The implementation of the 'spatial planning' approach is considered in Chapter Four.

Whatever the precise implications for planning, there are clearly broad changes in the management of the public service context within which planning sits, and the idea of fragmented networks of governance help us to understand that. There is some debate about what is driving those changes. Frequently the 'spectre of globalisation' is raised (Driver and Martell, 2000). Newman (2005) sees the governance shift located in broader patterns of economic and social transformation, with complex social issues such as environmental change eluding traditional approaches to governing. Healey (2006) talks about the drive of experiences of 'government failure', difficulties in delivery, a lack of resources to deliver expectations, a growing criticism of capacity and motivation of government bodies, and overall major shifts in economy, organisation of social life and social values (especially environmental ones) putting pressure to transform government agendas and practices.

Within the geography discipline, governance theory is often concerned with issues surrounding spatial restructuring due to changing economic conditions (Painter, 2000), and Allmendinger and Haughton (2007) talk about the 'motor of globalising capitalism'. Such work is most frequently liked to the 'Regulation School' (MacKinnon, 2001) and the idea of change in economic regimes of accumulation following the 'crisis' of Fordism (Goodwin and Painter, 1996). Seen from this perspective, the immediate postwar welfare state was characterised by the 'highly centralised, bureaucratised states of the Fordist-Keynesian era' which 'converged around the national scale' (Brenner, 1999, p 439). During the late 1970s, a crisis in capital accumulation occurred, and policy makers became increasingly concerned with industrial decline, reforming the welfare state and economic globalisation (Brenner, 2004): the Fordist 'sociospatial fix' (MacLeod and Goodwin, 1999) had begun to dissolve. The response was a re-scaling of the state and the growth of 'governance' (Brenner, 2004). This present era is usually described as 'post-Fordist'. These changes can be seen at the local government level (see, for example, Painter and Goodwin, 1995 and Goodwin and Painter, 1996). Prior (2005) understands planning reform through a regulationist interpretation, seeing the reform as a short-term institutional fix caused by wider changes in the structure of the economy. Elsewhere, Hay (1995) offers an interesting critique of such work, and is concerned about 'economic determinism' (see also Allmendinger, 2001b). Nevertheless, these approaches offer a strong analytical underpinning to our understanding of state modernisation processes that form the focus of this book.

Despite the large body of work associated with understanding this reconfiguring or new division of power associated with governance, there remain some areas requiring further examination (Newman, 2005). The changes have not been even or unidirectional, and there is no clear dualism between a former government of hierarchy to a new governance of competition and partnership. Indeed, the postwar welfare state was not an overly neat and simplified hierarchy but had long involved an interaction between professional, bureaucratic and managerial regimes. There is therefore a continuing need to explore what happens when differing models of governance coincide as governments draw on a multiplicity of different policy approaches, 'not all of them readily compatible with each other' (Newman, 2005, p 4). Similarly, while the governance literature tends to focus on change, 'paradoxically, questions of change in the mode or style of governance tend to be under-theorised' (Newman, 2005, p 4). Finally, 'theories of governance that focus on self-steering capacities of networks and partnerships tend to marginalize issues of agency and individual, institutional and state power' (Newman, 2005, p 20). Through the focus on the role of planners at a time of change in state governance of the planning system and local government, this book is intended to make a contribution to such areas.

Neoliberalism, planning, and the planner: collaborator or resister?

In Chapter One, we introduced the recent and ongoing programme of planning reform pursued by Labour administrations in power in London, Cardiff and Edinburgh, and continued by the UK Coalition and Scottish National Party (SNP) governments, as well as the wider local government and public sector modernisation agendas into which these planning reform agendas fit. The latest round of planning reform is nothing new, there having been a concern about the economic costs of planning during the 1980s, attempts for more efficient public services in the 1990s, and now a focus on burdens on business (Carmona, 2007). Indeed, Durning and Glasson (2006) saw planning as having passed through a turbulent period, with a correspondingly diminished professional status, in the 1980s. They cite Ward (1994), who conceptualised planning reform through the crisis in the Keynesian welfare state. Yet the planning reforms of the last 15 years are more significant than those of 1980s (even if wider public sector reforms were far-reaching, the planning process remained relatively unscathed by the end of the decade despite the institutional context, the role of the state and planning's professional status having been affected). These latest reforms can be understood in terms of the government to governance shift, and through the normative frameworks of new public management and the third way, through the ideology of localism and through the lens of neoliberalism.

Overall, there are clear linkages between the neoliberal, new public management, third way, localism and governance frames, and one can easily draw on all five to understand the modernisation of the state (of which planning reform is a part), but there are also clear differences. The third way, for example, is highly normative in both conception and usage, and thus offers little analytical strength, while the new public management framework does assist in conceptualising public sector reform but again, is a concept that is explicitly normative. These concepts are more about trying to shape reform than understand it. It is also debatable how much the third way really represents the Labour Party while in office as the UK government, just as the ideology of the Coalition government is an ongoing topic for discussion.

The governance and neoliberal frameworks are more analytical in their usage (although there are some criticisms that work associated with governance tends towards the descriptive). Indeed, work concerned with neoliberalism appears to offer the stronger analytical foundations for understanding what is driving, beneath the surface, the processes of public sector and planning reform in contemporary Britain. We would argue strongly that there has been a deeper hegemonic neoliberal structure underpinning the reforms of the state, including planning, that we have been seeing in the UK in recent years. Nevertheless, this book is concerned less with analysing the impulses behind such reforms and more with the role of planners in their implementation.

For our purposes, the brief outlines above are sufficient to help us to understand and contextualise the ongoing process of planning and public sector reform pursued by central and devolved governments in Britain over the last decade. More importantly, however, while there are clear implications for public sector professionals inherent within each, these five frames alone do not tell us enough to fully consider the place of planners in the reform process.

How have planners responded to the changes? And what perceptions do they have of the changing roles they have to perform? Very few planners record their emotional attitudes towards either their work as they are progressing it, or the context within which they are positioned. But clearly they are bound to possess deeper values that either chime or strike against the imposition of new agendas and ideologies. Planners are not neutral participants within a technical or administrative service; they are at the front line of ensuring that either the reforms are implemented or prove to be unworkable. To what extent do planners embrace planning changes, particularly if the newer agendas transpose planning activities into more customer-focused, more participatory and more performance-measured roles? Do planners resist the changes, or might we view them as collaborators in the ongoing reform of the state and public sector? These are the questions we seek to answer in this book.

THREE

The planner within a professional and institutional context

Introduction

The British planning system essentially comprises of a tripartite administrative arrangement, between the political, the judicial and the professional (Regan, 1978). The professional component rests on the assumption that planning is a technical and rational activity, involving the development and application of policies by qualified planning professionals and the deployment of skills gained through formal education and training. Indeed in Britain, membership of the planners' professional organisation, the RTPI, is only awarded to an individual following the successful completion of an accredited university programme, a period in planning practice and peer group assessment of credentials.

The judicial component features the laws or rules of the planning process, which are – to some extent – rigid in their application. Therefore, parliamentary statutes and case law determine how the planning system is to be operated by professional officers. Judicial influence also ensures a greater degree of consistency and predictability within the process and little room for flexibility. The political element rests on government agencies carrying out the planning function, and relies on democratic representation and the encouragement of public opinion. Frequently this results in a conflict between the political and the professional, since politicians can usurp the planner's advice and relegate his or her judgement to one of less importance. This is particularly true of the development control process where decisions on future development are usually considered by planning officers and determined by local politicians, partly on the basis of the professional's advice. Although this is intended to give rise to a stable partnership in the local planning process, it also encourages the possibility of politicisation as politicians refuse to accept professional guidance.

Conflicts between the two parties are difficult to resolve; democratic representatives rely on popular support for their views, planners seek legitimacy from laws, policies, professionalism and good practice. Over the years and in times of problems, it has frequently led the professionals to retrench behind a protectionist guard and to emphasise the role of the expert in local government, or even to deploy tactics themselves to ensure their advice is acceded (Tewdwr-Jones, 1995, 2002). As Hillier (1993, p 90) has remarked:

> Without substantial political power of their own, planners may feel threatened by political pressures.... [P]lanners may succumb to pressure and recommend the policy outcomes which they perceive as the least bothersome for themselves, whilst still appearing to hide behind a neutral, technical facade of rationality.

Very few planning professionals feel the desire to sit back occasionally and assess their role within the planning system, to consider what the reason is for what they are doing, or examine in detail their relationship with councillors of the planning committee, or the changing nature of the local state. Local government practice has provided little – if any – opportunity for development control officers to consider why planning exists, or to question the wider purpose, role and values of planning. The development control process is indecorously assumed to be a valid activity inherent in the commitment of individual staff and the output of each planning department. Planning theorising by the practitioner is, according to Nicholson (1991), an intellectually demanding task, superfluous to the requirements of the job, that may all too easily be abandoned. This should be of no surprise to social scientists. The chasm that exists between the academic and practice sides of the planning profession has been apparent for three decades or more (Allmendinger, 2001a). The practitioner is not interested in the development of an adequate theoretical base to guide decision makers. As McConnell (1981, p 74) remarks:

> A problem with the relationship of planning theory to planning practice of which development control is an excellent example, is that well experienced Planning Officers seldom have to ask themselves what the reason is for what they are doing.

Planning achievements manifest themselves in physical form. They are apparent in the conservation of historic buildings and areas, in the designation of green belts and in the attraction of new housing, retailing or employment developments. None of these achievements ever emerge as a consequence of advancements in planning theorising, as practitioners are only too eager to point out (Poulton, 1991). The officers, who have in some instances the arduous task of liaising with a whole range of different actors over the same development proposal, are forced to dispense with the background information and merely provide the hard facts of each case, to highlight the possible achievements or impacts on the ground. Inevitably, development control decision making in Britain often appears to be divorced from theory, devoid of values and dominated by technical information.

There has clearly been a move away from the postwar consensus of the Fordist welfare state, which is the period when the planning system emerged in its current public sector form in Britain (Reade, 1987; Hall and Tewdwr-Jones, 2011). But the postwar planning world is not just about the planning system; it also about the planners, a welfare state profession during the modern era and within public sector bureaucracy. It is therefore important that we consider how we can conceptualise planners as well as the reform processes. In this chapter we consider how we can think of planners as professionals, as neoliberal subjects and as SLBs. These approaches all differ in the amount of agency attributed to the frontline planner. Following this overview, we also consider the institutionalist approach and suggest that this offers the most useful way of understanding the role of the planner and the relationship between the important structural forces considered in Chapter Two and their own agency in implementing reform processes.

The professionals: planners as technical experts

Public sector planners are frequently understood through reference to their status as professionals, having undertaken approved qualifications and gained membership of a professional society (in the UK this is usually through the RTPI) (Underwood, 1980). There is some discussion surrounding what constitutes a profession, with Middlehurst and Kennie noting that the term 'professional' is neither uncontentious nor static (2001, p 50; see also Ferlie et al, 1996). A variety of new professional organisations, such as town planning and social work, emerged simultaneously to the welfare state. These led to refined conceptions of professionalism compared to older occupations such as law or medicine (Johnson, 1972).

Although the detail may be fluid and contested, there is general agreement that a key feature of being a professional is expertise. A professional will exert a degree of control, or even a monopoly of practice, over a certain body of expert knowledge (Abbott, 1988;

Ferlie et al, 1996), hence Weber comments that professionals bring knowledge to the service of power (quoted in Johnson, 1972, p 15). There are usually clear boundaries set by the profession about what their area of expertise is, alongside standards of training, entry and accreditation (Abbott, 1988; Ferlie et al, 1996). Most importantly, they exercise autonomy and discretion: professionals are expected to exercise discretionary judgement in their field and this is often expected to be exerted by the individual specialist (Lipsky 1980, p 14; see also Ferlie et al, 1996; Becher, 1999; Middlehurst and Kennie, 2001).

Autonomy is exercised at the individual level and also at the collective level, as the profession controls the conditions of practice:

> Three main forms of autonomy may be distinguished. These are: political autonomy, the right of the professions to make policy decisions as the legitimate experts; economic autonomy, the right of the profession to determine remuneration; and technical autonomy, the right of the profession to set its own standards and control performance. (Ferlie et al, 1996, p 169)

Alongside this, professions have traditionally been seen as marked by a sense of altruism, integrity and trust (Johnson, 1972; Swain and Tait, 2007). Rueschemeyer (1983) talks of professions having struck a bargain with society, adopting higher recruitment standards, ethical guidelines and internal controls in exchange for relative autonomy and material rewards through good wages and social status. Box 3.1 shows how the Monopolies Commission defined professionalism in 1970.

A variety of approaches have been adopted to study the professions, with a traditional sociological approach identifying traits of professions such as expertise and autonomy (Freidson, 1984, quoted in Rydin, 2003). This approach asserts that the professions are a special category of occupations with unique attributes (Carr-Saunders, 1928, and Goode, 1960, both quoted in Dietrich and Roberts, 2001). Indeed, until the 1960s the professions were largely viewed as positive influences within society. Durkheim (1992) saw the professions as the socially responsible guardians of moral authority and the public good, characterised by an altruistic pursuit of public service (Johnson, 1972; Campbell and Marshall, 2005).

There has, however, also been considerable academic critique of professions. Shaw is widely quoted as writing that all professions are conspiracies against the laity (1932, cited in Becher, 1999, p 13), and by the 1970s, a growing critique was emerging. Becker (1970) describes

Box 3.1: Defining a profession

Monopolies Commission (1970) definition of professions:

1. Practitioners apply a specialist skill enabling them to offer a specialized service

2. The skill has been acquired by intellectual and practical training in a well-defined area of study

3. The service calls for a high degree of detachment and integrity on the part of the practitioner in exercising his [sic] personal judgement on behalf of his client

4. The service involves direct, personal and fiduciary relations with the client

5. The practitioners collectively have a particular sense of responsibility for maintaining the competence and integrity of the occupation as a whole

6. The practitioners tend or are required to avoid certain methods of attracting business

7. The practitioners are organised in bodies which, with or without state intervention, are concerned to provide machinery for testing competence and regulating standards of competence and conduct.

Source: Cited in Becher (1999, p 7)

professions as a folk concept, contending that what may be labelled the symbolic attributes of a profession are not adequately reflected in the realities of occupational life (quoted in Becher, 1999, p 7). Marx himself was interested in the links between professionals and the class structure (Johnson, 1972), and a Marxist critique questioned the social standing and political influence of the professions (Freidson, 1983; Campbell and Marshall, 2005). A growing image of professionalism as a form of occupational control attempting to control a market for their expertise and exert undue power and influence emerged, with professionals criticised for their monopolistic power and closure (Johnson, 1972; Larson, 1977, quoted in Becher, 1999; Dietrich and Roberts, 2001). The privileged role of professionals to understand the public good and have a more highly developed ethical sense of service provision was heavily questioned (Freidson, 1983; Campbell and Marshall, 2005; see Chapters Six and Seven, this volume), with alternative propositions that professionals actively imposed their definitions of the public good

(Johnson, 1967, quoted in Abbott, 1988). More recently, economic liberalists and public choice theorists have joined more left-wing colleagues in this critique, seeing professionals solely as self-interested groups characterised more by a desire for monopolised power than a sense of the public good (Olson, 1978, and Larson, 1984, both quoted in Rydin, 2003; Derber et al, 1999, quoted in Becher, 1999; Campbell and Marshall, 2005).

Such stringent critique has led to some recent scholarly defence of professionals (see, for example, Freidson, 2001). Burrage and Torstendahl (1990) are concerned that the critics of professions are frequently unable to point to an alternative which would lead to higher ethical codes and moral positions, while Middlehurst and Kennie (2001, p 65) argue that there are numerous benefits to society and the economy of professionalism and of those activities commonly associated with professionals, including economic and service delivery advantages. Campbell and Marshall suggest there might be altruistic goals, even if these are not always achieved in practice:

> While it is certainly true that individual professionals do not always act altruistically, the ethos of a profession as a whole may be constructed in this way, that is, to uphold certain values and standards of behaviour that should represent the norms of those who aspire to be members of that occupational group. (2005, p 210)

Aside from the extremes of altruism and self-interest, an alternative stream of neo-Foucauldian work seeks not to criticise or defend professions per se, but instead to understand them as communities of discourse (Campbell and Marshall, 2005), and as socio-technical devices helping render realms of affairs governable by articulating social problems and the means of solving them (Johnson, 1993; Rydin, 2003).

There is, however, an important differentiation within the institutional framework of professional practice that is vital for considering any models of professions (Johnson, 1972). Some professionals clearly work in contexts that are strongly directed by the state (Rydin, 2003). Glazer (1974), Becher (1999) and Reade (1987) distinguish between traditional professions such as law or accountancy, and the 'semi-professions' (Glazer) or the 20th-century bureaucratised public service professions (Reade, 1987) such as nursing, social work or town planning. A number of sources suggest that these semi-professions, the offspring of the welfare state, have less independence, status and power because they are too reliant on the patronage of the state (Reade,

1987; Freidson, 1992; Kirkpatrick and Ackroyd, 2003). Scott (1966, cited in Davies, 1983) argued that the notions of professionalism and bureaucracy were diametrically opposed, so the welfare state professions were inherently diminished by their public sector context. Others, however, showed that in practice professions and bureaucracy could unite as bureau-professionalism, with expert knowledge becoming embedded as bureaucratic knowledge (Johnson, 1972; Hunt and Shackley, 1999; Rydin et al, 2007). Indeed, Clarke and Newman outline how bureaucratic administration and professionalism were together the two key modes of coordination constituting the postwar public service organisational settlement, drawing on the Fabian ideology of knowledge and expertise as positively valued and of the state as a neutral power standing above society:

> Just as bureaucratic administration promised impersonal fairness, so professionalism promised disinterested service. Bound by professional values and codes, the professional placed his or her skills and expertise at the state's disposal in the pursuit of social improvement. (1997, p 7)

Professionalism is closely linked to public sector reform, particularly through the New Right's critique of professions as inhibiting competition and economic liberalism while using a professional ethic to mask their true practices (Miller and Rose, 1991, quoted in Broadbent et al, 2001; Marquand, 2001). The Monopolies and Mergers Commission even reported on the undue control exercised by professions (1986, quoted in Rydin, 2003). There is strong neoliberal opposition to professions, and their tendency to stress rights based on citizenship as opposed to rights linked to ownership, and a salient feature of new public management has been its criticisms of public sector professions (Kitchener et al, 2001; Kirkpatrick and Ackroyd, 2003). New Labour's attitude toward the professions was, at best, ambivalent and, in power, Labour sought to reform the public sector by attempting to place public sector professionals on tap rather than on top, by standardising practice and introducing more coercive forms of regulation and audit (Boyne et al, 2001, p 2).

Alongside this, there has been an apparent decline in the trust the public hold in government, institutions and professions to uphold the public interest (Swain and Tait, 2007), and this has resulted in new forms of control based on surveillance, notably the technologies of performance of inspection and performance measurement (Dean, 1999; Rose, 1999; Sanderson, 2001). It is questionable, however, whether these new audit systems actually rebuild trust or further drive a decline in trust (Power, 1999). In local government, this has strongly been felt through initiatives such as Best Value (Allmendinger et al, 2003b), which can be seen as a threat to professional autonomy since targets potentially restrict discretion. The reaction of planners to targets is considered in Chapter Five, this volume.

Generally, new public management-inspired reforms have seen the emergence of new organisational forms, roles and cultures, and have aimed to strengthen the power of managers relative to frontline professionals (Ferlie et al, 1996; Sanderson, 2001). Accounting and accounting logic have become tools of control over professions (Broadbent and Laughlin, 2001). Barrett (2004) argues discretion and autonomy, the traditional hallmarks of professionalism, are curtailed by public sector reforms and the emphasis on audit and targets, but Ferlie et al suggest that professionals adapt to reform and retain autonomy in their core tasks (1996, p 7). Indeed, Broadbent et al (2001) believe that the fundamental rationale for professionalism remains, and Kitchener et al conclude that professions are robust in the face of management-led change, and wonder whether deep change in the supervising of professionals is possible at all (2000, p 225). More generally, Ferlie et al (1996) highlight that some professions, particularly accountancy and law, have actually gained through new public management reforms, and there is thus no simple one-way process of de-professionalisation at work in the public sector. Instead, there has been a broad change in the role and functions of professions per se (Allmendinger et al, 2003b, p 765).

We have seen, then, what constitutes a profession, and how public sector reform has had a heavy impact on professionals generally. More specifically, planners traditionally see themselves as welfare state professionals (Rydin, 2003), able to be understood through classic notions of professionalism (Eversley, 1973; Underwood, 1980). Yet planners have also been critiqued as an organisationally and intellectually weak profession (Evans and Rydin, 1997, quoted in Rydin, 2003, p 171). The professional body has a relatively small membership and there is a strand of thought that suggests planners lack a distinct expertise or skill set, and tend to be swayed by fashions (Broadbent, 1977; Reade, 1987; Rydin, 2003; Swain and Tait, 2007). Over the years, planners have been criticised for being a profession marked by muddled policy making (Lindblom, 1959; Campbell, 2002), for being sinister servants of capital interests (Harvey, 1978; Fainstein and Fainstein, 1979; Campbell, 2002) and for being indifferent to difference, exercising flawed expertise (Young, 1990; Campbell, 2002). The result has been a call to replace the expert professional planner with a more collaborative or deliberative practitioner, a community facilitator of collaborative planning (Forester, 1989; Healey, 2006). This Habermasian-inspired approach has been criticised for being too utopian, impractical in practice and power-blind (Richardson, 1996; Tewdwr-Jones and Allmendinger, 1998; Hillier, 2000; Chettiparamb, 2007).

In general, it appears that understanding planning as a profession is a useful way to understand the role of planners and the impacts of planning and public sector reform. Rashman and Radnor (2005) suggest that professionalisation in local government might even undermine the intentions behind central government reform, and Fudge and Barrett (1981) also see understanding professionalism as of central importance for policy and implementation issues, yet understanding planners through this framework alone would mean questions of their agency were insufficiently conceptualised.

The subject of neoliberal reform

As professionals, planners can be understood as objects of the reform process which sees such groups as in need of culture change, there being a need for change in professional identities to realise the reforms (Davies and Thomas, 2003). A quite different perspective, however, sees public servants such as planners as subjects shaped by the neoliberal reform. We outlined in Chapter Two how neoliberalism is frequently understood through the Foucauldian concept of governmentality (Dean, 1999; Larner, 2000), with a focus on the process of rolling back the state and instituting control at a distance. Seen through this perspective, the trick is the creation of self-regulating 'subjects' able to operate a regulated autonomy since they have internalised the goals of government (Rose and Miller, 1992; Newman, 2005; Rydin, 2007).

This framework is often used to analyse how citizens have been recast as consumers and how the public become citizen-subjects engaged in their own governance (Clarke, 2005) but can equally be applied to public servants. The reforms are thus understood as about actively creating and mobilising a new form of professional and so produce consent to the programmes of restructuring (Clarke and Newman, 1997). New public management can therefore be understood as a new disciplinary technology, an identity project enacted at the level of the individual and functioning to inculcate public sector professionals with new attitudes and values (Davies and Thomas, 2003). New forms of knowledge and power become linked to individual subjectivities and new subjects are constituted: government encompasses not only how we exercise authority over others, 'but [also] how we govern ourselves' (Dean, 1999, p 12). For Dean, such a theoretical approach is good because it provides a framework linking questions of government, authority and politics with questions of identity, self and person (1999, p 13).

While Foucault promoted the idea that identity and self are socially 'crafted rather than fixed and essential, many accounts of NPM are overly deterministic, portraying individuals as passive recipients, reacting to a given NPM imposed upon them' (Davies and Thomas, 2003, p 685). While some work adopting this approach is interested in contestation, not simply viewing neoliberalism as a top-down impositional discourse but instead interested in how the techniques of neoliberalism reconstitute spaces, states and subjects in varied, contradiction-laden forms (Larner, 2003; Larner and Le Heron, 2005), there is often a tendency to overplay the uniformity and totality of control in many accounts of managerial reform (Rosenthal, 2004). The danger in such an overly deterministic approach is that it can downplay the level of individual agency possible in responding to reform processes. Rather than being a closed managerial ideology which effectively produces new managerial subjects through disciplinary and surveillance processes that subject individuals to new forms of power and control, there is an active struggle for compliance in practice, and spaces are presented for alternative meanings and forms of practice (Clarke and Newman, 1997). As Davies and Thomas put it:

> Tensions, contradictions and internal flaws are revealed as the individual reflects on her or his self in conjunction with the subjectivizing forces of NPM.... Individuals may challenge the subject positions offered by dominant discourses in a constant process of adaption, subversion and re-inscription of the meanings these discourses offer. (Davies and Thomas, 2003, p 685)

Similarly, Clarke and Newman (1997) outline how neoliberal restructuring is often met both by articulated resistance and passive dissent.

Through this conceptual framework, one might view public sector professionals as both objects of change and subjects through whose agency change is delivered. Although popular in the modern academy, this approach is not without its critics. In fact, a key issue arises here for a project centred on the implementation of reform processes:

At the core of the arguments about the outcome of these changes lie competing views about the relationship between structure and agency. These raise questions about how far people are coerced or constrained, and how far they can determine their own actions, shape their own agendas, form their own definitions of reality, and identify and pursue their own interests. (Clarke and Newman, 1997, p 84)

MacKinnon (2000) argues contemporary governmentality literature finds it difficult to accommodate the possibility of contestation and resistance, and Rosenthal (2004) finds little sense of agency in such work. A sense of agency emerges as a key theme in this book. An alternative view, which focuses rather more on the agency of frontline public servants such as local authority planners, is the idea of street-level bureaucracy.

Bureaucracy at the street level

Arguably, the people most impacted by planning reform are the frontline local authority planners who need to change day-to-day practices and routines. It is these planners, the rule intermediaries, who are at the coalface. They can either be viewed as collaborators or opponents in the planning reform process, and we can consider them through the perspective of being frontline public servants. Although there is a managerial hierarchy within a local authority planning department, planners at all these grades regularly come into contact with the public, and senior staff take all delegated planning decisions, on the basis of case work by junior colleagues. Thus even planning managers remain, in a sense, on the front line. Barrett and Fudge see frontline staff as key to implementing public policy, which depends on understanding:

> ... the administrative structures and the way in which individuals respond and behave in bureaucratic organisations, involving issues such as accountability, rewards and incentives, organisational and professional cultures and limits of authority and control. (1981, p 6)

Frontline work is frequently characterised as uniquely pressurised, with low resources, increasing fragmentation of service provisions and ever higher expectations from the public (Gaster and Rutqvist, 2000). There has been considerable concern that just as frontline public sector work has been transformed and degraded by some elements of reforms, so have frontline professionals been largely ignored by the central elite policy makers responsible for reforms (Jones, 2001).

In fact, this conception of central–local relations is challenged by Rhodes' (1999) work on policy networks. In this, Rhodes shows connectivity between policy specialists and professionals in the same policy sphere at central and local levels regardless of institutional affiliation. He suggests that intervention by central government does not equate to pure control, and that power is constrained in policy networks based on interdependence between members. Other authors refute this, suggesting that pluralist relationships do not themselves reflect a pluralist power structure and that central government players can draw on far greater powers and resources than local government officials (Sullivan and Gillanders, 2005). Beyond the debates about the nature of power, however, this debate also highlights the issue of the agency of frontline officials.

Lipsky's (1980) conception of conception of street-level bureaucrats (SLBs) has been influential, although Proudfoot and McCann (2008) suggest their negotiation of discretion and constraint, their organising discourses and their practical impacts have all been understudied. Lipsky defined SLBs as 'public service workers who interact directly with citizens in the course of their job, and have substantial discretion in the execution of their work' (1980, p 3). A typical SLB in Lipsky's conception would be a police officer or social worker. Lipsky sets out typical working conditions of SLBs (see Box 3.2), which, he argues, heavily shape their practice. In particular, high expectations matched with low resources result in informal rules frequently being established to help manage workloads.

It is interesting that in defining SLBs, Lipsky (1980) highlights the professional context and discretion aspects, particularly in seeing discretion as key to the agency and influence of SLBs as it is the tool through which they can negotiate the constraints and pressures inherent to their practice (Proudfoot and McCann, 2008, p 248). Lipsky suggests that SLBs often engender controversy because of 'the immediacy of their interactions with citizens and their impact on people's lives' (1980, p 8), and highlights the importance of SLBs because their actions 'actually constitute the services delivered by government' (1980, p 3):

> I argue that the decisions of street-level bureaucrats, the routines they establish and the devices they invent to cope with uncertainties and work pressures, effectively become the public policies they carry out. I argue that public policy

Box 3.2: The work conditions of SLBs

Common working conditions of SLBs:

1. Resources are chronically inadequate related to the tasks workers are asked to perform

2. The demand for services tends to increase to meet the supply

3. Goal expectations for the agencies in which they work tend to be ambiguous, vague or conflicting

4. Performance oriented towards goal achievements tends to be difficult if not impossible to measure

5. Clients are typically non-voluntary, partly as a result, clients for the most part do not serve as primary bureaucratic reference groups.

Source: Lipsky (1980, p 28)

is actually made in the crowded offices and daily encounters of street-level workers. (Lipsky, 1980, p xii)

Controversy frequently arises because SLBs 'must be dealt with if policy is to change' (Lipsky, 1980, p 8), highlighting their centrality to the implementation of any reforms to public services (see also Hill, 2004). A defining feature of SLB working conditions is the constant need to interpret and implement new policy, often without sufficient resources or guidance. This means that policy is best studied where it is enacted rather than where it is drafted, because:

> ... the decisions of street-level bureaucrats, the routines they establish, the devices they invent to cope with uncertainties and work pressures, effectively become the public policies they carry out. (Lipsky, 1980, p xii)

In offering such a conceptualisation, Lipsky offers a decidedly bottom-up approach to implementation theory (Hill and Hupe, 2002). Lipsky is not without his critics, for example, those within the Implementation Studies field (after Pressman and Wildavsky, 1979), who prefer a more top-down interpretation (Jordan, 1995). Indeed, Pressman and

Wildavsky's own work falls into this category and is more concerned with prescribing remedies for policy processes by advising how policy makers can exert greater control over policy implementation as opposed to the more bottom-up approach of Lipsky, which sees implementation as 'inevitably a product of negotiations between actors who, in real world situations, have to make compromises and choices between conflicting policy objectives' (Allen, 2001, p 149; see also Barrett, 2004).

More recently, Taylor and Kelly (2006) have criticised Lipsky's model of SLBs as outdated since the rule-making capacity for frontline professionals has been much reduced both by audit and targets and by customer ideals and participation. This leaves a more limited room for discretion and hence a liberation for frontline workers from the dilemmas of street-level bureaucracy. Taylor and Kelly see this reduced discretion as a central goal of new public management since professionals being able to re-interpret policy at street level might be an obstacle to public service reform, but their analysis is slightly muddled. For example, they reject Lipsky's relevance due to reductions in frontline discretion, but elsewhere suggest that the idea the professionals once had considerably more discretion (the so-called golden age) is a myth. Overall, Taylor and Kelly (2006) suggest that while frontline professionals can still have personal beliefs (value discretion) and might still need to deal with unexpected and complex situations, there is less scope for personal rule setting to manage workloads and hence reduced ability to influence (and effectively make) policy:

> Discretion should not be regarded as static. However, for the time being the street-level policy making discretion observed by Lipsky is, for the most part, over. (Taylor and Kelly, 2006, p 640)

This analysis is questionable. The discretion of SLBs has always been curtailed by pressures from the public, from management and from law. Lipsky called it 'relative autonomy'. While there is no doubt that new public management reforms have increased managerial control and reduced professional discretion, this does not necessarily mean the SLB concept is without continuing relevance. There is, however, clearly scope for further consideration of the nature of discretion at the front line of public services, such as planning. Many local authority planners would recognise the working environment Lipsky sketches, and the focus on the agency of these actors appears helpful given the discussion about the degree to which new public management-style reforms subjugate public sector workers. Proudfoot and McCann believe SLB resonates with what Rose (1999) calls the 'how' of government, since 'it is the practices and subjectivities of individual state actors that constitute regulation and enforcement' (Proudfoot and McCann, 2008, p 350). It also highlights the importance of a continued focus on the actual implementation of public policy through empirical study (Exworthy and Powell, 2004; Schofield, 2004).

An implementation-focused agenda seems important for better understanding planning reform. As Schofield and Sausman write:

> The reality of policy initiatives is experienced by the frontline professionals and public servants who do not generally make up policy elites. If the elite system has no feedback mechanism by which to monitor and access the policy reality, the whole arena of knowledge capture based on experience is lost. (2004, p 245)

Thus, despite the importance of such a view from the coalface, a number of authors point to a lack of empirical evidence from the front line (Broadbent and Laughlin, 1997). As Pratchett and Wingfield suggest, there is often:

> An almost implicit assumption that the bureaucracy of local government and the people who staff it, have remained passive participants in the relentless process of change. Little attention has been paid to the effects of recent changes and on the perceptions and values of local government employees. (1999, quoted in Allmendinger et al, 2003b, p 777)

This appears to be a particular problem in the case of planning, where authentic accounts of life at the front line are few and far between (Kitchen, 1997). This book attempts to provide some evidence of the reforms as seen at the front line, and does so through an understanding of planners as SLBs.

Structure and agency: an institutionalist perspective

Major reforms are clearly having an impact on both the structures of the planning system in Britain and the wider public sector context within which it sits. In considering the response of planners to these reforms, a heavily contested question about structure and agency arises (as already noted by Clarke and Newman, 1997). The neo-Foucauldian perspective sees the reforms in terms of external forces acting on individual subjects, while Lipsky would offer quite a different perspective, with his SLBs having considerable agency. Frequently, however, 'theories of governance that focus on self-steering capacities of networks and partnerships tend to marginalize issues of agency and individual, institutional and state power' (Newman, 2005, p 20). Indeed, as Allen (2001) notes, the policy studies literature tends to focus on policies and procedures rather than the important role of individual personalities in policy implementation networks. As he puts it elsewhere, 'structure never quite succeeds in smothering agency' (Allen, 2001, p 164).

While agency is important, the state modernisation process clearly involves major reforms to the structures of the planning system and public sector that appear to be driven by strong underlying structural forces. A key issue of how best to conceptualise the role of planners in such change therefore arises. In studying local government modernisation, Vivien Lowndes uses the framework of institutionalism (see Lowndes, 2001 or 2005), arguing convincingly for its appropriateness in the face of the conceptual challenge of competing narratives of change of local government that highlight both resistance and acceptance of new public management-style reforms. Institutionalism refers to:

> ... the embedding of specific practices in the wider context of social relations that cut across the landscape of formal organisations and to the active processes by which individuals in social contexts construct their ways of thinking and acting. (Healey, 1999, p 113)

It is about focusing on both the formal rules and structures and informal conventions that embody and shape societal values, power relations, interests and identities (Lowndes, 2001).

This new institutionalism emerged during the 1980s, particularly from the work of March and Olsen (1984), as a reaction to the dominant behaviouralist and rational choice perspectives then prevalent in political science which were undersocialised and reductionist, seeing institutions as simply the aggregation of individual behaviours and ignoring the importance of identity and socio-political values (Peters, 1999). It is less a theory and more a conceptual framework (Lowndes and Wilson, 2003), and although originating in political science, this institutional turn has taken many different forms (Jessop, 2001), including historical, rational choice and sociological institutionalism (Hall and Taylor, 1996). In contrast to the old institutionalism which apparently conflated institutions and organisations and assumed structure fully determined behaviour, these various forms of institutionalism instead share a common view of institutions as 'the norms of behaviour and routines of practice embedded in particular histories and geographies' (Healey, 2006, p 324). Indeed, in this context, institutions are not simply administrative and political organisations, but 'the rules, norms and practices that structure areas of social endeavour' (Coaffee and Healey, 2003, p 1982). These are formal (for example, structure plans) and informal (for example, professionalism) rules, customs and conventions that guide and constrain actors' behaviour by determining appropriate behaviour (Lowndes and Wilson, 2003). As the rules of the game, institutions constrain behaviour and change only incrementally, yet as processes, must also be sustained over time (Peters, 1999; Lowndes, 2001, 2005).

Central to institutionalism is an attempt at understanding the relationship between the individual and the setting for determining behaviour (Peters, 1999). In this context, this is understood not through a simple one-way relationship between institutions and actors but instead as a dialectic relationship with actors being shaped by their institutional inheritance and also helping shape it. As a consequence, actors are both framed by forces imposing structuring imperatives on social relations, but also themselves actively constitute and change those structures, making and remaking institutions on a daily basis (Healey, 1999, 2003, 2007b). Structure is not external to individuals but instantiated in their practice (Lowndes, 2005).

Institutionalism therefore draws on the work of Giddens (1976, 1979; Jessop, 2001) and his meta-theory of structuration (Parker, 2000), which is an attempt to articulate a process-oriented theory that treats structure (institutions) as both a product of and a constraint on human action (agency), and thus brings together structure and agency. Giddens (1984) rejects the dualism that treats structure and agency as logically exclusive, and argues they are mutually constitutive. He proposes that social organisational structures influence agents' actions, but that these structures do not themselves exist independently of those agents: the 'duality of structure' (quoted in Yates, 1997).

Although there have been some critics of the structuration approach (see Archer, 1982; Haralambos and Holborn, 2000; Jessop, 2001), structuration has been particularly central to the sociological institutionalist perspective (DiMaggio, 1988, 1991; Barley and Tolbert, 1997). Indeed, of the various strands of institutionalism, it is sociological institutionalism, as promoted by Healey (see, for example, Healey, 2006), which is of interest here. Sociological institutionalism is particularly concerned with shifting attention away from the design of projects and policies and towards their impact on identities, knowledge resources and cultural assumptions, focusing on how concepts and discourses become embedded in practices (Gonzalez and Healey, 2005). There is a particular concern with the role of institutions in sustaining identities and practices and the way rules, norms, routines and discourses are created, become embedded and may then again be questioned (Healey, 2007b). The focus is very much on the process of creating meaning and the relevance of values in defining institutions and guiding behaviour (Peters, 1999). There is an emphasis on social constructivist and relational perspectives on the practice of governance, with individuals seen as 'networked within social units' (Del Casino et al, 2000).

The traditional sociological concept of the institution is as ideal types (the church, the family, the village), whereas in more recent sociological-institutionalist approaches institutions are sets of chronically reproduced rules and resources which constrain and facilitate social actions and also bind social actions in time and space, so that more or less systematic action patterns come to be generated and reproduced (Jessop, 2001; Coulson and Ferrario, 2007). Drawing on its structuration routes, sociological institutionalists hold that organisations and the individuals who populate them are 'suspended in a web of values, norms, beliefs and taken-for-granted assumptions that are at least partially of their own making' (Barley and Tolbert, 1997, p 96). Indeed, through an institutionalist account, the power of structuring forces is not seen as some kind of external force but instead actively constituted through the social relations of daily life:

> These power relations are not outside us. They are part of us, they exist through us. Through our relational webs, we continually reaffirm them, modify them, challenge them. We interpret rules, we make resources work in new ways. (Healey, 2006, p 66)

The result is that, 'the patterning of social life is not produced solely by the aggregation of individual and organizational behaviour but by institutions that structure action' (Clemens and Cook, 1999, p 442), and hence, 'institutions set bounds on rationality by restricting the opportunities and alternatives we perceive and, thereby, increase the probability of certain types of behaviour' (Barley and Tolbert, 1997, p 94). In some strands of new institutional theory, there is an emphasis on the power of existing institutions – as the rules and norms of social actions – to limit the possibility of new forms of social agency (Barnes et al, 2007).

We can therefore understand institutions as acting as symbols of meaning, conveying a sense of how their members should behave – for example, the profit maximisation of a bank or the altruism of a charity – and the result is that organisations are not explained simply through the task being performed or the resources available, but also by the symbolic dimension:

> The fundamental perspective ... is that institutions are systems of meaning and that their behaviour and the behaviour of individuals within them depend upon the meanings incorporated and the symbols manipulated. (Peters, 1999, p 102)

It is important to note, however, that actors can be seen as located at once in a proliferation of different institutions, each with their own value and meaning systems (Tewdwr-Jones, 2002). Therefore an actor in local government may be influenced at once by political, managerial, professional bureaucratic and constitutional rule sets that interact in complex ways (Lowndes, 2001, 2005).

This understanding of an interaction across an institutional matrix with distinct rule sets that may change at different rates and in different directions highlights how an institutionalist framework can help us understand public sector reform processes. An institution may result in decisions by individuals being framed in a certain way, for example, membership of a profession may mean problems and evidence are perceived in a particular professional manner (Peters, 1999). Attempts at reform may prove difficult as new institutions are hijacked or resisted by those benefiting from existing arrangements or seeing new rules as hostile to their interests. Institutional entrepreneurs may exploit ambiguities in the rules of the game to protect (or further) their own interests (Lowndes, 2005). More generally, new rules will be adapted to local environments, organisations and groups that may all have capacity to absorb co-opt or deflect new initiatives (Lowndes and Wilson, 2003). New and old institutions will also often have to coexist, frequently in tension, and change necessarily involves deinstitutionalisation and reinstitutionalisation as there are attempts to eliminate old value systems and to replace them with new ones. Indeed, a key idea in institutionalism is sedimentation: current practices are built on those of the past, so that current practices can be influenced by layers of values and understandings left from earlier times. Thus, institutions are temporal and cumulative (Peters, 1999).

New institutionalism has been criticised for simply stating the obvious, that change is hard to control and for over-emphasising contingency (Lowndes and Wilson, 2003), but overall the sociological institutionalist perspective, drawing on Giddens' concept of structuration, appears to offer a powerful way of thinking about individuals, organisations and change over time. It helps explain why institutional change is not simply a reflection of broader changes in the global space economy, because actors and organisations involved in reform processes exert their agency through their understanding of their cultural, social, political and economic contexts. You cannot simply read off behaviour from theories about structuring processes because 'agents are subject to conflicting structuring forces and are inherently creative and inventive in their responses' (Healey, 2003, p 109), but nor is agency entirely unrestricted; individuals are neither autonomous nor automatons as powerful forces shape our lives, presenting opportunities as well as constraints (Healey, 2006). Seen through this light, a manager cannot change existing work structures single-handedly, for example, but instead workers must enact those reforms (Yates, 1997), and while new innovations such as Best Value involve the establishment of new rule sets and conventions that shape behaviour, transforming governance is not just about formal changes in law and organisational structure but about transforming deeper frames of reference and cultural practices which structure how people make sense of their collective worlds and engage in day-to-day routines (Lowndes, 2005; Healey, 2007b). Such an approach has clear applicability to the planning reform context and appears a powerful frame for understanding the reaction to planning reform by planners at the coalface, and their role in enacting those same reform processes.

Planning reform: a peopled process

Rein and Schön (1993) discuss the problem of 'framing' in policy situations, a topic that is particularly appropriate in analysing both the role of the planner and the development control process. Framing is the phrase used for the integration of facts, values, theories and interests in decision settings. It acknowledges that decisions are formulated on the basis of judgement and values, in addition to technical criteria, and that such decisions vary between individuals and situations. But as Rein and Schön (1993, p 147) acknowledge:

> Framing is problematic because it leads to different views of the world and creates multiple social realities. Interest groups and policy constituencies, scholars working in different

disciplines, and individuals in different contexts of everyday life have different frames that lead them to see different things, make different interpretations of the way things are, and support different courses of action concerning what is to be done, by whom, and how to do it.

The problem for the policy analyst is how to identify and act on these different frames when they are essentially dependent on personal motivation, on the subconscious take-it-for-granted world of individuals. Irrespective of the number of advice notes, good practice guides, and complaints emanating from business and the public, it is not possible for planners to standardise or uniform framings in policy settings. But it is possible to focus on the methodology used in policy framing, on the problems associated with frames and on the reasons why frames are formed in particular ways. In policy and decision settings, individual frames of analysts form the principal issues for conflict and argumentation. Rein and Schön identify these policy and decision settings in two categories: either cooperative – where inquiry into problem issues are meaningfully and effectively assessed – or politically – where differences in opinion are acknowledged between those undertaking the inquiry process and attempts are made to minimise the costs of the win or lose game. Although the former realises the best chance in decision settings for conflict to be transformed into cooperation, it is extremely difficult to achieve in practice. The latter possibility, for individuals to recognise each other's differences and reach best agreement in the light of them, masks the fundamental underlying differences in the formulation of those varying opinions in the first place. But in decision settings, this is probably the most likely problem-solving technique: discussions take the form of negotiation and debate.

There are no real victories in these situations, only temporary ones, since the underlying differences in the individuals' conflict remain unchanged. These underlying differences are further exacerbated in situations where the legitimacy of individuals' frames are brought into disrepute for some reason. In such cases, the relationship between the individuals in the decision settings suffer a breakdown, and questions of legitimacy and credibility unfortunately dominate the issues.

The problem of policy framing between individuals is compounded due to the clash of legitimacy associated with the components of the system. On the one hand, the professional basis to planning takes the form of the technical skills and the decisiveness of objective analysis. On the other, the political basis to decision making requires the professional's role to effectively be subsumed under the necessity for democratic accountability. The planning officer becomes the adviser, a channel of communication between technical criteria and the political process.

Planning reform is much more than just the structures and the changes made by government to the system. Government is a peopled process and planning reform not only has an impact, but must also be put into practice by, frontline planners. These planners at the coalface can be conceptualised as professionals with distinct agendas, as neoliberal subjects, and as SLBs with distinct autonomy, discretion and individual frames. Each of these perspectives can bring valuable insight, and a great deal of useful work has been done considering how neoliberalising reforms can constitute particular subject positions, but there appears to be some evidence supporting the ability of frontline professionals to exert agency in reform processes, although this autonomy is restricted. In trying to frame our understanding of the implementation of planning reform, an institutionalist perspective thus appears to be of great use, helping us to focus on the various rule sets which structure the response of actors to reform processes, but which can themselves be changed through the practices of those actors. It is this approach that frames our work.

FOUR

Process: implementing spatial planning

Plan making process reforms

Although the key underlying principles of the British planning system have remained static since 1947, namely LPAs formulating some sort of plan envisaging policies to manage land use in their areas 15-20 years into the future and then determining applications against these plans and other 'material considerations' (Allmendinger, 2011), there have been some concerted efforts to reform the scope of, and process for preparing, plans since the turn of the century. Naturally these process reforms have captured the attention of practitioners and academics alike, as they cut to the heart of planning practice. The most notable reform over the last two decades has been the introduction of the LDF system of Local Plans in England in 2004, which has explicitly been associated with the drive to move British planning practice from a 'land use' to a 'spatial planning' approach.

On 13 May 2004, the Planning and Compulsory Purchase Bill received royal assent and became law (HMSO, 2004a). The key part of this Act for local authority planners in England was the introduction of a new system of Local Plans, the LDFs, which came into force with the commencement of regulations later in the year on 28 September 2004 (HMSO, 2004b). Keith Hill, then Planning Minister, called the 2004 Act 'the gestation of an elephant', and commented that planning was being put 'back in the driving seat' (cited in Brindle, 2004). Initial hopes were high, with a Public Service Agreement that all LDFs would be in place within three years. However, as we saw in Chapter One, just 22 core strategies (one component of an LDF) were in place by March 2008 (out of 396 English LPAs, including counties that plan for minerals and waste matters).

Something had clearly gone wrong with this flagship component of New Labour's planning reform agenda, which attempted to radically alter the process through which development plans were created in order to modernise a system seen as outdated and ill equipped to ensure delivery on the ground. During the research interviews (conducted in two waves in 2005 and again in 2007/08, as LDFs were being first implemented), the comments by Brian, a planner, were quite typical of the sentiments expressed by many planners:

> "I think the ideas behind planning reform, to make the system more transparent, more accountable, speedier, engage the public more, all those things are entirely laudable and something that we would all want to aspire to. Unfortunately despite those laudable aims it hasn't quite worked out like that. I don't think the government has achieved any of its aims to be quite honest. As far as both the profession and public are concerned the system is far more opaque than it used to be, is more confusing than it used to be, as far as speed is concerned I think it's slower than it used to be, or certainly slower than it needs to be, and no, I don't think it's any more transparent."

Brian spoke in the manner of someone who had genuinely supported the idea of reform but had been severely disappointed by the results. He reflected strong feelings about the LDF system that came across frequently during the course of the research on the legacy of New Labour's reforms.

The main focus of this chapter is on the reaction of frontline planners to the new LDF system in England, since this represents the local spatial planning system with which there has been most progress. We avoid such a distinction between England, Scotland and Wales elsewhere in the book because it is about how local authority planners, as public sector professionals at the coalface, respond to the various reforms having an impact on them, rather than assessing any one nation's reform policy, and because the other key reform agendas are markedly similar between all three territories. But in the case of policy planning, the English reforms clearly go furthest and, crucially, were the only ones actually being implemented at the time of the original research project.

As argued in Chapter One, a considerable literature exists outlining the nature of these broad planning reform agendas, but there has been much less academic examination of the reaction to them from local authority planners. With regard to the plan making reforms that are the subject of this chapter, Shaw and Lord write that 'whilst there has been much discussion and debate as to what spatial planning is, or should be, less attention has been given to how it will be achieved' (2007, p 63). The RTPI and the government did commission a report from University College London (UCL) and Deloitte in 2006 to gather evidence from emerging practice to set out 'effective practice in spatial planning' (Morphet et al, 2007; Morphet, 2011). The government also sponsored a research programme called Spatial Plans in Practice (SPiP), and this report was published in June 2008 (Baker Associates at al, 2008). We consider these further later.

The quotation from Brian, above, gives cause for concern that the achievement of reforms, such as the introduction of spatial planning locally, may be difficult. Brian suggests something may have been problematic about the way the planning reforms were implemented: "it hasn't quite worked out like that". In the first and main section of this chapter, we set out how planners at the coalface reacted to New Labour's plan making reforms, and what this evidence can tell us about the implementation of spatial planning.

Reaction to New Labour's reforms

To gauge broad opinion, the research survey (conducted in summer 2006) simply asked planners whether or not they thought that, on balance, the reform agenda to the planning policy process under way in England after 2004 was a good thing, and whether they thought the reforms helped (or would help) achieve the objective of speeding up and simplifying the planning system. Figure 4.1 illustrates that opinions were evenly split on whether or not planning reform was a good thing, while Figure 4.2 shows that a strong majority (63.1 per

Figure 4.1: Did respondents think that the planning reform agenda was a good thing on balance? (*n* = 535)

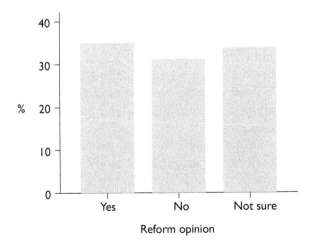

Figure 4.2: Did respondents think the planning reforms would help the objectives of speeding up and simplifying the planning system? (*n* = 535)

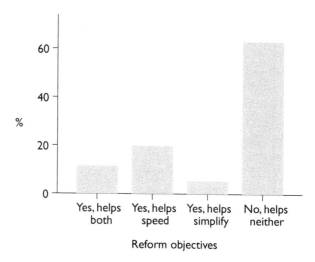

Reform objectives

cent) of respondents doubted that the reforms would help either speed up or simplify planning.

A planning reform Likert agreement on the survey examined these opinions in greater depth by asking planners how much they agreed or disagreed with a series of statements referring to the planning reforms. Table 4.1 illustrates the results. The Likert statements included both positive and negative statements about planning reform that had been used by interviewees during the initial interviews. As Table 4.1 illustrates, it is not simply the case that people were more likely to agree with just positive statements and disagree with negative statements (or vice versa). Instead, a majority of planners seemed to either disagree that the reforms had improved planning outcomes or were undecided on the matter, and yet a majority also either supported the reform agenda or were undecided on the matter. The statements with the strongest agreement were that 'the resource implications [of the reforms] have been underestimated' (by some margin) and 'the reforms increase red tape', while those with the strongest disagreement were that 'the reforms are part of a coherent agenda' and 'the reforms make me consider changing jobs'.

In trying to further analyse this data, we compared the general opinion on the reforms to age, gender and job focus. It was noticeable that there was no significant relationship between a planner's gender or job focus and their opinion on their reforms; there was, however, a significant relationship between a planner's age and opinion. A cross-tabulation revealed that the percentage of people who did not think

Table 4.1: Summary of responses for Likert agreement measuring how much respondents agreed or disagreed with statements relating to various aspects of the direct planning reforms on a scale of 1 (strongly disagree to 5 (strongly agree)

Likert statement	n	Median	Mode	% strongly disagree	% disagree	% undecided	% agree	% strongly agree
The reforms improve planning outcomes	525	3.00	3	7.8	31.0	41.1	19.0	1.0
The reforms increase red tape	524	3.00	4	1.9	9.4	19.7	45.4	23.7
I feel stressed by the reforms	527	3.00	4	5.1	30.3	21.5	36.0	7.0
I feel well informed about the reforms	525	3.00	4	5.5	31.1	18.6	42.1	2.7
The pace of change is too fast	528	4.00	4	2.1	31.2	27.2	31.8	7.6
The resource implications have been underestimated	528	4.00	4	1.3	2.8	9.8	44.9	41.1
The reforms have not been radical enough	528	3.00	2	5.7	39.0	32.8	17.6	4.9
I support the reform agenda	528	3.00	4	6.4	17.2	33.1	40.7	2.5
The reforms make me consider changing jobs	524	2.00	2	12.6	44.8	18.7	18.1	5.7
The reforms have raised the profile of planners	529	3.00	2	5.3	38.0	23.1	30.6	3.0
The reforms increase interest in the planning system	527	3.00	2	8.0	36.2	22.2	30.9	2.7
The reforms are part of a coherent agenda	528	2.00	3	15.0	37.5	37.7	9.5	0.4

the reforms were a good thing increased markedly with age group while the percentage of people not sure one way or the other decreased with age group. In other words, older planners were more likely to oppose the reforms and younger planners were unsure. A chi-squared test showed this relationship between reform opinion and age was statistically significant ($p \leq 0.018$, df = 6). It is possible that this pattern is due to the fact that older planners had worked with the old systems for longer, so were simply more used to them. But one interviewee suggested that the post-2004 spatial planning approach represented a return to the approach of the 1970s; MacDonald calls spatial planning a return of the 'pre-1979 idealism' of planning (2007, cited in Morris, 2007, p 15). Older planners might thus be more resistant to reform as they had seen different planning approaches come and go, which had consequently bred cynicism.

Support for the ideals of spatial planning

As the survey results show, there was some concern among planners that the spatial planning reforms were not achieving their objectives and might not be, on balance, a good thing. Despite such concerns, there was support for the overall reform agenda: more survey respondents agreed or strongly agreed (43.0 per cent) than disagreed or strongly disagreed (23.6 per cent) that they supported the reform agenda (see Figure 4.3).

This may be linked to the fact that there was some comment in interview that the old development plan system needed to change. There was mention of numerous out-of-date old-style Unitary Development Plans (reflecting the 2001 Green Paper; see DTLR, 2001a), and a feeling among some that practices had become irrelevant. Ray even commented:

> "I think land use planning as we had it in the 1980s was very blinkered, quite a technical thing in a bad way. Now we are more open, more comprehensive, more cross-cutting, the LDF is more cooperative than anything ever before."

There was also some degree of support for the proclaimed aims of reforms that Mark called "well intentioned". David stated:

Figure 4.3: Opinion on whether respondents in England supported the reform agenda (n = 528)

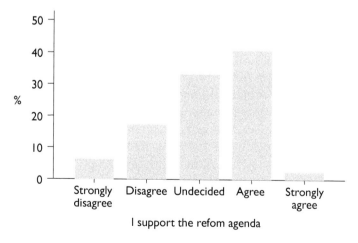

I support the refom agenda

"The spirit of the reforms, the move to create local development frameworks which are more responsive, interactive is great."

In the light of such perceived need for change and support for the aims of the LDF system, those who disagreed may well be reflecting on the practical difficulties encountered in the early stages of the LDF system rather than on the aims as a whole. In addition to support for the overall reform agenda, there was also some support for certain elements of the new spatial planning system.

There was quite strong support for the idea of a spatial planning approach that the LDF embodied. Asked whether or not they thought local spatial planning documents were useful tools, 51.8 per cent of survey respondents agreed or strongly agreed that they were (Figure 4.4). This is supported by the interview data, with many planners commenting supportively on the fact the LDF was a specifically spatial, as opposed to more traditional land use, approach. Many of these were quite forthright in their praise, for example:

"The whole spatial planning approach, it's patently good that the council as a whole should try and coordinate their activities." (Daniel)

Matthew elaborated more, and called it "hugely exciting":

Figure 4.4: Opinion on whether spatial planning documents were useful tools (n = 529)

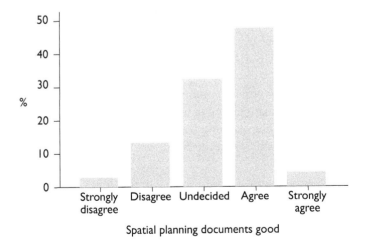

Spatial planning documents good

"I think the thing which excited everybody is the spatial nature of what was local planning, which will now be our Local Development Framework. Hugely exciting, hugely interesting. And that has addressed a lot of the traditional frustrations of planners"

It should, perhaps, be unsurprising to learn that there was some support for a spatial planning approach, given that it makes planning more key as a service for coordinating the delivery of local aspirations. There was also some support expressed in interview for the sustainability approach being promoted as part of the reforms:

"I think the government agenda of a plan-led, sustainability-based system, was actually quite logical and thought through. I think the statutory aim of, you know, the statutory purpose of sustainable, of having sustainable development, is a good thing." (Daniel)

Alongside this, support was also expressed by some of the interviews for the idea that the LDF system was about delivery, about the centrality of a strong evidence base in underpinning LDF documents, and about the nature of having a folder of different documents that could be updated independently rather than one long single document.

Finally, there was support (perhaps unsurprisingly) for the idea that planning was now being seen as a service more central to local authorities than a narrow, regulatory part of local government. For example, David explained that:

"Planning is being seen as a major way of delivering change, achieving vision and of getting connection between spatial delivery of services and improved environments that, that meet political aspirations and community needs."

But there was some concern among other interviewees of not being able to meet raised expectations of planning being centre-stage. Michael stated that he thought planning was now seen as very important, but highlighted how that also meant increased expectations:

"I mean planning, in my career, has waxed and waned in its importance in the eyes of government and particular environment ministers; now it is, planning is seen as very important. Now clearly, with that also, you know, has come some important expectations in terms of the service that we provide."

This final feature that some planners liked about LDFs was thus somewhat of a double-edged sword.

Overall, there appeared to be support for the idea of planning taking a spatial approach, coordinating the spatial implications of activities from across (and beyond) the authority, with a focus on delivery and the physical format of having a portfolio of different documents within the LDF. The note of concern expressed by Michael was, however, by no means the only issue raised with respect to the introduction of the LDF system.

Difficulties implementing the LDF system

Despite the support for some of the principles and objectives of the LDF system, there was a tangibly strong feeling among the planners interviewed and responding to the survey that there were a number of problems with how the new system was working in practice, and that some of these were fairly significant. This issue was raised during the initial interviews, and the most striking evidence of the difficulties came from the spectacular failure to meet the original Public Service Agreement, as already mentioned (see also PINS, 2008, quoted in Baker Associates et al, 2008). This research was conducted immediately following the implementation of the system, as the problems were first coming to light.

There was some concern expressed by survey respondents that the LDF system was not improving outcomes (see Figure 4.5). At the heart of the problems seemed to be the idea that the new LDF system was too complex, as David stated:

> "... we've replaced a, well, a reasonably labour-intensive complex system with another labour-intensive and complex system."

Thus, as Daniel phrased it, the intentions were right, but "the machinery is wrong". Lucy was a little more expressive than most, but the sentiments seemed quite typical of the view among local authority planners:

> "Planning reform, absolutely dreadful. They've made an already difficult and complicated system in England worse,

Figure 4.5: Opinion on whether respondents in England thought the reforms improved outcomes (n = 535)

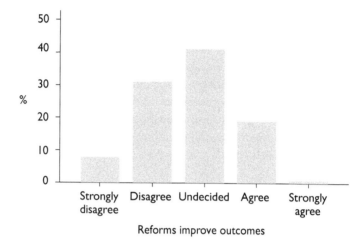

which was almost impossible, and I think they've made it worse; the wheels are coming off the system. I don't think district authorities are going to be able to develop and deliver the LDFs."

The cause of these difficulties seemed to centre round too much process, and problems with complexity. In terms of process, there appeared to be a clear concern about the bureaucracy of the LDF system. A strong majority of 69.1 per cent of English respondents agreed or strongly agreed that the reforms had actually increased red tape (Figure 4.6), despite apparent government aims of streamlining the plan making process.

What this means can be understood with reference to the interview material. Paul evocatively spoke of an "absolute nightmare" due to too much process, while Barry talked about the "bureaucratic extreme":

"Well there are lots of things that are sensible but it's taken to the bureaucratic extreme. So writing a project plan is perfectly sensible but one that now is so complicated that you have to revise on a regular basis and you've got the Government Office crawling over your every typo, every crossed T and doted I, it's process-driven rather than output-driven."

Figure 4.6: Opinion in England on whether the reforms had increased red tape (*n* = 524)

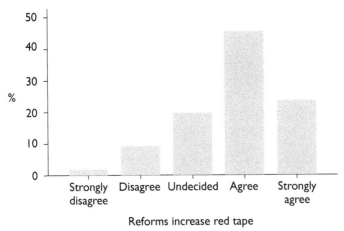

What this appears to be concerned with is that there are more stages to go through when producing LDF documents, more time working through matrices and more documents to be produced, with precise criteria on what sections each document must contain. The result is focusing more on actually producing the documents, rather than thinking about the content of the plans and the outcomes they are meant to achieve:

> "I mean it's quite ironic isn't it, that when you go through the process and it's such a relief when you've produced something, you tend to forget, well, you know, the important thing is actually the content of the document, not having gone through all the processes." (Simon)

Daniel spoke of a "deadly combination" of too much process and too little clarity about aim:

> "There's a, there's a sort of deadly combination of over-control in terms of process and vagueness of aim. So, erm, they're over – there's this monstrous over-complicated, over-controlling process, which, you know, have hundreds and hundreds of steps and components and interrelating bits and connections that they haven't really thought of. But, at the same time, when you sort of try and get a handle on what it's actually all for, it's not at all clear."

The apparent result of this was that documents were produced that few people ever even read.

The concern expressed by interviewees was not just, however, that the LDF system was too focused on process, but also that those processes were themselves problematic. Brian talked about how the processes were time-consuming and cumbersome, and was dismayed at what he saw as having to clear "so many hurdles". A particular concern seemed to be the sustainability appraisal process. Almost all the interviewees raised this. David raised a general issue with the process, which he found to be too resource-intensive:

> "The sustainability appraisals are incredibly unwieldy. They take a long time to do, they're very resource intensive and the end product, frankly, is a major turn-off for both our elected members and our stakeholders and communities."

Other interviewees described the process as too "tick-box", while Margaret was extremely negative of her experience of undertaking one particularly long (and, she claimed, of little practical use) sustainability appraisal:

> "I was just at the point when I was filling out your questionnaire, I was signed off for three months with exhaustion. I developed RSI through five hundred pages of fucking matrices for the SA [sustainability appraisal]."

There was a specific concern that the process was being inappropriately required for all documents, particularly Supplementary Planning Documents as well as Development Plan Documents, which Ahmed described as involving a "monumental" additional workload. Ahmed suggested that sustainability appraisals might be disproportionate, with the resulting documents hugely resource-intensive to produce but little noticed by the public. Some similar comments were made about the SCI requirements.

This negative view of the checks and balances was also raised more generally; there was concern expressed by some that there were too many checks by both regional and central government, despite the emphasis on deregulation, and concern expressed about the role of inspectors during the Examination in Public. The result of this was, apparently, that planners were becoming increasingly of a tick-box, risk-averse mentality:

—

"So, coming back to how it all impacts on us, it means that you're a bit sort of paranoid about, about, ticking every single box. If there's a long way of doing things, you know, if there's an onerous way of interpreting the regulations, then that's what you find yourself doing, because you don't want to take any risks at all." (Daniel)

Alongside concerns that the system was too bureaucratic through too many processes required to produce documents, there was concern that some of those processes were too complex. As evidence of this, Thomas offered the amount of guidance needed to explain the new system:

"You only have to look at the amount of guidance they're having to produce so we can understand it all, to indicate that there's something gone wrong here."

It is worth noting that Caron did not quite agree, commenting that the processes were all quite logical, but the balance of opinion among interviewees seemed to lie more with Thomas.

Linked to this was a widely expressed feeling that the LDF system was too full of jargon, which Margaret described as "Kafkaesque":

"As soon as you look at the terminology, LDS, LDF, LDD, DPD, SPD, you know you're in big trouble, because, you know, civil servants have been sitting there dreaming up a system that's going to be Kafkaesque. And just by looking at the acronyms you know you've got a major problem."

There seemed to be a feeling among planners that such jargon made it harder both to grasp the intricacies of the system and to explain the system to local communities. Jane was particularly concerned about this:

"We've been asked to go out to local parish councils to explain the new system, and you put up this thing that looks like a plumbing diagram and you explain it as simply as you can. And there's a stunned silence. And then they laugh at you. Then they come up afterwards and they pat you on the head and say 'you poor things'."

The result, according to David, could be community disengagement:

"The process is incredibly more complicated now. There's no way that the community and politicians feel engaged in the process. The documents are jargonistic, they're technical, they, they fit what the government has asked us to do but they're a million miles away from what the residents and members can relate to on a day-to-day basis."

Anne also noted that people would rather talk about issues than get to grip with the technicalities of the system. This would obviously constitute a serious concern given the government's objectives for increasing community participation through planning (see Chapter Six).

Complexity seemed to lead inevitably to a sense of frustration, stress and increased workloads for frontline planners. More planners agreed than disagreed that they felt stressed by the reforms (Figure 4.7), although opinion was fairly divided.

Those planners who spoke about this stress in their interviews were fairly expressive as to what was causing it. Mandy spoke of the LDF reforms as being "exhausting" and "like wading through treacle". There were concerns that the LDF system had greatly increased workloads for the policy planners:

"I mean my guys, girls and guys, are working jolly hard, you know, on it. And erm, it, with a new system, again the Local Development Framework, it takes a while to know how much, how much effort is appropriate." (Michael)

Figure 4.7: Opinion on whether respondents in England felt stressed by the reform agenda (*n* = 525)

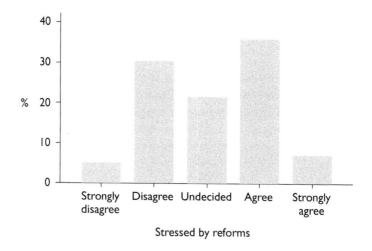

The stress this was causing was raised by three different interviewees, who talked of otherwise reliable colleagues going off work because of it.

In sum, there was genuine concern among frontline planners that the LDF system was not achieving the government's aims, or the generally supported aims of spatial planning, since the system was too focused on bureaucratic process, the processes were considered too cumbersome and the technical jargon hindered public engagement. The result was, apparently, increased stress and frustration for many planners at the coalface.

Causes of problems with Labour's LDF system

The data provide some evidence of what planners thought were the causes of the problems with the LDF system. Overall, it was suggested that the reforms had suffered from a lack of hands-on planners being involved in the design of the new system. George said the reforms had been "largely done to us rather than us being involved". Rob went further, specifically implicating civil servants in having made the new system more complex than it needed to be:

> "As with a lot of what the government does, I think the noble ideas are being mangled by civil servants, and especially by legal people, and translated into legislation that, under the banner of simplifying planning, has made it more complicated."

What one planner termed the "dead hand of the civil service" probably reflects a longstanding critique of the British civil service as "too generalist". This is unsurprising but not entirely fair, given that some qualified planning professionals are employed by central government. It echoes a wider imagery of central government as somehow too remote and out of touch with the realities of planning at the coalface and what reforms mean practically, on the ground. It also speaks to an idea that the planning profession should be driving the reform of planning itself, although it is not immediately apparent what sort of system this might have led to.

Implementation issues

From the research data, there appeared to be three specific issues that planners thought had caused the problems with the LDF system in practice. The first concerned implementation issues: the idea that

---

original proposals for the LDF system had been good, but that there was something after conception that had led to problems. Jane felt it was the fault of poor, rushed legislation:

> "There are logical and legislative inconsistencies. Woefully inadequate legislation, regulation, internally contradictory, desperately unclear, very badly written and drafted, which really doesn't make life easier."

More common was a feeling that the fault lay in what Neil termed the "struggle" to make the new system work on the ground. Julia specifically used the term "implementation":

> "It's obviously not been thought through beforehand, how you actually deal with the minutiae of implementation, you know."

There appeared to be a number of strands to the implementation problems.

First, some survey respondents felt that they were not well informed about the reforms. As Figure 4.8, indicates, more planners agreed than disagreed that they felt well informed about the reforms. What those who disagreed meant by this is hard to discern from the survey material, but interviewees were more forthright in saying that the problem was that the guidance from central government about the new system had been slow in coming. Matthew commented quite sharply:

> "I mean, the guidance didn't come out until six months into the process, terrific, bloody marvellous!"

Richard described late guidance as his major frustration:

> "I think our major frustration has been the lack of clear guidance and the way we've had to fumble around, really, to be perfectly honest, in, in actually understanding what it is the ODPM expects of local authorities. And I suppose, my honest opinion is that I'm not sure that they really know what they expect, and I'm being quite candid here: it, it feels like a make-it-up-as-you-go-along approach."

Anne gave the specific example of late guidance on the sustainability appraisal process meaning her team had had to start again with the

Figure 4.8: Opinion on whether respondents in England felt well informed about the reforms (*n* = 527)

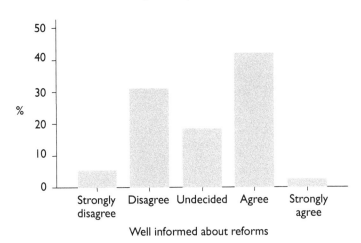

Well informed about reforms

process. Margaret felt this reflected the fact that while local authorities were tied to strict, centrally monitored targets on the time taken to produce their work, the same did not seem to apply to central government. Such a 'them and us' perception of central government appeared common among local government planners.

There was also concern that there had been poor guidance to the government's own agencies, with the planning inspectors initially appearing to planners to have widely divergent expectations as to what constituted a sound plan. More recently, delays in guidance and inconsistent advice were recognised by Baker Associates et al (2008) as a probable cause of some of the difficulties experienced putting spatial planning into practice. O'Toole (2004) notes that the information requirements of those on the ground implementing policy are often different to those of lawmakers writing the original policy, and this is still not fully recognised.

A second implementation issue appears to have surrounded resources. The survey data show very clearly that the overwhelming majority (86 per cent) of respondents thought that the government had underestimated the resource implications of implementing the LDF system, as illustrated by Figure 4.9. Twelve interviewees also specifically mentioned resourcing, Rob calling it the biggest issue:

"I think resources is of number one importance … we are spreading ourselves very, very thinly and it's the depths at which we can explore the issues that are being compromised, so I think resources are the biggest issue."

Figure 4.9: Opinion on whether respondents in England felt the resource implications of the reforms had been underestimated (*n* = 528)

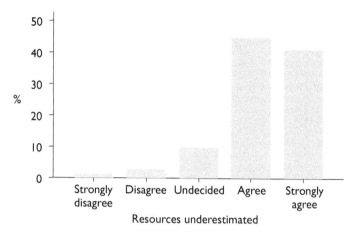

Some thought the LDF system needed more resources per se than the old-style Local Plans system it replaced, Daniel calling it "an enormously resource-intensive system". Some thought the information requirements and evidence gathering were the reason for resource issues, while Jo specifically mentioned the time and resources required to do sustainability appraisals on every document produced. For other interviewees, the concern seemed to be less the LDF system requiring greater resources per se, and more that it was simply a new way of doing things:

> "One of the biggest issues for me is making sure I've got the resource to deal with any change." (Paul)

Therefore the problems result from the fact that implementing any change on the ground necessarily takes resources, as staff have to learn new systems and ways of doing their jobs, but budgets are limited and the local government workload does not stop while people get to grips with new tasks.

These resource issues were apparently greatest for small, rural district councils where the policy team may only be a couple of officers. The LDF system does allow for authorities to club together to produce 'joint' documents, a provision specifically designed to help smaller authorities facing such struggles, but a variety of political and institutional factors seem to have led to a low take-up of joint working opportunities in the first few years of the system. Furthermore, some planners admitted that their authorities did not appear to fully appreciate that the LDF was not simply a 'new name' for the Local Plan but something combining elements of the former Local Plan and the former Strategic Plan and requiring consequentially greater resources and new skills to produce. Alongside this, there was apparently no transfer of staff or funding from county councils to district councils with the abolition of Strategic Plans, despite the fact the core strategy involved much work that would have formerly been done by the county planners.

All LPAs, not just district authorities, will have further been impacted by the fact that the government's PDG tended to focus on rewarding development control performance as opposed to plan making (see Table 4.2). Alongside this, with the government targets focusing on development control performance (see Chapter Five), the leadership of many authorities apparently focused more on development control (to avoid being 'named and shamed' by the government) and less on the policy side of planning. Combined, these factors explain why so many planners thought the resource requirements of putting the LDF system into practice were underestimated by government. Resourcing must be considered a major factor in explaining why authorities have experienced problems with the LDF system. These concerns chime with a wider trend for resources to be a key issue in the implementation of any policy: Hill (2004) outlines how there is a tendency in the UK for Parliament to pass legislation that local government must implement without adequately resourcing the policy implementation (despite the Regulatory Impact Assessment process). Indeed, Lipsky (1980) suggested that the struggle of working with chronically inadequate resources was a defining characteristic of street-level bureaucracy. More recently, the government's own consultants have acknowledged resource issues in implementing the new LDF system, which they see in terms of financial concerns (particularly surrounding evidence gathering costs), staffing concerns (particularly the recruitment and retention issues then prevalent in British planning) and skills concerns (particularly concerning understanding the new spatial planning approach) (Baker Associates et al, 2008).

Partly linked to these resource concerns was a third concern about unrealistic expectations, as Jim commented:

> "I think the early expectations were too high. The process of change from the local plan to the LDF requires you to do complete new plan from scratch in three years. With a lot of process. And for the first cycle, three years isn't enough. Every single local authority in the area is struggling. Not just a bit struggling, seriously struggling."

Table 4.2: History of the Planning Delivery Grant allocations

History of PDG (Planning Delivery Grant)	
2003–04	• PDG introduced • Based solely on performance against the time-based performance targets
2004–05	• Performance against development control targets, plan making performance, housing delivery in areas of high housing need, location of Enterprise Areas and performance at appeal
2005–06	• Two main portions of grant: one part for exceeding BVPI 109 targets (split between major, minor and other) and another part for performance improvement on DC time targets • A further element for high housing demand areas/growth areas receive a proportion of funding • 25 authorities in Pathfinder market renewal areas received £160,000 each • A further element for progress on e-planning (Pendleton scores) • £5,000 per Enterprise Area in an LPA area • A receiving authority's development control grant element is abated where the authority has a higher than national average number of its negatively determined planning applications overturned on appeal
2006–07	• Majority of grant (£49,504,151) for exceeding BVPI 109 targets (split between major, minor and other) • Further allocations (£20,686,199) made for improvements in development control performance • High Housing Demand and Growth Areas element • The 25 local authorities in Pathfinder areas each receive an allocation of £100,000 • A total of £20,799,900 is allocated for plan making to be divided equally between all authorities who meet the criterion • A total of £7.7 million is allocated for progress in e-planning • £1,743 per Enterprise Area in an LPA area
2007–08	• Majority of grant for exceeding BVPI 109 targets (split between major, minor and other) • A receiving authority's development control grant element is abated where the authority has a higher than national average number of its negatively determined planning applications overturned on appeal • 25 authorities in Pathfinder market renewal areas received £100,000 each • £1,743 per Enterprise Area in an LPA area
2008–09	• PDG replaced with HPDG (Housing and Planning Delivery Grant) • Housing element: all LPAs with net additional housing completions equivalent to at least 0.75% of their existing housing stock will be eligible for the housing element • Planning element has four components: demonstrating sufficient land for housing in line with Planning Policy Statement 3 (PPS3) (40%); delivery of Core Strategies and DPDs allocating more than 2,000 dwellings (50%) • Joint working on the production of DPDs (6%) • Publication of a Strategic Housing Market Assessment (4%)

Sources: ODPM (2004b, 2005d); CLG (2006, 2007c, 2008d)

Jim then linked this issue back to resource issues, highlighting the considerable resources required to produce the first of the new-style plans:

"I think you could easily have given people five years to do the first one because you've got to do all the background research from scratch. It's got to be robust, all those guidelines around soundness require you to start with good sound information."

The three-year timeframe emerged in an indicative programme produced by the then ODPM and was adopted as a central government Public Service Agreement. LPAs did have some freedom to set out their own timeframes in their strategies, but there was clearly strong pressure to conform to this three-year model. This strongly suggests that if central government had simply had 'lower expectations' to begin with, by giving authorities more time to produce the first round of the new LDF documents, then some of the perception of there being big problems with the new system would not have occurred as rapidly as they did.

Critiquing New Labour's approach

While some of the concerns associated with the LDF system surround the nature and implementation of the LDF itself, other factors strike a chord with a wider critique of New Labour's way of governing. First and foremost here is the criticism that there has been 'too much reform'. Mike spoke of this as an issue having an impact on all policy areas:

"... this government's obsession with change for its own sake, and it seems right across the board, not just planning but a whole range of other issues as well. As far as I can see it seems to have this need for constantly revisiting things, constantly revising things, to give the impression, presumably, of action."

Barry, meanwhile, directed his comments just at planning:

"Planning reform? It's just one thing after another, isn't it? There doesn't seem to be any real, clear direction where the government are going, where they want to go. There is no possibility for anything to settle down before there's one reform after another."

Both of these quotations are suggestive that reforms introduced by Labour administrations were taxing on frontline staff simply because there had been so many reforms, rather than anything to do with the individual reforms per se. As a result it was difficult for planners to get a grip on planning reforms since the field was undergoing continual change and reform.

The questionnaire data, however, show a more mixed view about the pace of change, with slightly more agreeing than disagreeing that the pace of change was too far (see Figure 4.10). Nevertheless, some planners clearly believed that the pace of change had been too fast, and that this had caused problems for implementing the reform agenda. Baker Associates et al (2008) suggest a constantly changing context can create uncertainty and make implementing the new LDF system more difficult. On a broader level, this also echoes with critiques of New Labour's reform agenda from beyond planning, as highlighted in Chapter Two.

A similar wider critique of New Labour has been that it suffered from a lack of 'joined-up thinking', and this was suggested numerous times as a reason for problems associated with planning reform. In the survey, 52.5 per cent of respondents disagreed or strongly disagreed that that planning reforms were part of a coherent agenda, as opposed to just 9.9 per cent agreeing or strongly agreeing (see Figure 4.11).

Lisa and Gerard both specifically used the term 'schizophrenic' when describing the mixed messages coming from government. Such mixed messages apparently led to a lack of clarity on the front line about the government's agenda:

"I'm never quite sure of what the precise planning reform agenda the government currently has." (Michael)

Figure 4.10: Opinion on whether respondents in England felt the pace of change had been too fast (*n* = 525)

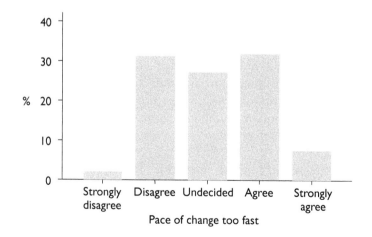

Figure 4.11: Opinion on whether respondents in England felt that the reforms were part of a coherent agenda (*n* = 528)

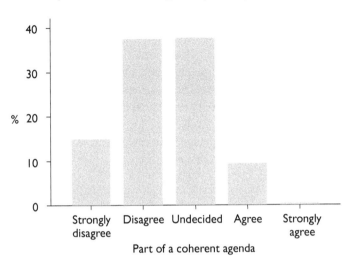

This links back to the idea that the government itself had not been 'joined-up' enough in its approach to planning reforms such as the LDF, as planner Jane mentioned:

"And I think what we're suffering from really is this government not being joined-up in its thinking ... we find ourselves, at local level, trying to resolve issues that really should have been sorted out elsewhere. For example, disputes between government agencies and the government."

In some cases, there had apparently been cases of conflicting advice from different arms of government, and several planners gave specific examples of this.

This may reflect differences of opinion between various parts of government, particularly HM Treasury and the then ODPM, as Allmendinger (2011) highlights. In a similar vein, there was some concern that there were conflicting messages coming from central government about the future of the planning system, particularly with HM Treasury critical of the planning system as an obstacle to business at the same time as the LDF system was being put into practice (MacDonald, 2007). Daniel outlined the result of this, at the front line:

"In a variety of ways, I think the planners are being pulled in too many different directions. There is a fundamental contradiction between, they expect you to be business

friendly, they expect you to do what communities want
and they expect you to deal with sustainable development."

Many of these competing agendas may simply reflect deeper tensions
running to the heart of New Labour and its 'third way' (see Freeden,
1999; Painter, 2005). A common critique is that, rather than being truly
a party of the 'third way', triangulating economic and social democratic
concerns, Labour was decidedly pro-market and pro-business (Cutler
and Waine, 2000; Cammack, 2007).

It was suggested in one interview, however, that it was not just central
government that had created mixed messages:

> "It's not just the government, it's the mayor, it's other
> organisations like CBI, CPRE, you name it, everyone's got
> an agenda, everyone's issuing guidance, making suggestions
> for reforms, it means, we talked about this the other day,
> more time is spent responding to other people's agendas
> than actually setting your own agenda." (Barry)

Barry succinctly highlighted the difficulties of contemporary
governance, with many functions no longer the sole province of local
government. The result was planners having to spend time reacting
to competing agendas that they felt had an impact on their ability to
implement reforms such as the LDF system smoothly, even though
one of the key drivers to the move to a spatial planning approach was
precisely to provide a forum for local 'joining-up'. Nevertheless, this
reflects wider concerns with the difficulty of integrating policy streams
in what Exworthy and Powell (2004) term the 'congested state', where
implementing new policies requires both vertical and horizontal
integration of objectives and action among a number of different
organisations. Therefore, despite New Labour's exhortations about the
importance of 'joined-up government', there was actually a growing
feeling of a lack of coordination for many local actors (Exworthy and
Powell, 2004). This does, however, reflect a longstanding concern far
pre-dating New Labour.

Politics of time

A final theme emerging in the interview data was that it was less a
case of problems with the reform and more just a case that it was too
early to fully evaluate the LDF system since the new approach would
take time to 'bed down' (this was in 2007). Such sentiment reflects

ideas that early expectations about the LDF system were, perhaps, too high, but that given time, the system would operate more efficiently. Tewdwr-Jones et al suggest that 'there is a real change in the system that may take a period of time to settle down' (2006, p 549). The danger of hyperactive reform therefore becomes that people are still learning one system and seeing how it works in practice when that system changes yet further. Schofield highlights the fact that 'in effect, public managers have to learn a range of new and detailed techniques in order to implement what are often ambiguous policy directives' (2004, p 283), and that is something that takes time. Such a conclusion is not, however, inevitable since it may be that if there is something fundamentally wrong with the mechanics of a new system, it will not bed down in time but could simply get worse.

Something that came across very strongly during the interview process was a genuine sense of disappointment and frustration with the LDF system. Feelings were much stronger on this than on just about any other issue discussed. As time went on, however, it appears that not only were planners getting more used to the new system, but also that central government acknowledged some of the problems and modified the LDF system. Planners were becoming aware of these forthcoming changes towards the end of the in-depth interviews:

> "I think the bottom line is that it's far too complicated and I think the government's realised this and it trying to simplify some of the LDF approach to make it less of sledgehammer." (Les)

The reforms involved a change to the regulations governing the production of LDFs, a new version of government guidance PPS 12 and a new online 'plan making manual' giving examples of good practice and talking planners through the stages involved in producing LDF documents (CLG, 2008a; PAS, 2008). These went live on 27 June 2008 (HMSO, 2008). Among other changes, they gave authorities greater discretion over the stages taken to produce Development Plan Documents; removed the need for sustainability appraisals for all Supplementary Planning Documents; and made it possible for an inspector to allow authorities to go back to a particular stage in the production of a Development Plan Document that was unsound, rather than forcing the LPA to go back and start the document again from scratch. A new Public Service Agreement target was introduced for local authorities to have all Development Plan Documents in place by March 2011, and additional funding to support this was made available through the new Housing and Planning Delivery Grant (HPDG), which focused on plan making rather than development control (CLG, 2008d).

The Coalition reacts

After 2010, the Coalition government embarked on yet another period of planning reform. Planners, already reeling from the ongoing wave of reform introduced by the New Labour government, reacted with disdain. But the new reforms represented what the Coalition termed a radical programme of 'localism', with a commitment to enhancing participation and the transfer of powers to neighbourhoods and citizens away from regional and local governance actors and government agencies. The Coalition's take on localism relates to whether elected local government is the level through which some of these measures are delivered, or whether local government is bypassed in favour of direct involvement and decision making by citizens, neighbourhoods and community groups.

Key criticisms of the Local Plan preparation system over the last two decades of the 20th century and first decade of the 21st century, as advanced by government, representatives of the private sector and other users of planning, are remarkably constant. The Coalition did not wait to judge and assess the 2004 and 2008 LDF reforms before embarking on the case for planning reform. The criticisms related to: the speed of plan preparation and an accusation that planning was overly bureaucratic and a constraint on business and growth; that it possessed a narrow focus on land use matters concerning the physical development of land and was unable to integrate with strategies of various organisations; that the quality and quantity of stakeholder involvement was poor; and that the public felt remote from planning decision making (The Conservative Party, 2010). Some of these criticisms are indeed genuine and relevant issues of concern, but some were repeated as assertions with little in the way of evidence to back them up. The Conservative Party's *Open source planning* Green Paper of March 2010 stated:

> The planning system is vital for a strong economy, for an attractive and sustainable environment, and for a successful democracy. At present, the planning system in England achieves none of these goals. It is broken.
>
> … we need a planning system that enables local people to shape their surroundings in a way that … is also sensitive to the history and character of a given location.

Our conception of local planning is rooted in civic engagement and collaborative democracy as the means of reconciling economic development with quality of life ... the planning system can play a major role in decentralising power and strengthening society. (The Conservative Party, 2010, p 1)

Although there is merit in some of these ideas, not least the idea of encouraging direct civic engagement and linking planning to issues of place and cultural identity, the criticisms towards a broken planning system seem a politically expedient viewpoint to justify further radical ideological reform without an adequate case being made for the necessity for change. The resultant legislation, the Localism Act 2011, abolished aspects of the national and regional spatial planning processes (although there has been quite a saga surrounding the abolition of RSSs, which has been handled in a somewhat cack-handed manner by the government; see Donnelly, 2011b; Millar, 2012), but retained LDF. At the level below districts and boroughs, a new neighbourhood level of planning was introduced to be instigated by new Neighbourhood Forums preparing Neighbourhood Plans, bringing the citizen directly into the planning process by transferring some power away from LPAs to a more localised scale (DCLG, 2011b; Holman and Rydin, forthcoming).

LDFs are required to conform to the provisions of a newly released National Planning Policy Framework (NPPF) of March 2012 (DCLG, 2012a) setting out the key issues and principles for the planning process to address, and which sought to rename them Local Plans. But they will also be required as an integrative tool on a range of strategic local matters and will continue to act as a way through which other non-planning bodies can be brought into the policy-making process. Despite the political commitment to enhance the neighbourhood level after 2010 alongside local government practices, frontloading for policy development will still be required. The Coalition government believes that it has set clear objectives to ensure faster, more inclusive and better-quality local plan making in future.

Criticisms have been directed in particular at who will be able to establish Neighbourhood Forums, whether they will have to reside in the neighbourhood concerned, and what legitimacy they will have to take decisions for a larger constituency when they will not be an elected body. There has also been concern at how any deliberations of a Forum, or the contents of a Neighbourhood Plan, will dovetail with the local authority's LDF, or the Sustainable Community Strategy and its local governance partners. The other concern relates to the fact that ministers have insisted that the contents of the NPPF de facto take priority at the local and neighbourhood scales where there is no up-to-date and relevant plan in place. LPAs have until March 2013 to ensure the LDF contents match up to the NPPF, otherwise the LDF will be deemed to be of less weight. The speed of preparation of LDFs will therefore be set back as a result of the conformity issue, and may also now additionally have to face in two directions simultaneously, as a bridge to national policy issues and as a strategic view for Neighbourhood Plans.

There are anecdotal accounts of a number of authorities slowing work on their LDFs prior to the 2010 General Election because of a belief that they would be abolished if the Conservatives gained power, and by the end of March 2011, just 98 LPAs had adopted 'sound' core strategies (PINS, 2011). The next year is likely to be an interesting time given the pressure now exerted through the NPPF to adopt Local Plans, but in a time when authorities are facing funding cuts and making staff redundant. 'Institutional entrepreneurs' (Lowndes, 2005) may be able to use local political fear of the results of not having an adopted plan to protect policy planning staff posts because of this, but it is likely to be a difficult time for many planners at the coalface. There have already been concerns among practitioners at the resource levels required to support Neighbourhood Plans, which LPAs are duty-bound to provide assistance to (Johnston, 2011; Smulian, 2012), and rapid progress with Local Plans in a time of a changing policy context is likely to be tricky.

Putting local spatial planning into practice: past, present and future

There was clearly a feeling among local authority planners that the implications of implementing local spatial planning were not sufficiently considered by the Labour government. Similarly, while it would be unfair to say that the planning academy tended to ignore the views of the front line – publications such as those by Morphet et al (2007) and Baker Associates et al (2007) are authored by planning academics who have gathered information from local government case studies (both for government consultancy projects) – there is clearly an implicit assumption in much published work that planning reform is simply about the policies as formulated by central government. A plethora of work (drawn on in Chapter One) outlines the legislation, policy and systems established by the reforms, but there has been little consideration of what happens when those systems are put into practice.

In one sense this implies a top-down conception of implementation whereby central government formulates a policy that is then put into practice. But it is actually more indicative of a view that almost totally ignores implementation considerations (top-down or bottom-up) altogether, apart from setting targets for local authorities to aim for. O'Toole (2004) notes that despite the acknowledged importance of implementation, and 25 years of scholarship in the area, lessons about basic change management have still not been learned. In this chapter we have attempted to interrogate the space in which the local spatial planning reforms were put into practice. Looking at New Labour's process reforms, the evidence seems to suggest there were significant difficulties in the implementation of the LDF, despite the strong support for central government's stated reform aims, and for ideas like spatial planning. This has been noted elsewhere:

> There seems to be considerable enthusiasm for the changes which spatial planning has brought about. Some planners told us that this was the kind of planning that they had always wanted to practice from the earliest days in their careers and that they now felt more fulfilled in their work. (Morphet et al, 2007, p 29)

There is, however, a feeling that in practice the reforms did not fully meet the stated aims.

The most pressing concerns were that the implementation was not adequately resourced, that the reforms actually led to increases in bureaucracy and that the reforms did not always seem to be part of a coherent agenda. Particular concerns were that the LDF system was over-engineered and too process-driven. These difficulties were blamed on such factors as the role of an ill-informed civil service, late guidance and inconsistent advice from Government Offices, insufficient resources, early expectations being too high and there being too much reform in too little time. Despite the commonality of views expressed by planners working across the country, we see a distinct sociology of the reform in that older planners seemed more resistant to the reforms than younger ones.

The difficulties experienced implementing the LDF system are well recognised, and the CLG subsequently made changes to the system (CLG, 2008a). It is interesting to note, however, that there appear to be a variety of opinions as to where the problems lay. Planners at the coalface clearly believed (perhaps unsurprisingly) that the problems were external to them, for example, late guidance from government or insufficient resources. The government's commissioned SPiP research, however, seemed to lay the blame more squarely with planners:

> It is clear that achieving the objectives behind the reforms is reliant on a cultural change in the way that professionals conceive what plans are for, and how they are prepared. Many authorities point to insufficient resources in terms of people, but the gap is increasingly about skills. The skills needed to make spatial plans ... are not those that have been emphasized in the profession for the last two decades. (Baker Associates et al, 2008, p 10)

This accords with the longer-standing concern for a 'culture change' in planning (Inch, 2010). Shaw and Lord (2007) seem concerned about factors inherent to the introduction of the new system, such as 'information overload' and 'procedural uncertainty', while Morphet et al (2007) were particularly concerned about the role of Government Offices.

The reality of where 'blame' lies for the slow progress on LDFs by local authority planners probably involves some combination of all these factors: the approach of individual planners, local leadership and council 'buy-in', available resources, speed of introducing a radical new system and the guidance to accompany that (with some factors varying by location). Pressman and Wildavsky suggest that 'the essential constituents or any policy are objectives and resources' (1979, p 182). While the original objectives for the LDF system seem clear (if a little complex), the resources needed to implement the new system did not seem to have been sufficiently accounted for by central government. Only after several years of slow progress did policy planning become a focus for grants through the HPDG, and this rewarded those authorities with adopted core strategies rather than supporting those who had been struggling with them. This contrasts with other areas of planning reform, such as public participation, where the resources seem to have been less of an issue than tensions within the wider policy arena, meaning a lack of clear objectives (see Chapter Six, this volume).

Whatever the causes, in so far as a target for all LDF documents to be in place within three years of the start date for the new system has been spectacularly missed, one could ask, has this been an example of 'implementation failure'? Mazmanian and Sabatier (1989, quoted in Hill and Hupe, 2002) talk of implementation failure if the outputs of a process are not consistent with original objectives, and Hood and Dunsire (1978, quoted in Hill, 2004) talk of 'implementation gaps' when there are shifts of policy between the initial objectives and the final outputs due to difficulties with implementation. And in a sense, yes, there does appear to have been a failure in the implementation of the LDF policy in so far as the initial targets were not met. There is also some evidence to suggest why, contained in this chapter and other sources. Indeed, Wolman (1981, quoted in Exworthy and Powell, 2004) argued that such implementation failure would occur without clear objectives, mechanisms to achieve those objectives and resources to fund the implementation.

But such a question is probably the wrong one to ask. We are now seeing widespread adoption of core strategies, and CLG adapted its own policies to aid this, clearly partly due to feedback from the front line. Indeed, part of the problem appears to have been that initial government and planner expectations were simply too high. Nadin comments that 'It may take some years and further iterations of development documents before real fundamental change is realized' (2007, p 56), and Pressman and Wildavsky (1979) suggest that professionals do gain new skills, but not as fast as new policies come in. More fundamentally, however, the 'implementation failure' thesis has traditionally been associated in implementation studies with a top-down approach. DeLeon writes that 'talk of "implementation failure" risks making explicit, normative judgements' (1999, quoted in Hill and Hupe, 2002, p 10), since it suggests a simple model of implementation involving frontline staff passively implementing policy made by a small section of central government without any change to that policy or factors influencing it during the course of implementation. This is quite distinct from the ideas about SLBs, as discussed in Chapters One and Three. As Barrett and Fudge (1981) commented, if implementation is about putting policy into effect, then any compromise involved in doing that is 'failure', but if implementation is about 'getting something done', then compromise is not 'failure'. In so far as CLG compromised around the LDF system, it is clear that getting something done, namely, implementing a new local spatial planning model in English local authorities, is what mattered more than the precise mechanics of the process.

More generally, in looking at the response of frontline planners to the implementation of local spatial panning, we can see a number of key themes emerging. The roll-out of modernisation appears to raise questions about resource implications, about the skill and capacity of frontline staff and about time. In particular, with regard to questions of time, there are issues about how long it should take new systems to 'bed in', and whether reform is better implemented as ongoing or periodic modernisation. Through the institutionalist lens, we can also see that the implementation of new approaches to plan making sediment against layers of values and understandings left from earlier times and earlier systems (institutions being temporal and cumulative, as Peters, 1999, notes), and inevitably practice on the ground will therefore differ from what the designers of new policies may have intended. We develop these themes further in Chapter Eight. The planning reform agenda has involved much more, however, than just implementing a new process, a new spatial planning approach. In order to fully understand the planning reforms from the perspective of local authority planners, we need to explore some of the other major reform elements that have an impact on local authority planning. The next chapter considers the impacts of managerialism of planning through the efficiency agenda, and most particularly, through audit and targets.

FIVE

Management: the efficiency agenda, audit and targets

Growth of an 'audit society'

Just as the growth of local spatial planning, examined in Chapter Four, has been the major reform for policy planners, so the growth of auditing and targets appears to have been the major reform facing development control planners over the last decade. Michael was quite clear on the impact of targets for his professional life:

> "Yes, well they've had a very, very significant effect on the job, there's no question. I mean if I had to say, if I had to say the most significant impact on the last six years for me, it has been the targets."

This comment was common. At first sight, just as spatial planning apparently increases the role for the professional planner, so the growth of a central government target setting and performance auditing agenda might seem to restrict it, reducing autonomy and discretion. As we saw in Chapter Two, this can be conceptualised as a response to declining trust in public sector professionals to guarantee value for money and secure the 'public good' (Swain and Tait, 2007). There is therefore reason to believe planners might respond to such an 'audit explosion' (Power, 1999) in a wholly negative way: 'The processes of organizational change demanded by NPM and its auditing agencies produce varying forms of conflict and resistance' (Power, 1999, p 97). Through examining the data on how frontline planners responded to New Labour's centrally driven agenda of targets and inspection, this chapter interrogates this diagnosis of simple resistance, before considering the continued currency of efficiency for local government and planning.

In Chapter One, we outlined the growth of the target and inspection regime that this chapter is concerned with, and how, for planners, the most important target across Britain over the last decade has been that measuring the speed of processing applications. There is little specific literature on performance management in planning (Carmona and Sieh, 2005), and few accounts published by frontline planners themselves (Kitchen, 1997). Houghton (1997) suggests this is due to a lack of reflexivity in planning. This is in contrast to other public sector professional domains. For example, a number of serving frontline police officers have written books (PC Copperfield, 2006; PC Bloggs, 2007) and online blogs (Inspector Gadget, 2008) which offer a highly negative account of centrally imposed targets due to the apparent huge distortions that they cause. Much of this negative discourse is reflected in the broader academic literature about auditing and targets.

There are perceived problems about defining objectives for public services (Power, 1999), and it is argued that auditing and targets tend to concentrate on mere economy and efficiency, rather than democratic accountability impulses or other specific public service objectives (Lane, 1997; Power, 1999; du Gay, 2000; Andrews et al, 2003). Local authorities often have a wide variety of stakeholders with conflicting views, which are not easily captured by indicators (Jackson, 2001; Boyne et al, 2002a), and there is a tendency for these to focus on processes rather than outcomes (Sullivan and Gillanders, 2005). There are also concerns that targets, in particular, tend to be unsophisticated and reductionist (Carmona and Sieh, 2005) and restrict public dialogue (Power, 1999; Boyne et al, 2002b). Carmona and Sieh (2004, 2005, 2008) highlight planning as a particularly difficult context for performance measurement due to the range of uses and desired processes and outcomes, and because it is very difficult to isolate the value added by the planner.

A further concern is that quality becomes solely about conformity with the targets and audit processes (Power, 1999; Sanderson, 2001; Barrett, 2004; Rashman and Radnor, 2005). Ball et al even suggest that central performance management could actually 'impede the development of deeper cultural change' (2002, p 15). As well as issues with the targets themselves, there are concerns that targets cause distortions and 'dysfunctional side effects' (Power, 1999; Hood, 2007; McLean et al, 2007; Carmona, 2007; Carmona and Sieh, 2008). The net result can therefore be that while performance on the targeted aspect of a service improves, overall there are negative consequences as the non-targeted aspects of performance suffer (Boyne and Chen, 2006). There are also suggestions that:

> When a measure becomes a target, it ceases to be a valid measure. Performance indicators are subject to gaming, in the sense of hitting the target but missing the point. (McLean et al, 2007, p 114)

Instead of increasing trust and improving performance overall, a number of scholars suggest that the systems of auditing are more a top-down national agenda focused on central control (Houghton, 1997; Power, 1999; Ball et al, 2002; Carmona and Sieh, 2008). Indeed, the growth of audit is often understood by conceptualisations that draw on Foucault's ideas of governmentality, as introduced in Chapter Three (see, for example, Rydin, 2007). Beckford asserts that 'the only way to solve the problem of quality in the service sector is simply to employ trained, educated staff and grant them the freedom necessary to do the job' (2002, p 278), and there has been concern that Best Value focused too much on performance management and too little on people management, leading to worse staff relations within local authorities (Higgins et al, 2004).

Despite such negativity, Grace argues that audit and inspection are powerful instruments for achieving better public services, from which 'significant benefits' have flowed (2005, p 576). In planning, Carmona and Sieh (2004) suggest that performance indicators in planning have effected change in organisational capacity and structure, and led to introducing new systems. It has also been argued that performance management has helped encourage best practice and focused minds, encouraging a more reflective approach (Power, 1999; Carmona and Sieh, 2008). Likewise, it is argued that indicators have increased accountability (Grace, 2005), strengthening managerial accountability to the public interest (Boyne and Chen, 2006). A further strand in the literature suggests that it can be argued that there is nothing wrong with targets that focus on process since optimum processes might lead to optimum outcomes (Carmona, 2007), although this is very much open to debate. It is also suggested that some might see distortions as acceptable if the overall effect is improvement (Carmona and Sieh, 2004).

In its widespread use of targets, New Labour was obviously convinced that the overall impact would be positive. Professionals from a number of professions, such as healthcare and policing, dispute this through their first-hand accounts. In planning, there is less literature on the topic generally, and very little in the way of frontline accounts. Empirical research data therefore provides a vital insight, and insight which has a continued currency given the continued drive for an 'efficient' planning system being pursued both by central (in particular) and devolved government in Britain.

Strong reactions to New Labour's targets

Local authority planners under New Labour held some strong views on targets – the survey (conducted in summer 2006) revealed fairly clear trends in opinion about targets (Table 5.1). The statement with the strongest agreement is that 'targets are too obsessed with speed', something with which almost 90 per cent of respondents agreed or strongly agreed. There were also strong majorities agreeing that 'auditing and targets have increased the amount of stress for planners' and that 'auditing and targets have altered the way people work'. At the other end of the scale, over 83 per cent of respondents disagreed or strongly disagreed that 'targets correctly assess the quality of planning outcomes', over 70 per cent disagreed or strongly disagreed that 'targets restrict scope for professional discretion', and almost 60 per cent disagreed that 'auditing and targets have improved our relations with the public'.

Table 5.1: Summary of responses for Likert agreement measuring how much respondents agreed or disagreed with various statements relating to auditing and targets on a scale of 1 (strongly disagree) to 5 (strongly agree)

Likert statement	n	Median	Mode	% strongly disagree	% disagree	% undecided	% agree	% strongly agree
Auditing and targets have improved the performance of the service	599	3.00	4	4.5	25.5	22.9	43.4	3.7
Auditing and targets have raised the profile of planning in the council	599	4.00	4	3.5	26.5	16.7	47.1	6.2
Auditing and targets have increased the amount of stress for staff	599	4.00	4	0.0	3.5	9.2	57.4	29.9
Auditing and targets have altered the way people work	597	4.00	4	1.2	7.0	12.4	63.8	15.6
Auditing and targets have improved our relations with the public	599	2.00	2	10.7	48.4	31.1	9.5	0.3
Targets should be abolished	601	3.00	2	0.0	42.9	29.0	15.6	12.5
Targets are too obsessed with speed	600	4.00	4	0.0	7.0	3.2	46.5	43.3
Targets restrict scope for professional discretion	601	2.00	2	22.0	49.9	13.1	13.8	1.2
Targets correctly assess the quality of planning outcomes	600	2.00	2	39.8	43.3	10.7	3.8	2.3
Targets place too much emphasis on applicants	597	3.00	3	0.0	28.0	38.0	25.5	8.5

The factors that lay behind these trends can be discerned using the interview material (from the interviews conducted in 2005 and again in 2007–08), which we review later in this chapter. Initially, however, we wish to examine any significant relationships within the survey data.

Within the target regime, as noted in Chapter One, there are some post-devolution differences between England, Scotland and Wales. The percentage of major applications determined in 13 weeks, or minor or other targets determined in eight weeks, is a longstanding measure that has been audited by government in all three territories. But it is in England, through these planning targets becoming part of the Best Value indicator set and linked to financial rewards though PDG, that there has been the greatest emphasis on the targets. There is some suggestion of this geography in the literature (see, for example, Andrews et al, 2003).

While it is clear that there are some differences between England, Scotland and Wales, analysis of the questionnaire data shows no significant relationships between location (in terms of nation, or in terms of region within England) and opinion on any one of the 10 items on the Likert agreement (using chi-squared tests). In other words, the opinions about the targets show similar trends in all parts of Britain. Given this, we do not break up my detailed examination of the reaction of planners to the targets in the remainder of this chapter geographically, and do not think it is a central determinant of attitudes about targets.

That said, the interview material suggests that there is some national geography to the impacts of the targets on the professional life of the planner. This can be understood as differences in emphasis, but not trends in opinion. For example, in Wales, there has been close monitoring of the processing performance by the Welsh government but no financial rewards. In Scotland, there has been less emphasis on meeting the targets and no PDG at all. Comments in the research interviews reflected the literature (see, for example, Downe et al, 2008). The result of this differing approach to targets in Scotland was apparently that authorities did not consciously try to push performance. Nevertheless, analysis of the survey data suggests certain sociological factors are more important than these geographical factors in determining reaction to the targets.

The targets are partly driven by the desire to effect a culture change in planning, thus it might be expected that planners who had been in the profession longer, and are thus more engrained in its culture and bureaucratic practices (Hull, 2000), might be more resistant to targets. The survey data were examined to see if there was a significant relationship between age, gender or job focus and opinion on any one of the 10 items on the Likert agreement (again, using chi-squared tests). There was no significant relationship with gender. In Chapter Four, we saw that older planners were more likely to be resistant to the new local spatial planning systems. No such relationship was found with relation to targets; there were no significant relationships between opinion on any one of the Likert agreement statements and respondent age. More surprisingly, there was no significant relationship overall between job focus and opinion. Development control and policy planners often work closely together, which may explain why reactions are so similar, even though policy planners in interview tended to say targets had an impact on development control colleagues much more than on them.

There was, however, a significant variation by job seniority in responses to four of the statements about targets.[1] Cross-tabulations clearly indicate that planning managers were more likely to agree that targets had improved performance than less experienced planners. Several possible reasons why are evident in the interview data. However, senior planners were also more likely to disagree that targets improved relations with the public and were more likely to agree that the targets restricted discretion. Thus, while there was a strong relationship between job seniority and attitudes to targets, this was not simply a more positive view. Planning managers, like their junior colleagues, can hold both positive views of some impacts of targets and negative views of other elements. In the next section, we examine the most commonly cited negative consequences of the planning targets during the New Labour years.

Perceived problems with the targets

As Table 5.1 suggests, there were some strong concerns surrounding the targets expressed in the survey responses, and the interview data also contain a number of complaints about the targets made by planners. Brian was quite succinct:

> "If you're not careful you'll end up valuing the measurable rather than trying to measure the valuable."

Paul even went so far as to comment that targets were "one of the worst things to happen to planning in many years". He then raised concerns about the relationship between speed and outcomes. Many of the complaints raised by planners echo longstanding concerns from beyond planning about central government targets. Overall, these concerns fell into four broad categories: ideological concerns about the targets, complaints that the targets measured the wrong thing, complaints that there was too much emphasis placed on the targets, and complaints that the current target regime had led to unintended consequences. Since these closely reflect material already considered at length in existing academic literature, we offer only a brief consideration of each.

Some of the most cutting criticisms of the target regime came from those questioning the ideological impetus behind the targets. Although only discussed by five interviewees, strong feelings were expressed. There was concern that targets represented a mistrust of local government by central government, and suggestions that there was an 'unhealthy' central government obsession with targets. Margaret went further than any other planner in discussing what lay behind this target culture, her opinion of which had been influenced by a recent documentary she had seen on television:

Margaret: "One of the ideas was what came out of America – of course, it always comes out America – is that people aren't capable of working towards the common good. They will only work towards what's in it for them."

Interviewer: "So this was someone's idea."

Margaret: "Yes it was a psychopath, needless to say. John Nash. And it only works for psychopaths and economists, you know, and everybody else would work towards the common good. But all this thing was set out on the assumption that people need motivation because they will not work towards the common good, they will look at what's in it for them. So therefore you bring in targets. And you bring in targets and people will be motivated and work towards targets. And I think targets are the most dangerous thing that the government ever brought in."

Margaret therefore implied that the targets were a result of a philosophy that argued that people could not be trusted to work for the common good on their own. Although she was the only planner to go so far in exploring target culture in her interview, this reflects the academic critique of public choice theory (see, for example, Hay, 2007).

More common, however, was the sense that the targets were being driven by the desire to ensure that planning was both more business-friendly and also run according to a more "business-like culture", as Richard put it. Three planners all mentioned Conservative former Environment Secretary Michael Heseltine, and his comment in 1979 about planning locking jobs in filing cabinets:

"I think we've been singled out as a department dragging our feet and holding up business. What did Heseltine say? That we were tying up jobs locked in filing cabinets. So we've had it in the neck since then, haven't we?" (Mandy)

Such commentary doubtless reflects pressure being placed on government to speed up the planning system by certain business interests (see Chapter One).[2]

Much more common than any attempt to unpick the ideological impulses behind the targets were concerns surrounding the specific impacts of the targets on planning. A key concern was that there was something wrong with the targets themselves because of their focus on speed, their apparent blindness to outcomes and their impacts on the professionalism of planners. With regard to this focus on speed, the survey statement about auditing and targets that elicited the strongest feeling was 'targets are too obsessed with speed'. Some 89.8 per cent of respondents either agreed or strongly agreed with this statement, with not a single respondent, out of 600, strongly disagreeing (see Figure 5.1).

This survey data thus presents a fairly unambiguous message: New Labour's target regime was too obsessed with speed as the sole measure of planning performance. In the interviews it was suggested time and again that the targets were too centred on speed alone, and that this could have an inverse relationship with quality:

Figure 5.1: Opinion on whether 'targets are too obsessed with speed' (*n* = 600)

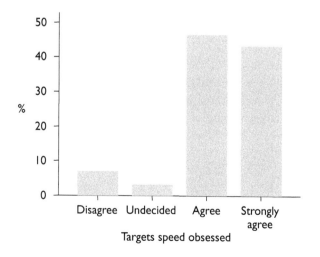

"It's put huge pressures on us as officers because we are so target-orientated, so target-driven and I think on occasions that has been at the cost of quality ... some discretion definitely needs to be in place when you've got important schemes. But it's a fine balance." (Patrick)

Andrew developed the theme when he suggested that in the longer term planners would be judged in terms of what was actually built on the ground rather than the time taken to process an application:

"Quality of the decision is the important thing, rather than the target. Yes it mustn't drag on for months and months and months, I agree ... but if an application goes over a week because you're trying to get an improved landscape scheme or a highways improvement, I don't see the problem, at the end of the day you're judged on what is built not how quickly you can turn it around."

This was a common critique.

The statement about targets with the second strongest feeling in the Likert was: 'the targets correctly assess the quality of planning outcomes'. Some 83.1 per cent of respondents either disagreed or strongly disagreed with this statement, as Figure 5.2 illustrates. The

Figure 5.2: Opinion on whether 'targets correctly assess the quality of planning outcomes' (*n* = 600)

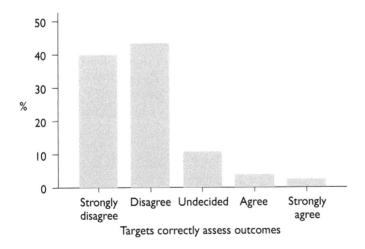

interview material provides further evidence of what outcomes planners were concerned about:

> "The point that I make, and I've made it to the Assembly, is that when you walk down the street and you look at a good quality, well-designed, well-placed, strong material building....What it won't have labelled to it is how long it took for the consent to be given." (Phil)

During interviews it was clear that planners saw their role as broadly shaping the development of local areas in line with the desires of the local community, and the constraints, opportunities and needs of the local environment and economy. For a development control planner, like Phil, an ideal outcome was therefore a well-designed building in the right place, but there was clear concern the targets did not capture such outcomes.

There was also concern that the targets were leading to resources being concentrated on processing applications quickly rather than achieving good outcomes. The implication was often that the planner actively added something to development proposals when they were being mediated through the planning system and that that was a process that needed a certain amount of time. The argument is that the whole reason for having professional planners process applications is that they are able to exert judgement and actively improve applications. Thomas therefore felt the targets were diverting planners' energy from their proper purpose:

> "So we've turned what should be an important and interesting and rewarding exercise in adding value to the scheme, making a difference to the scheme, improving the trees, saving the building. That's what planning is about, that's the purpose of it. And from the planning officer's point of view that's what should be rewarding but they haven't any time and energy to do that. All their energy is consumed in ticking the boxes and their time runs out because – time runs out!"

The statement "time runs out" is particularly evocative, but the comment about box ticking highlights a further concern about the current target regime: its bureaucratic nature.

There were comments about "endless form filling", and Les said that the Best Value indicators had created excessive bureaucracy and had been a "humbug". Simon, meanwhile, said that some of the recommendations on how to improve performance could be rather mundane, focusing on ensuring they had sufficient rubber stamps and ensuring "that every piece of paper that comes in to the authority is date stamped." This image of planning being somehow reduced to the completion of endless paperwork was further developed in some of the other interviews, with targets having apparently made the job a "boring treadmill". What this seems to suggest is that the targets somehow de-professionalised planning by reducing it to a 'tick-box exercise', where there was nothing more than a 'treadmill' of work 'under the cosh'. Thomas was clear about this reduction of the role of the planner and was particularly concerned about the impact on newer planners:

> "What I'm concerned about is that particularly among the younger planners who are sort of coming into the process, just see the job as a piece of paper processing. It's all about making sure that all the forms are filled in.... At the end of the day you've then got to, having spent a lot of time ticking boxes, you've then got to watch a clock."

There was some support for this in that one of those younger planners, Gwilym, stated that:

> "I like being a development control officer. What motivates me is the eight-week period. I'm quite competitive when it comes to the eight-week period."

So the target was what motivated him, just as Thomas had feared. This was by no means a universal feeling (see Chapter Seven), but it lends support to concerns within the profession about the impacts of the targets (see, for example, Swain and Tait, 2007). Such concerns have been reflected in the professional press (see Figure 5.3).

A third key area of concern was that there was simply too much emphasis placed on the targets. Wyn felt there was a danger you might miss the wider picture, while Mandy expressed concern that the time-based targets had become a way of life:

> "What impacts have targets had on you? It's just become a way of life. It's become, I think we're so entrenched now and people don't question it now."

Figure 5.3: Suggestions of a colonising target culture in *Planning*

Source: Cowan (2007b)
Reproduced with permission of Rob Cowan.

Linked to this was the concern that there were no reductions in targets and their auditing even if an authority performed well. Richard was disappointed at this, commenting that, "we've done enough to deserve a bit of a break, really". This runs counter to what one might expect: Rydin (2007) suggests that good performance should allow some release from central government scrutiny, what Vincent-Jones (2002, cited in Rydin, 2007) terms 'responsibilised autonomy'. Although there was no specific survey question linked to this issue, the feeling that there was too much emphasis on the targets seemed widely spread within the profession, particularly in England.

Finally, there was a strong strand of thought evident in the data that argued against the targets because of the consequences – unintended by central government – that they were having locally. Roger spoke about the inevitable distortions associated with the time-based processing indicators:

"If you just have a process-driven indicator, speeding up planning applications, you'll end up with huge distortions in the planning system.... People will sacrifice the output quality and the actual achievement of some benefit for the community, just for the sake of pursuing that single objective. And, while one half of me always feels I'm glad that planning has not got a plethora of performance indicators, another half of me gets very irritated that the ones we have, are so poor, so process-driven, and really don't address the fundamental issues of, what are you trying to achieve here, you know?"

Others spoke similarly about the 'game playing' that occurred due to the targets. Thomas discussed the consequences of such 'game playing':

"It's having a corrupting effect on the service partly because planning authorities play games. They say, no, we're not accepting this planning application; it hasn't got everything with it. Now before BVPIs came along, before the Planning Delivery Grant came along, we would just say, all right, we'll take it in…. Now it doesn't actually help the developer at all, it makes our statistics look good but it doesn't help the developer. At the other end of the process you get a situation whereby consultations have run on and you're unhappy about certain aspects of the scheme but the eight-week deadline is looming. You then have to make a decision as to what you should do. Should we carry on processing the application? Should we approve it or should we refuse it? Now in a lot of cases, too many cases I suspect, we are making a decision before that scheme is ready. We're either refusing an application which with another round of negotiations could be okay or we're approving something which really could be improved but we've run out of time."

Thomas suggested a number of unintended consequences that the time-based processing targets were having. Each of these deserves some further examination. If we follow a planning application through its lifespan, from germination to development, from the pre-application to the discharging of conditions stages, then the data suggest problems at just about every stage. At the first stage, there is evidence that some authorities were making planners focus on the actual processing of applications so much that there was no time to engage effectively with developers at the pre-application stage:

"Some authorities have taken the view that they've got to concentrate on meeting their targets, and they will not have any pre-application discussion with developers … that is actually counterproductive." (Dick)

Once applications were received, a number of interviewees reported that they felt like they were rushing applications, without being able to give due consideration to all the issues. Mandy expressed concern about the possible implications of such rushing of applications:

> "In 20–30 years' time do we turn around and look at what happened and think, 'Oh God we've re-created the 70s'. Do you know what I mean? Because we've rushed decisions through."

This clearly returns to an idea that the professional planner could somehow add something extra, if only there was sufficient time to do so. Such a framing is unsurprising, given that the profession is likely to seek to justify why a qualified professional is needed to process applications rather than just an administrator.

What the professional can add might be related to the ability of a planning officer to negotiate changes to applications prior to the granting of planning permission. Numerous planners reported in interview that they felt that as a direct result of the targets they could no longer negotiate as much as they would have liked:

> "You know we do not negotiate, we've pretty much stopped negotiating on planning applications.... Once you get the application, we're into determining, the consultations, determining, and that's the way we managed to hit our targets." (Michael)

This lack of negotiation was, apparently, leaving planning officers with two key options to meet targets: either passing applications that were not fully up to scratch, but applying conditions to the planning permission; or refusing applications within the target time. Derek discussed the use of conditions:

> "I think that in a sense what can happen is that ... officers do is do as much as they can in two months and then everything they haven't dealt with they put on as conditions and try to cover it that way. All that that does is when you come to monitor the thing you suddenly find you've got all these conditions you're trying to sort out and sometimes you have conditions that you can't resolve. They really should have been sorted out before you ever granted the consent."

This use of conditions was unsatisfactory because of the time they then took for the developer to discharge them and for the planning authority to certify that they had been discharged (time that was not counted within the government's target).

In terms of refusing planning applications, George related how it was common practice now to refuse applications within the timeframe, even though this might mean it would take longer to deliver development overall:

> "Get it within the eight weeks, get it within 13 weeks, get it in within the 16 weeks, bang it through. Or refuse it, we shouldn't do, but we have done. And then the fresh application it takes twice as long to get the permission, whereas if we just let it go beyond those, you know, 13 weeks, then you've negotiated something and got it say, in 15 weeks, whereas… it's taken us 30 weeks. But statistically we've done well. So that's a frustration."

Others made similar comments, and suggested it meant they were providing a poor service to the public. Indeed, if the result of this refusal was that a further application then required processing, it can hardly be claimed that the resultant process was more efficient.

There was even evidence of planners actively putting pressure on developers to withdraw applications or face refusal. Dick provided a direct example:

> "We've had two sets of amendments while the application's been running…. We've now got to the point where we're up against the 13 weeks, prospect of another set of revisions coming for re-advertisement, we're saying no, this, this isn't on, we're going to, if you don't withdraw this application we're going to refuse it…. Now the developer's absolutely incensed by this but we're under so much pressure that we can't afford not to do that, so it's the law of unintended consequences."

These unintended consequences were blamed squarely and directly on central government by a number of interviewees.

Overall, there appears to have been a feeling of regret within the profession, with planners reporting that over-burdensome targets aimed at improving planning restricted the quality of service that they could provide due to the unintended consequences. This probably explains why a strong majority of survey respondents (59.1 per cent) disagreed or strongly disagreed that 'auditing and targets have improved relations

Figure 5.4: Opinion on whether 'auditing and targets have improved relations with the public' (n = 599)

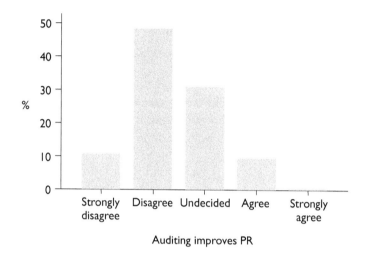

with the public' (compared to just 9.8 per cent who agreed or strongly disagreed) (see Figure 5.4). Since targets are supposedly about regulating local government services in the interests of the public taxpayer, this was a stinging criticism.

A final unintended consequence concerns the fact that a majority of interviewees spoke about the targets having increased job-related stress. The survey data provides strong evidence for this, with a large majority of 87.3 per cent of respondents agreeing or strongly agreeing that 'auditing and targets have increased the amount of stress for staff', compared to just 3.5 per cent disagreeing and none at all strongly disagreeing (see Figure 5.5). Interview data provided further evidence of the effects of 'relentless figures' making the job "a nightmare", as Rob put it. Several planners tied targets directly to problems with job satisfaction, while others raised a link between target-induced stress and retention. This was noted by an Audit Commission study in 2002 (2002). A typical comment here was that by Margaret:

> "Nervous breakdown! No, exhaustion. I was signed off. One guy in DC [development control] has been off several months. Two of our senior planners in DC left. They, one of them, made a party political speech when he did leave. Said he was leaving because he was sick to death of government targets."

Figure 5.5: Opinion on whether 'auditing and targets have increased the amount of stress for staff' (n = 599)

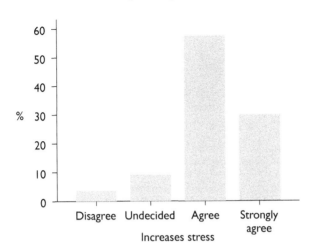

Such lived experience provides a powerful narrative. Nevertheless, it is worth noting that the survey data suggested that the majority of planners were not considering leaving the profession because of any elements of planning reform.

We therefore see that the targets were having a number of 'unintended consequences'. Many planners believed targets were actually leading to them providing a worse service to the public, as well as demoralising them by increasing the stress of the jobs. There was also concern that the targets somehow de-professionalised development control planners, perhaps by reducing discretion, perhaps by making them 'box-ticking administrators'. Allmendinger (2011) also notes this, and the link between the targets, stress, de-professionalisation and recruitment and retention problems for development control planners. These concerns reflect more widespread criticisms of target culture seen in the academic press and across the public sector professions, but they do not represent the full story of how planners were reacting to targets, as the next section will show.

Making targets work for you

One of the most striking survey results was that when asked whether 'targets should be abolished', most planners did not agree. Just 12.5 per cent strongly agreed and 15.6 per cent agreed (28.1 per cent totalled) compared to some 42.9 per cent who disagreed (see Figure 5.6). This finding is somewhat surprising, given the strong criticisms of the

Figure 5.6: Opinion on whether 'targets should be abolished' (*n* = 601)

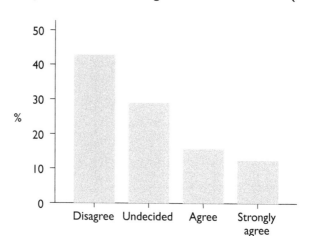

targets already discussed. In interview, only one planner thought that targets should be abolished outright (Margaret), and one thought they had once had a role but now needed "retiring" (Les). Other planners were more supportive both of targets specifically, and of the idea of processing applications expeditiously.

A number of planners commented specifically that there needed to be some sort of target, Alistair saying "you couldn't just leave planners to do their best" and George commenting:

> "No, I don't think I would actually get rid of targets, no because otherwise what are we going to do? I know I've said I think there's too much central government control, but I don't think there's anything wrong with a bit of basic standards that they expect you to adhere to…. Otherwise authorities can have a tendency to slip back into complacency, there is that risk."

These two quotes tell us quite explicitly that these planners did not themselves believe that planners as a group, or local authorities generally, would necessarily serve the best interests of applicants or the public if left to their own devices. Therefore, despite the criticisms of targets already discussed, there was no strong support within either the survey or interview data for abolishing targets altogether. Indeed, there was support for the idea that there should be some sort of target. A number of responses to the survey and interviews indicate why this should be: there was belief both that targets could be useful in themselves and also that targets could be used by planners, particularly planning managers, for their own gain.

A number of planners thought that the targets had actually improved the way planning worked, and that some speeding up of planning was necessary. In other words, targets had achieved their stated purpose. The survey data shows that more planners agreed than disagreed that the targets had improved the performance of the service (see Figure 5.7). The interview data show that a number of planners thought that planning needed speeding up, that timeliness was important as a part of quality of service and that the targets had helped that happen. Boyd commented that when New Labour had introduced BVPIs:

> "I think the system probably did need some sort of incentive, some sort of speeding, there's stories of applications taking years to go through."

There was also a comment that the public did want a faster planning service and this had been achieved to a certain extent through New Labour's targets.

Not only were there financial rewards (through PDG) for authorities that met the targets, but there was the threat of government intervention for authorities missing the targets by a large margin – the so-called Standards Authority designation:

Figure 5.7: Opinion on whether 'auditing and targets have improved the performance of the service' (*n* = 599)

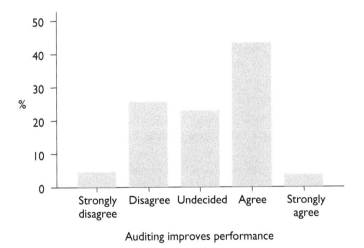

Auditing improves performance

"We were a Standards Authority a few years back and we've obviously that ... that focused our minds very much on what we've been doing and how we were delivering our messages." (David)

In other words, the sanction and reward system linked to the targets had worked, to some extent (although note that many planners would argue that the unintended consequences already discussed would mean that the overall life of a planning application was unlikely to be much quicker than it was before the targets). Tony went further. He said that speed was important, and that the targets were vital to ensuring timely determination:

"My personal view is that targets on determining applications are in themselves not unreasonable because obviously having things determined quickly is important to applicants ... however well intentioned you are there are all sorts of things that become part of the professional routine and that isn't necessarily always serving the needs of other people. Any institution in a sense works to benefit itself rather than the people who are using it or supposed to be benefiting from it. I think it probably is necessary to have targets."

As well as speeding up planning, some planners also thought the targets had altered working practices. The survey data show that 79.4 per cent of responding planners agreed or strongly agreed that 'auditing and targets have altered the way people work' (see Figure 5.8). This implies that the targets had been successful in terms of another objective, introducing a 'culture change' in the profession, involving new practices and conceptions of planning and the role of planners. This does not, of course, show whether planners thought that this altering of the way they worked had been a good thing or not. Many planners would likely point to feeling that they were now providing a worse service, as already discussed. A significant number of interviewees, however, stated that they believed that the targets had cut inefficiency and sharpened their approach.

Some of the interviewees clearly thought that planners needed to change some of their practices. David spoke of the need for planning to become more performance-driven:

Figure 5.8: Opinion on whether 'auditing and targets have altered the way people work' (n = 597)

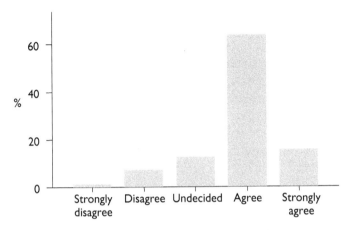

Auditing alters the way we work

"Where we were before we entered a performance-driven culture was that we probably spent far too much time on almost fruitlessly chasing levels of quality and detail that were of marginal benefit to the area and its community and we needed to refocus our resources, given the changes and the, the kind of push that, I think, everyone wanted to make in terms of regeneration. So, yeah, we had to grow up, we had to change."

Martin also refuted the idea that speed and quality were in an inverse relationship:

"Well I'm inclined to think that some of these places where they never met any of their targets, it was because they weren't organised. They didn't know what they were doing, they didn't get on with it and they were using the cover of making a better decision to cover up this inefficiency. Now, I look round here and I see people make speedy decisions, getting on with it, and actually probably making at least as good decisions as those who can't keep up with it."

Alongside this suggestion that cutting inefficiency could allow quality and speed to both be achieved were suggestions that the targets had helped sharpen up planning because they were useful tools, in ways that those implementing the target regime would have probably intended. These included introducing a more project management-type approach and allowing comparability of local authority performance. Several planners spoke of how the targets had helped stop slippage of application processing. There was also talk of the targets allowing an authority to see how it was doing relative to others, something Martin appreciated as he felt it allowed him to learn whether his team's practices were good or not.

Alongside the negative 'unintended consequences' already discussed, there also appeared to be some positive 'unintended consequences' of the targets. Jack spoke about the eight-week target helping to manage expectations on the public side about how long the application would take to process (although he felt the 13-week target did not achieve this because it was unrealistic). A similar positive consequence (from the viewpoint of most planners and, probably, central government as well) was that the targets had apparently increased the delegation rates for processing applications, so planners were empowered to determine more applications themselves rather than simply making recommendations to elected members. Paul felt this meant they focused, correctly, on "strategic applications, rather than having neighbour disputes played out in the public arena".

These increases in delegation rates as a result of the targets may help explain why so many planners – 71.9 per cent – reported on the survey that they did not feel that the targets had restricted their scope for professional discretion; indeed, in a sense it was helping

Figure 5.9: Opinion on whether 'targets restrict the scope for professional discretion' (n = 601)

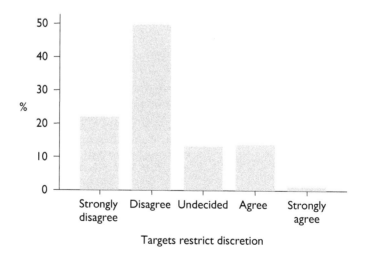

Targets restrict discretion

increase it. Figure 5.9 illustrates this result, which is striking because as we have already seen, the targets did restrict the amount of time planners spent processing applications and the way in which they did that. We suspect that several factors combined to produce this result, in addition to the increased delegation rates: first, the planner could still recommend whatever decision they liked so long as it was in the decision time (refusal within target was still successful from the government's perspectives), but second, there was some evidence that planners had actually been using the targets for their own benefit, as outlined in the next section.

Targets you can use

Research data suggest that planners had been making use of the targets with respect to resource issues and managing staff, applicants and objectors. The interview data provide strong evidence that many planners supported the targets as they enabled them to bring extra resources into the planning service, both from government (particularly through PDG) but also internally. Linked to the latter is the idea that the targets made planning matter more to the council leadership (political and officer). The idea that the targets might be used to lever in extra funding to the planning department was specifically mentioned by 15 interviewees, making it the single most commented-on feature of targets (alongside that they increased stress for staff, also mentioned specifically by 15 interviewees). One key theme here was that if you performed well on the targets, there was a financial reward from central government in the form of PDG. Anna offered a flavour of the sums involved:

> "We've brought in over a million, well over a million, it's probably a million-and-a-half now, on PDG, we wouldn't have done that before this. That's a lot of money for a district."

It therefore seems as if the targets were being used by planning managers to bring extra resources into their services through PDG.[3] Jim saw this as a major positive due to past inadequate resourcing:

> "Planning has been pretty much just bubbling along for the last 20 years, the culture change that we're seeing is down to the fact that there are real opportunities being created

by being target-driven. We're having to employ the right number of planners, that's brought a lot of new people in."

Jim spoke about "the opportunities created by being target-driven". This linked to comments mentioning not only the direct reward of PDG, but also an understanding of that by the council leadership. The survey data show that some 53.3 per cent of planners agreed or strongly agreed that auditing and targets had raised the profile of planning within the council (see Figure 5.10). The interview data suggest a number of reasons why, beyond PDG. This included the fact that the targets could be used to gain, or at least safeguard, resources locally. Patrick pointed out that the targets had been essential in protecting a reasonable budget for planning:

"It's difficult for councils. They've got so many competing things. If you look at a unitary authority like ours, when the councillors have got a choice to close a school or put a million pound into planning, what are you going to do? You're going to keep the school open and say to the planners, 'I'm sorry, we've got no resource for you'.... So what it did, by introducing targets and rewards, they actually put us on an equal footing to things like education, highways and social services, which was again fundamental, absolutely fundamental."

Figure 5.10: Opinion on whether 'auditing and targets have raised the profile of planning in the council' (*n* = 599)

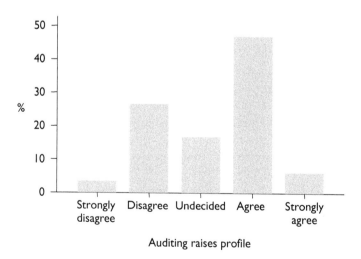

Auditing raises profile

Anna spoke similarly, calling planning the 'Cinderella service' compared to competing local authority functions.

Further interview evidence suggested that the targets were not just useful in terms of safeguarding resources for planning, but also in terms of setting out what resource planning should have within the council:

> "They'd say, 'Look you're responsible for that, this is your directive, we want you to determine 80 per cent of the applications in eight weeks, and get the development plan.' Fine, okay, and then I could go to the chief exec and say, 'Look I've got this target, this is the resource I think I need to do that'." (James)

Other, similar examples given in interview demonstrated targeted performance being used not just to safeguard, but also to gain resources for planning departments. A number of interviewees spoke of how councillors and chief executives were concerned that planning should achieve a good performance against the targets. Simon said the targets had changed what councillors wanted from the service:

> "They have had a substantial impact, because previously in the development control service, the view of members was that it was a function of the council to negotiate acceptable schemes with developers, however long that took. Now, they take the view that they want us to be one of the top performing authorities in terms of speed of decision making."

Furthermore, under the BVPI system in England, the planning indicators did not just count individually, but each local authority was also given an overall score based on performance against all targets – the CPA score. This score seems to have mattered to council leadership teams, and Dick explained that because planning performance could have an impact on the overall CPA score, poor performance (or the threat of it) could be used to get extra resources into planning.

This overall argument, that targets could be used to lever in extra resources to planning, and raise its profile, is reflected in the literature, with Carmona commenting that: 'If no attempt is made to measure the performance of planning, then planning will have a hard time making the case that it is a service worthy of public investment' (2007, p 4). This linked to a theme evident in the interview data that everyone had targets, so planning should not be left out. It was almost as if having targets was seen as a badge of legitimacy, confirming planning's importance within the bigger public service. In part, this could be symptomatic of a wider pervasive new public management-type culture where the subjectivities are such that no alternative is even perceived. But it may be more conscious ideas about the status of planning (targets confirming the importance of planning) and about the ability to bring in, or at least defend, resources.

One further way, evident in the interview material, that the targets appeared to be being used by planners was in terms of management within planning departments. Patrick, a planning manager, talked about how the targets allowed him to "monitor everything":

> "It means I monitor everything. I can literally press a button and I can tell you precisely where we are at any one particular point in time in terms of our performance, on any of the categories of development. I can tell you how many applications a particular officer has got on their desk. I can tell you how they're performing individually per month, per week, per day, if I need to. It's forced us to develop systems and mechanisms to monitor exactly what's going on. I think actually it's made us better managers."

This idea that the targets had 'forced' the introduction of systems that enabled him to be a better manager is both a notable consequence of the targets, but may also help explain the earlier observed correlation between seniority within the planning profession and views on the targets. This growth of professional managers actively managing colleagues' performance is not unique to planning (see Fitzgerald and Ferlie, 2000).

Several times during the interviews, it was suggested that the targets could also be used to manage, or exert control, over applicants and developers:

> "We, I think, are, we are less prepared to accept poor quality applications and then negotiate improvements. You know, we are more prepared to say, 'Thank you, this is just not good enough, you can either withdraw it or we'll refuse it, go away and come up with a better scheme'." (Simon)

Similarly Patrick said that before the targets he would have negotiated at length, but now he felt empowered to tell applicants that they had submitted "rubbish" and should go and learn to "improve themselves". Martin even joked that:

"The development industry has been crying out for years for speedier decisions. So they've got one now: refusal."

This apparently applied not just to applicants, but also to consultees and objectors: Rob said that the targets enabled him to cut back the 'endless say' that the public wanted on everything:

"I mean, the public want to have endless says on everything. And they'll want to continue to have says, especially if they don't like the answer or the recommendation that the council makes. Now, I don't think there's necessarily anything wrong with speed, 'cos it's the wider public interest that we're trying to achieve."

The comment about the "wider public interest" is indicative of the idea that those objecting to most planning applications did not represent the wider public interest, something we explore further in the next chapter.

Overall, the data show that planners seemed to be actively using New Labour's targets to lever in extra resources and recognition for planning, and to manage more junior staff, applicants and objectors. This may all help to explain why there was no strong support for the idea of abolishing targets.

Continued currency of 'efficiency' under the Coalition government

Since the Coalition government took office in May 2010, the regime of performance management, targets and measurement has continued, but in a less stark way. In Opposition, the Conservatives had been scornful of the overt bureaucracy of the local planning process, and stipulated a determination to scrap a considerable amount of red tape. On assuming office, the Coalition has retained the 8- and 13-week targets for determining planning applications, but has scrapped the CPA and the HPDG, the incentive element of the performance measurement regime. Simultaneously, ministers remain concerned at the costs of the planning system and the impact of delay, but have largely couched their concern in the context of the need for economic recovery and growth, and the potential effect delay has on the business community. In Scotland and Wales, performance measurement has been retained. It seems likely that the management of the planning system through performance assessment will still occur for the foreseeable future, albeit one where the incentives of good performance are not rewarded back to local planning authorities in the way that they had been up to 2010.

Nevertheless, although there may be a reduced emphasis on targets as a tool for managing planning, the efficiency of planning (like many other public services) has remained a high priority for government.

> "We are going to tackle what every government has identified as a chronic obstacle to economic growth in Britain, and no government has done anything about: the planning system." (George Osborne, Budget speech to the House of Commons, March 2011)

The reference to the problems of the planning system, as outlined in George Osborne's Budget statement in 2011, was remarkably familiar to Parliamentarians and students of political science alike. In fact, Mr Osborne's contention that no government has done anything to tackle the obstacle of the planning system conveniently sweeps aside vast swathes of government legislation and policy statements going back over 30 years. The New Labour government passed three Acts of Parliament[4] and innumerable changes to secondary legislation, and produced planning statements that promised to 'do something' about planning. They even commissioned Kate Barker, the Monetary Policy Committee member, to produce two detailed Treasury reports on the matter: one on planning and economic growth in 2004, and the other on planning and housing development in 2006 (Barker, 2004, 2006).

Labour and HM Treasury in particular had identified planning as the key barrier to enterprise and economic development. These sentiments echo the words of George Osborne and members of the Coalition government since 2010. But perhaps what is more interesting is the fact that they are virtually identical to the words of Michael Heseltine as Environment Secretary and Geoffrey Howe as Chancellor when the latter announced the establishment of Enterprise Zones for the first time in 1980 (Thornley, 1991). The Thatcher government then embarked on an eight-year policy of systematically deregulating most of the *local* planning system while simultaneously parachuting in pro-economic growth *central* policy initiatives. Government Circulars 22/80 (DoE, 1980) and 14/85 (DoE, 1985b), and the *Lifting the burden* White Paper (DoE, 1985a), told local planners to make economic growth and job creation the number one priority when determining planning applications for new development, over any local concerns.

A little reading of political and planning history will reveal a great deal of all political parties' commitments to 'do something' about the planning system almost as though it is a tedious broken record. The Chancellor was therefore making the wrong statement; he needed to ask why, despite these legislative and policy initiatives from Conservative, Labour and Coalition governments, was the planning system still viewed as an obstacle to development? And who viewed it as such? The Barker reports produced a wealth of facts and opinions from the business community about the pros and cons of planning. Yes, delay and overt bureaucracy did feature in the responses, and the fact that some LPAs were more efficient than others in responding rapidly to unlock business opportunities. But business leaders also stated that they welcomed the certainty provided by the planning system, allowing phased release of land for development, creating scarcity, of course, and also in some cases a positive approach to change. There was little evidence for planning being portrayed as an 'obstacle', despite politicians and certain sections of the media continuing to peddle the fact. So why do we have this continued vilification? Perhaps it relates to the fact that in 2010 only 87 per cent of planning applications nationally were given planning permission? Or that some of the 'failed' 13 per cent just happen to be in the green belt, National Parks and in other important landscape areas designated, appropriately enough, by central government?

So what has happened over the last 30 years? Two matters stand out that tend to continuously compromise the planning deregulatory initiatives of all governments. And both suggest that in planning things happen *despite* government, not *because* of it. The first concerns the form of local economic growth enabled by a pro-growth agenda and the designation of Enterprise Zones. Studies of the first period of Enterprise Zone designation in the 1980s showed that most of the jobs created originated from non-zoned areas, that is, the zones were successful in attracting development but at the expense of other areas, not as new business start-ups. According to the Work Foundation, 80 per cent of jobs came from other places, at the cost for the Zones of £23,000 per job (Thornley, 1991). Furthermore, the form of economic growth was not manufacturing, creative industries, business services or life sciences as perhaps successive ministers hoped for, but rather short term in nature or out-of-town retailing developments. Box goods shopping stores, such as hypermarkets and DIY stores, flocked to the Zones in the 1980s, enticed by cheap taxation and little planning control compared to that for the towns. These projects, although objected to by LPAs in order to protect the vibrancy of high streets, still met the employment-generating requirements of central government's policies. These projects then caused problems for town centres commercially and the life of towns, which needed addressing eventually in the 1990s through a change in planning policy away from out-of-town stores in favour of town centres.

The second concerns the local planning system itself. When Nicholas Ridley, another former Environment Secretary, attempted to deregulate the local planning system in the 1980s in favour of housing development and commercial property projects in the name of fostering national economic growth, he received an almighty backlash from the Conservative-voting Home Counties, concerned about the imposition of policies and the fact that their voices locally were not being listened to. Central government ministers often seem to forget to their cost that the local planning system that they dislike and label so much as an economic barrier nationally is, in point of fact, not only about giving out planning permission for new economic development. It also serves as the governmental and management process locally and on the ground to deal with environmental and countryside protection, and is a bulwark in favour of local democracy and expressing views of support or objection (Bruton, 1974).

Planning supports economic growth, environmental protection and local public participation. A government deliberately shifting that delicate balance in favour of economic growth in the national interest will sooner or later find opposition on the ground, project by project, from representatives acting in the local interest. The latter 1980s represents a period when ministers learned the hard way how not to go about skewing local planning against localised interests. And so we come full circle to the post-2010 period. The Budget statement of 2011 set out a new agenda for local planning:

1. All bodies involved in planning to prioritise economic growth and job creation

2. A new presumption in favour of sustainable development – the default answer for local authorities to new development proposals is always 'yes'; in reality this is not new, but makes it more explicit

3. The retention of controls over the green belt, but the removal of nationally imposed targets on the use of previously developed land; the implication here is that if you don't build on brownfield sites in town and city centres, you build on greenfield sites on the edge of towns – not all edge-of-town land is designated in planning law as green belt (this proposal was subsequently amended)

4. Certain use classes change, with time limits on applications (12-month processing maximum) and pilot auctions of planning permission on land

5. The establishment of an initial 21 Enterprise Zones, featuring 100 per cent discount on rates, reduced planning restrictions, new superfast broadband and the potential to use capital allowances in zones. Local Enterprise Partnerships, rather than individual local neighbourhoods or authorities, to come forward and make proposals; a further eight Enterprise Zones have since been designated

6. Businesses to be allowed to bring forward Neighbourhood Plans and Neighbourhood Development Orders, not only communities themselves (HM Treasury, 2011).

Most of these policies have been tried and tested before by previous governments, with outcomes very different from those imagined by their sponsors. What makes these policies vastly more interesting is how and where they support localism, the 'Big Society' and the provisions of the Localism Act 2011, which attempts to reconfigure the local planning system towards neighbourhood matters (see Chapter Six). The continued currency of the 8- and 13-week application processing speed targets is notable here – this appears to be the only measure of planning performance central government is really interested in – and a proposal was made in 2011 to impose an overall 12-month limit for processing an application as well as sanctions for local authorities performing poorly (Smulian, 2011b). In 2012, Communities Secretary Eric Pickles announced that planning powers could be taken away from local authorities and given instead to the central Planning Inspectorate if councils 'living in an economic la la land' continued to show a record of slow decision making. Asked if this contradicted the UK government's own localism policies, he replied this was 'muscular localism' (quoted in Wintour, 2012). The spectre is raised that if planners cannot show themselves to be 'efficient', they may just be by-passed altogether.

Targets: restricting *and* empowering professionals?

There is no doubt that over the last decade, various central government audit processes, most particularly the system of NI targets, had a massive impact on local authority planners across Britain. While there is clearly a geography to auditing and targets, particularly post-devolution, the reactions of the profession show similar patterns in all parts of Britain. In sum, while we see some ideological concerns about the very idea of targets, much more common is a feeling that the time-based processing targets are wrong, focusing too much on speed at the possible cost of quality and ignoring outcomes. There is also some feeling that targets somehow de-professionalise planners, making them administrators, and a feeling that too much emphasis has been placed on NIs. Furthermore there are very strong feelings that the targets are distorting planning practice through a range of unintended consequences, so that the service offered to all users of the planning system is actually worse overall. This accords with what Power (1999) terms 'colonisation', where audits are effective in unintended ways with side effects possibly actually undermining overall performance.

This range of reactions is what might have been predicted from the literature, particularly that covering the experience of other frontline public sector professionals such as the police or NHS staff. CLG's own research suggested that 'there is a lack of statistical evidence that [the unintended negative consequences were] ... a widespread problem' (2006, p 4), but that does not negate the reality of the reactions being expressed directly in the research, and the feeling of strong negative consequences associated with the targets, particularly in England.[5] The story, however, is not so simple. Strikingly, in the survey, just 28.1 per cent of respondents agreed or strongly agreed that targets should be abolished. There was some opinion expressed that the targets had worked, that planning performance needed improving and targets had helped, as well as the fact that targets could be used to level in extra funding to planning, to raise the profile of the service and to help the management of staff, applicants and NIMBYs (not in my backyard). There was also some talk of everyone having targets in the public sector, so planning needed targets too in order to gain sufficient recognition of its value and importance.

We therefore have a range of positive consequences balancing the negative, and helping explain the surprisingly small number of planners who seemed to want to get rid of NIs for planning. There was certainly some correlation between reaction to targets and job seniority in the survey, in particular with more senior staff being less likely to agree with abolishing targets. Interestingly, research done by the Killian Pretty review (Killian and Pretty, 2008c) found that, statistically, there was no correlation between authority size, the amount spent on planning services, the number of applications received and performance against national targets. The missing factor explaining performance might therefore be linked to leadership. Carmona and Sieh (2005) comment that key officers can have a strong influence over performance. It also makes sense that more senior officers might look more positively on a tool that can be used to lever in extra resources to their departments, while more junior staff might simply feel more stressed trying to meet the targets day to day. Nevertheless, the senior staff surveyed were actually more likely to think the targets were restricting discretion. In other words, there are planners at all levels who could see positive and negative consequences of the performance management regime. Few planners, however, made suggestions for alternatives to the processing speed targets to measure planning.

More broadly, it is clear that the performance management regime for planning has been very much a central government-driven phenomenon. This raises issues about to what extent these processes act to create a certain subject, a certain type of planning professional. The reaction of planners at the coalface to targets further illustrates that frontline staff can react to central government agendas in complex – perhaps even perverse – ways. It is not simply a case of acceptance, or indeed resistance, but a more nuanced process of working within an overall framework, complying with what must be complied with but actively trying to use that framework to further the professional planner's own ends. Indeed, there is some evidence that targets do not just act to restrict the professional planner but also, in certain other ways, empower them. This top-down imposition can actually create a space for staff to try to pursue their own agendas. There was evidence of alternative visions of planning remaining resilient and of targets being used in ways their designers may not have envisaged.

This may be because governmental priorities around 'efficiency' and the obsession with the speed of processing planning applications do not seem as deeply embedded in the discourses and professional identity of planning as they were among government, and some local authority senior managers. There is clearly some active contestation of the idea that planning is just about processing applications quickly, and little evidence of any great inculcation of new attitudes and values about planners' purpose being solely the efficient processing of applications in a business-friendly manner. This fits with the institutionalist frame: the interaction of new audit procedures and a culture of efficiency with existing local government processes (Imrie and Raco, 1999) and professional identities (Campbell and Marshall, 2005) – a clash of institutions and 'rule sets' – produces tensions but also a common range of broad positions adopted by frontline planners. Once again, we also see the tension within the reforms between central control and the encouragement of local autonomy, responsiveness and diversity (as noted by Davis and Martin, 2002). A key, and ongoing, tension appears to be between objectives for both speed and participation for planning. The next chapter explores the issue of public participation in planning.

SIX

Participation: planners and their 'customers'

Participation and active citizens

During the research on New Labour and planning reform, the topic of public participation cropped up in conversation.[1] "Ah", said the planner, "when I was doing my planning course we had a Canadian planner come to chat to us, as they were ahead of us in terms of public participation in those days. He told us how terrible it was, that the only thing they could get done was plant trees, because nobody objected to that, and that seems to me a danger of where we are headed in this country." The planner then smiled wryly before adding, "well actually in the last couple of weeks I have had several letters from local residents complaining that decomposing leaves from trees along the streets are falling onto their cars and damaging the paintwork. So we can't even plant trees any more."

The image of almost a 'tyranny of participation' from the eyes of a planner is fascinating given how efforts at making British planning more participatory have formed a central part of the planning reform agenda promoted by central and devolved government in Britain under both Labour and the Coalition since 1997 (Kitchen and Whitney, 2004; Gallent and Robinson, 2012). As reviewed in Chapter One, this seemingly pro-participation agenda is in conflict with other government priorities (see also Baker et al, 2007). Given these tensions, there is a clear need to explore what planners at the coalface think about public participation.

Just as the requirements of targets present a 'top-down pressure' on public sector professionals such as planners, so participation presents a 'bottom-up' check on their discretion (Taylor and Kelly, 2006). Participation is not the only such bottom-up check, however. As introduced in Chapter One, there has been a rise in the use of the language and ideal of 'the customer' across public services in recent years, particularly in the local government context in which planning sits. This idea of 'the customer' grew from John Major's 1991 'Citizen's Charter' (Bolton, 2002) and continued under Labour administrations, the ideal of the customer being central to new public management (Clarke, 2004). There has been a clear attempt to create a 'customer-oriented' bureaucracy (Korczynski and Ott, 2004). Swain and Tait draw on Rose (1999) to conceptualise the logic of customers as part of a wider process of neoliberal reform that sees bureaucrats as impediments to the working of the free market and so in need of change: 'One way of doing this was not to govern bureaucracy better but to transform the very ethos of the public sector' (quoted in Swain and Tait, 2007, p 240). It also leads to new modes of citizenship (Raco, 2007).

This rise of 'the customer' has been widely commented on in general literature about public service reform, but has clearly had an impact on local government planning specifically. Kitchen writes that planning is an activity with customers, but suggests that 'for the public sector this is a more recent idea which in some circles was resisted because planners saw themselves as being responsible for a general public interest which was by definition superior to individual interests' (2006, p 101). This raises clear questions about how the customer discourse has been implemented in planning. Indeed, Rosenthal and Peccei (2006c) highlight the importance of a context-specific understanding of the deployment of consumer discourses; elsewhere they write that:

> The 'sovereign customer' is seen to demand great individual attention, flexibility and novelty in the provision of services, as well as goods.... Service quality has thus become a major management preoccupation....A key problem for managers is how to ensure appropriate behaviours on the part of front-line workers: those employees who actually meet the customer and deliver the service. (Peccei and Rosenthal, 2001, p 831)

There are, therefore, questions about how much planners use the term 'customers' and what the implications of the customer discourse are for local government planning, and these have important links to relations between planners and the public. In this chapter we consider, in turn, evidence relating to how planners have reacted to the ongoing efforts to make planning more participatory and more customer-responsive over recent years.

Conceptualising participation

The topic of public participation in planning has received considerable academic attention over the years, and there is still lively debate around the idea (Alfasi, 2003). Within this debate, there is even contestation about the very definitions of 'public' and 'participation' (Thomas, 1996; Barnes et al, 2003). Discussion of participation is often understood with reference to Arnstein's 'ladder of participation' (Arnstein, 1969). This ladder represents not just a classificatory device; there is also the underlying implication that the higher rungs are somehow better.

In general, debate in the planning literature is broadly split between those seeking a more participatory planning and those questioning its implications in practice. There are arguments on both sides of the debate about the effectiveness of public participation in planning, and whether there should be more of it. The arguments are both theoretical and practical, with a debate between those who consider increasing dialogue will lead to better decisions and those who argue that participation is a form of governmentality. The central theoretical debate thus often draws on Habermas, on the one side (see, for example, Healey, 1997), and Foucault, as well Nietzsche and even Machiavelli on the other (see, for example, Flyvbjerg, 1998).

Rydin and Pennington suggest that 'within the literature on environmental policy and planning, public participation is usually considered an unalloyed good' (2000, p 153). Those supporting a more participatory planning justify this through rationales of building 'institutional capacity', social, intellectual and political capital and community cohesion (Healey, 1997; Innes and Booher, 2004; Taylor, 2007). It is argued participatory planning can better capture the pluralism of values and knowledge (including lay knowledge) in a modern society whose preferences have not been properly captured by the technocratic bureaucracy (Myers and Macnaghten, 1998; Coburn, 2003; Petts and Brooks, 2006). Democratic rationales are offered (Bedford et al, 2002; Innes and Booher, 2004; Taylor, 2007), arguments are made around improved policy outcomes and implementation (Rydin and Pennington, 2000; Taylor, 2007) and arguments around empowering and educating citizens (Lowndes et al, 2001b). The strongest proponents of a more participatory planning argue for 'collaborative planning' based around an inclusionary, deliberative approach and drawing on a Habermasian concept of a deliberative democracy (Innes, 1995; Healey, 1997, 2006; Forester, 1999a).

Drawing on Foucauldian critiques of power, a critical interpretation argues that in practice participation fails to live up to these persuasive theoretical and professional ideals (Ellis, 2004). Barnes, Newman and Sullivan are concerned that much of the participation literature is highly normative, and comment that 'The practices of public participation, while appearing to be empowering, may be a new form of domination' (2007, p 70). Those on this side of the debate argue that in practice outcomes are not always beneficial for the public interest due to the dominance of certain interests, an emphasis on short-term objectives and reproduction of existing power structures (Campbell and Marshall, 2000; Bedford et al, 2002; Hillier, 2003). There is concern about the difficulty of achieving consensus in the face of existing power structures (Flyvbjerg, 1998; Tewdwr-Jones and Thomas, 1998; Pløger, 2001) and the unrepresentativeness of those involved in planning public participation exercises (Thomas, 1996; Campbell and Marshall, 2000; Rydin and Pennington, 2000; Bickerstaff and Walker, 2001). There is also evidence that those who do get involved tend to promote individual rather than collective interests (Campbell and Marshall, 2000; Warburton, 2002). Thus collaborative planning 'assumes a unified, coherent voice that is seldom realised in practice' (Barnes et al, 2007, p 199).

These arguments are well versed. There is, however, a large gap in the literature, and that is an overview of how planners as a professional group are reacting to the ongoing drive for participation (and indeed, the tensions between this and other government objectives). This is despite some of the literature suggesting planners have a key role in making planning more participatory. This is a striking absence since the role of the frontline planner is clearly so important in implementing public participation and other policies. Indeed, the concerns raised in the literature are not simply abstract or theoretical; they are materialised in and through the experiences of planners at the coalface. Their testimony provides a way of exploring the seriousness of those concerns, and whether perception matches discourse. Some of the existing literatures do portray an implicit picture of what planning professionals think about the participation agenda, but all too frequently this is without much supporting evidence. There is usually an assumption that planners have a negative attitude to participation, hence a number of authors call for the necessity of fundamental change in planning practice, with calls for a 'culture change' in planning to further promote collaborative approaches (Healey, 2003; Gonzalez and Healey, 2005). Such calls reflect a wider concern about overcoming the professional cultural barriers and institutional inertia to further encourage meaningful participation (Taylor, 2003; Petts and Brooks, 2006). Coulson (2003) and Jones (2002) also note that adequate skills and commitment by professional staff are vital to the success of public participation.

A cursory examination might support the analysis that there needs to be a culture change in the profession. Cartoons in the professional journal and news magazine of the planning profession, *Planning*, offer a tongue-in-cheek yet informative image (see, for example, Figure 6.1) which suggests a certain scepticism – or perceived scepticism – about public participation among planning professionals. If such alleged hostility of planners to participation is true, then it could mean they are an obstacle to equitable and efficient public participation. There is currently insufficient evidence, however, to conclude this. Tewdwr-Jones and Allmendinger argue that 'collaborative planning fails to incorporate adequately the peculiar political and professional nuances that exist in planning practice' (1998, p 1975), and there is a pressing need to get beyond a cursory examination of the attitudes of planners to public participation.

Figure 6.1: A tongue-in-cheek comment on the view on public participation from within the planning profession

Source: Cowan (2004)
Reproduced with permission of Rob Cowan.

Debating the customer ideal

Just as public participation has been the subject of considerable academic debate, so the possibilities and limitations of the customer concept in public service provision have been widely debated (see Rosenthal and Peccei, 2006a). At the simplest level, those in favour see the 'front line' as a see saw, which should be tipped more towards 'the public' than towards 'the bureaucracy' (Gaster and Rutqvist, 2000). Osborne and Gaebler (1992) argue strongly for the legitimacy and potential of the customer concept for the public sector. Alford (2002) sees significant complexities in re-positioning public service users as customers, but also significant possibilities, and Rosenthal and Peccei outline how:

> The customer concept is seen capable of driving a more effective social exchange between government and the public – wherein public sector organisations offer more accessible, respectful and flexible treatment/provision in return for greater compliance and cooperation from individual recipients of their services. In this view, the customer concept can enable public administrators to do their job more effectively and can contribute to active and responsible citizenship. (2006a, p 661)

The majority of the literature, however, takes a much more negative stance to the theory and practice of using the customer concept in the public sector. There are several different strands to the critique. One strand simply sees public administration as a distinctive form of activity with different ethical-political characteristics to the commercial sphere (du Gay, 2000; Rosenthal and Peccei, 2006b, 2007). The customer concept is unsuited to the public sector and attempts to introduce it amount to the 'Disneyisation' of service work (Bryman, 1999, quoted in Korczynski and Ott, 2004), bringing with it discomforting commercial values (Bolton, 2002). A second strand contends that the customer concept in the public sector is a sham, part of the 'enchanting myth of customer sovereignty' (Korczynski and Ott, 2004, p 580), because the necessary conditions of individual choice, exit and power are illusory (Rosenthal and Peccei, 2007). A third line of critique seems to have the opposite worry about what happens when public sector organisations respond to the preferences and demands of individual users:

> Here the customer becomes a danger to himself and others. He is an usurper of proper political accountability … and a likely corrupter of his alter ego, the citizen, whose true embodiment is one of collective responsibilities as well as rights.… His damage is not limited to the citizenry but extended also to public sector workers. Here, in an echo of the sovereign of the reformers, the customer takes on an active and demanding image – but not for good. This is a figure that now knows to get up and complain and in the process, has become an aggressor, a threat and a drain to public sector workers. (Rosenthal and Peccei, 2007, p 208)

Such critique can clearly be seen in du Gay's (1996) analysis of the customer discourse as a threat to frontline staff and a danger to the wider collective citizenry, and similarly in Bolton's (2002) account of hospital patients behaving differently and in a more demanding manner towards nursing staff.

There is also debate around the very definition of the term 'customer'. While it is generally agreed that 'a customer is an individual who has bought, or is buying a good or service from a service organization' (Korczynski and Ott, 2004, p 582), applying the term to the public sector raises a host of issues. Table 6.1 illustrates a range of differing conceptions of 'the customer', which is a contested concept vested by various (and sometimes conflicting) attributes by different authors (du Gay and Salaman, 1992; Rosenthal and Peccei, 2007). On the whole, however, the literature regarding the mobilisation of the customer discourse in the public sphere tends towards the theoretical, suggesting (as Rosenthal and Peccei, 2001, highlight) that there is a need for greater situated study of the implications of actually implementing the customer concept at the front line of public service.

This debate about the applicability and implications of applying the customer discourse to the public sector contains very little that considers the planning sphere (Kitchen, 2006). What literature there is tends to focus on the difficulty of defining just who 'the customer' of public sector planning is:

> There is often no clearly identifiable client or, perhaps more appositely, the client/professional relationship is diffuse with the consequence that the obligations that the professional might be required to meet are diverse and sometimes conflicting. (Campbell and Marshall, 2005, p 210; see also Campbell and Marshall, 2002; Allmendinger et al, 2003b)

Table 6.1: Defining 'the customer'

Conceptual frame	Associated concept of 'the customer'
Neo-classical economics	Someone at the centre of the narrative, imbued with sovereignty and rationality and likely to rationally chose the lowest cost option
Total Quality Management	Someone who expects quality as well as price
Critical Sociology	Someone who consumes and through doing so connects with 'the cultural', particularly with the prevailing discourses of neoliberalism and enterprise
Entrepreneurial governance	A figure of agency and self-reliance
Critics of neoliberalism	A 'dupe' who has gained some trivial agency in their dealings with public sector workers but has traded off more significant value

Source: After Rosenthal and Peccei (2007)

Swain and Tait (2007) highlight that this distinguishes planning from other professions such as medicine, law or teaching. Nevertheless, Kitchen argues that planning does have customers, in terms of 'a well-understood relationship of entitlement between customer and provider' (2006, p 102), but that there is a range of different customers with different needs and interest.[2] He does, however, then go on to suggest that planning as a public sector activity is not only about meeting the needs of a series of sectoral customers as there can be a need to override sectoral interests.

A further issue with the customer concept in planning is how to deal with conflict between the interests of different groups who might be defined as 'customers' (Kitchen, 2006). Such conflicting demands are not unique to planning (see, for example, Painter 2005, on the customer discourse in the criminal justice arena), but do very much characterise the nature of planning (and, in a sense, define the reason for its very existence). Kitchen (2006) suggests the solution is to try and satisfy as many customers' needs in any given situation as practicable, without duping any of them. Despite this, the very nature of planning raises a host of difficulties for the application of the customer discourse. For example, Korczynski and Ott suggest it is important for frontline workers to display 'pro-customer empathy' (2004, p 588), but this may be difficult in the planning arena, where a developer may well be proposing something hugely damaging to the interests of the local community. Similarly, Gaster and Rutqvist (2000) argue that within the customer concept, public services should understand and do their best to meet the needs of citizens, as formulated by citizens themselves, but do not consider what happens if these citizens are themselves in dispute (such as a neighbour dispute).

The applicability of the very term 'customers' to planning is therefore, at best, troublesome. Despite the comparative longevity of the term, the centrality of the customer concept to new public management and the fact that authors question its impact on the public sector ethos mean that it is important to consider how frontline planners use the term as part of a study of the implications of reform on the profession. Both the customer concept and moves to increase participation raise key questions about the relationship between planners and the public, and the purpose of the system. In this chapter we use empirical evidence to consider, first, the reaction of local authority planners across Britain to New Labour's participation agenda, then, similarly, explore data about how planners think about 'customers', then turn our attention to some of the recent policy moves by the Coalition government in England, before drawing some general conclusions about planners, the public and reaction to reform in this sphere.

The planner's perspective on participation

Tensions in the participation paradise?

As we saw in Chapters One and Five, there is a (commonly, but not universally) perceived tension between government objectives for planning to be both speedier and more participatory. This was something that several planners commented on during the interview process (in 2005 and 2007–08); for example, Dick called it a challenge:

> "I think that's, that's one of the greatest challenges actually. That, you know, we're being pulled in two directions, which I think are incompatible. We're been told we've got to engage more and try and achieve consensus, and yet we've got to deliver more quickly. I don't think those two things are compatible."

The impact of the tension seemed to be that, when it came to a forced choice between participation and a time limit, speed would win out, as Matthew highlighted:

> "You've got, you know, your whole driven LDF process is tightly driven that you can't afford to exceed standards [the minimum consultation levels set by government] by a great deal, or it will screw up your whole programme. And … this is about going the extra mile to do that extra bit of consultation with those very difficult to reach groups. And you can't be time constrained because you don't know how long it will take to get into some of those communities."

Other interviewees highlighted an apparent difficulty in the need to both spend time undertaking participation with all stakeholders as part of the LDF process (indeed, without it, the document would likely be found unsound) but also to try and get these documents produced expeditiously.

For its part, the Labour government suggested that frontloading participation, as they termed it, would reduce objections later in the planning process, saving time in the important late stages of dealing with a planning application or the plan making process. There was actually some support for this view among the questionnaire survey respondents, with a narrow majority of 50.1 per cent of respondents (to the 2006 survey) either agreeing or strongly agreeing that 'frontloading can save hassle later in the process' (see Figure 6.2). These results are not, however, replicated in the interview data, where there typically was a feeling that the government was somehow naive:

"So you know a lot of work has been put into it, and so far it has, it hasn't had the desired result because the government have this idea that if you consult and talk enough to people you'll win them round. And therefore when you publish your plan you won't have too many objections. I think that's incredibly naive, particularly with, with controversial proposals for major development. You will not persuade people that your arguments will be fine by talking to them long enough." (Dick)

This argument that the ideal of consensus may be naive accords with Hillier, who comments that, 'in the reality of practice, many planning strategies and/or disputes do not end in harmonious consensus' (2003, p 38). Whether or not frontloading principles are promoting consensus or not, there was clear evidence of concern among local authority planers about tension between speed and participation objectives.

Figure 6.2: Opinion on whether 'frontloading' can save hassle later in the process (n = 595)

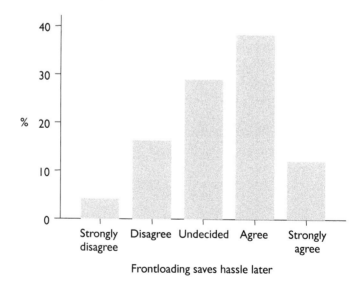

Frontloading saves hassle later

Richard went on to comment that even if it did not result in consensus, participation was still important and worthwhile. This feeling that public participation was something that it was right to do, but that brought difficulties in practice, is reflective of the broader divide in the data on what planners thought about participation. Their responses tended to fit into arguments made for participation on the one side and difficulties raised concerning participation on the other. Some of the planners did seem to fit neatly into one or other of these categories. Mike was clearly more on the side of finding difficulties with public participation:

> "It's not important to me personally at all quite frankly. I could do without the buggers."

On the other hand, Daniel was emphatic in his support for participation:

> "Well I regard it as, it's absolutely vital. I think sort of the old style of hierarchical, you know, things emerging from the darkened rooms is absolute poison and it shouldn't have happened then and certainly shouldn't be happening now."

The majority of planners, however, did not fit neatly into either category. For example, Michael could be said to be entirely on the fence:

> "There's a sort of a love/hate relationship on public participation."

In the next sub-section, we examine the arguments planners made in support of participation, and then, following that, we examine the concerns they raised about it.

Arguments favouring participatory planning

Despite the apparent heterogeneity of opinion, the questionnaire data contain some clear patterns, with similar issues raised between those seemingly more pro-participation and those seemingly opposed, as shown by Table 6.2. Interestingly, further analysis of the questionnaire data using cross-tabulations to see if certain categories of planner were more likely to consider that public participation exercises were useful finds no significant relationship whatsoever between age, gender, geographical location (particularly with concern to location in England, Scotland or Wales) and job seniority against opinion of the usefulness

Table 6.2: Summary of responses for Likert agreement measuring how much respondents agreed or disagreed with various statements relating to public participation and planning on a scale of 1 (strongly disagree to 5 (strongly agree)

Likert statement	n	Median	Mode	% strongly disagree	% disagree	% undecided	% agree	% strongly agree
More public participation is needed to improve planning	599	3.00	2	5.5	38.7	21.7	26.5	7.5
Public participation exercises are useful	601	4.00	4	1.3	14.3	21.1	53.2	10.0
In practice, public participation is dominated by NIMBYs	601	4.00	4	0	15.0	15.0	47.8	22.3
Being involved with public participation exercises is easy	600	2.00	2	15.8	57.0	14.7	11.7	0.8
'Frontloading' can save hassle later in the process	595	4.00	4	4.2	16.3	29.1	38.3	12.1

of participation. This suggests no trends of, say, younger planners being more likely to be pro-participation despite the fact that participation is being given increasing prominence on the curriculum of most planning courses. Therefore it may be that practical experience of participation practice is more important than training in determining views about public participation.

There was one significant relationship found, however, and that was between the job focus and the view of whether public participation was useful. Performing a chi-squared test produced a strongly significant relationship ($p \leq 0.012$ df = 6, no cells with an expected count less than 5). A cross-tabulation clearly showed that development control planners appeared less likely to view public participation as useful than policy planners. Although the questionnaire data cannot alone show causality, this relationship does ring true with our general impression of the interview material. The link may well be that development control planners were more likely to be involved in the most high-pressured, time-limited, reactive participation events when it was often too late for the public to have too much influence due to policies for deciding the principle of development already having been agreed in the development plan. Furthermore, planning managers were most likely to consider participation useful. Speculatively, this may reflect that they have a more strategic overview in their positions, greater experience of participation or even that they want to appear more supportive of government policy in the hope of career progression. Nevertheless, a majority of all respondents, whatever their job foci, agreed that public participation exercises were useful. Similarly in interview, all but four (out of 53) in-depth interviewees said they felt participation was important to them personally. Several rationales were put forward by planners themselves in support of participation.

The first reason was that many planners reported a sense that it was morally the right thing to do. A number of respondents linked participation in planning to fundamental democratic ideals:

> "One of the things I like and I enjoy about planning is that it's a public, democratic, transparent process." (Sarah)

There was talk of participation as key to planning being a democratic process and even Lucy, one of the few 'openly anti-participation' interviewees, commented that:

> "I don't think participation is useful [in practice] but I do think democracy in planning is very important."

Brian went further and talked of participation as the morally right thing to do:

> "Participation is important for a number of reasons.... One is I think it's in a sense morally right to do so if you're planning for other people's environment and their future way of life."

James spoke similarly, noting that "we manage change on behalf of society". Indeed, it seems the link between participation and planning was so strong that it was almost inconceivable to do planning without some sort of participation, as Bill stated:

> "You couldn't do planning without participation. What you'd be delivering without participation would be some sort of quasi-legal that's saying to people: this is what you're doing, end of story. That is just not acceptable. Mean, the bottom line is, well, we are professionals, and we can have a good go at trying to get it right. It's patently obvious,

however, that we're humans and we'll not get it all right. And there are many good ideas out there."

While participation may be seen as intrinsically the right thing to do, the data also show that planners see it as something useful to do. In the survey, 63.2 per cent of respondents agreed or strongly agreed that 'public participation exercises are useful' (see Figure 6.3). Naturally this does not tell us why the planners tend to think public participation is useful. The interview data suggest a number of possible reasons.

Several interviewees stated that public participation could actually improve the outcome of the planning process. Brian commented that:

> "I think it actually improves the product, quite often people will know things, will have ideas that you as a planner don't have, either because you can't literally know everything particularly if you are dealing with a different area, and different people come at things from different perspectives so what you end up with is a richer response."

Ray even thought it was "dangerous" not to have reference to the public. This improvement seemed to stem from technical and political factors. One of the most important factors was that public participation

Figure 6.3: Opinion on whether 'public participation exercises are useful' (*n* = 601)

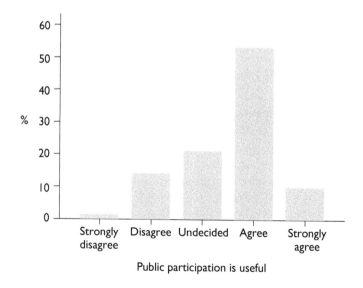

Public participation is useful

was seen as a method for ascertaining local knowledge that the planner was unaware of, as Derek happily admitted:

> "I think the public very often are aware of things locally that you are not, it has to be said. They're the ones in the local area who know what's happening, even what's likely to happen and who's thinking about what."

Alongside this deficit model justification was the idea that participation offered the opportunity to gain insight into the public preference for how the area should develop.

It may not simply be a case of planners lacking local knowledge or insight into local preferences, but rather that their knowledge is somehow restricted because modern target-driven planning was a 'conveyor belt':

> "As a planning officer you're on a conveyor belt dealing with applications largely if you're in DC and you can become very blinkered to that process and you think you've got a lot of experience … but you don't live at a site or not a site, you may not shop at that shopping centre, you may not go to that place and so on, people can bring new issues to the table that you haven't thought about." (Mandy)

This idea of planners being 'blinkered' is an interesting metaphor, given the Labour government's performance regime and the continued drive for efficiency. It is interesting to note, however, that planners usually maintain a monopoly on judging the legitimacy of such local knowledge, as discussed below.

A further rationale is the idea that participation processes can somehow add legitimacy and validity to the process:

> "Is public participation important to you personally? I suppose it is yes purely from the point of view that it can lend validity to your outcomes." (Gareth)

What is not entirely clear here is whether legitimacy is added as the public's attitudes have been better incorporated into the planning process through participation, or whether it is simply that allowing a chance for participation gives the appearance of validity, even if you ignore what is said (cf Cooke and Kothari, 2001).

Certainly Gwilym suggested that participation could add to transparency and allow people to see how a decision was reached, even if it was not the decision they might prefer:

> "If you've got transparency in your system they can see why, they can see the whole process all the way through and they understand again how we handle the process of applications, why we come to our final decision."

This hints at participation existing to allow the public to feel that they have been heard, even if their views are then ignored. This emerged even more explicitly during some interviews, for example, when Martin discussed public speaking rights at planning committees:

> "It's turned the first night when we do the public speaking, it's a sort of theatre really ... in the sense of everything being seen to be done and people getting it off their chests, everybody sitting there playing their part in this theatre and all having their go, I think it, it helps people feel happier with the decision even if they don't agree with it and even though it's usually too late to have that much of an influence."

The imagery of a theatre here is revealing, suggesting participation processes are somewhat of a performance. Such participation could be understood as a sort of therapy on Arnstein's ladder (Arnstein, 1969), allowing the public to feel they have been heard even if they are ignored. These mechanisms may provide an outlet for frustrations at development proposals people dislike, reducing resentments being expressed directly to the planner. Such use of participation as a tactic for absorbing criticism could explain planners' support.

We can, however, go even lower on Arnstein's ladder, to the level of 'manipulation'. Here there was some sense that participation could be used to convince the public of the planner's own (or more usually, their council or central government's) agenda. This was occasionally commented on in interviews, for example, by Brian:

> "If you can build that trust and build that cooperation what you will end up with is a plan more people will accept and then you don't end up with a battle to try and get it adopted."

Perhaps this was central government's agenda when it promoted a frontloading approach; certainly under Labour, centrally dictated housing targets in England were almost non-negotiable at the local level and thus a process that encouraged local people to be convinced of the worth of such development could be something central government would wish to encourage.

Such impulses may appear Machiavellian, yet may also be understood as coping strategies deployed by pressurised SLBs. However they are understood, there certainly appeared to be genuine support among many planners for an idea of participation as a useful source of local knowledge and as a fundamentally important process in a democratic planning system. But while there was some consensus among survey respondents and interviewees about the benefits participation could bring, there was also some consensus on difficulties associated with it, as we explore in the next section.

Concerns surrounding participation in practice

While no planners explicitly made philosophical arguments against participation (as opposed to some who made the argument that it was morally right, a democratic imperative), the practical concerns surrounding participation raised by interviewees actually go to the very heart of the debate surrounding participation. These concerns appeared to fall into four key themes, namely, the amount and the ease of participation, and the nature of who got involved and what they discussed.

A noticeable trend among many interviewees was a feeling that, while they might support participation, there was now enough of it, especially considering recent government pressures in favour of a more participatory agenda. Therefore, quite simply, Jenny stated:

> "I think we've got enough participation to be honest. I think there's enough already."

Boyd presented a reason as to why he felt that there did not need to be any more than at present:

> "There's a danger I think of having too much public participation and that schemes get hijacked or lose sight of the overall goal and get bogged down in the nitty-gritty of the sort of, I don't know, cracks in the pavement and dog mess worries and that bigger vision is, if you like, lost."

The imagery of being "bogged down", or as Mark put it, "snowed under by representations", is particularly telling of a wider attitude towards participation, which is that it is indeed in conflict with the other key government agenda, that of efficiency. Nevertheless, the many planners who did not want more participation were not anti-participation per se; they just wanted limits to it:

> "There is a line that has to be drawn, it's only another component of planning. Planning can't be driven by public participation, it's just got to be a part of it, in my opinion." (Shaun)

This attitude was evident in several interviews, but was not entirely supported by the survey data. Respondents were asked if more public participation was needed to improve planning. While more planners disagreed (44.2 per cent) than agreed (34.0 per cent), as Figure 6.4 illustrates, this was by no means a majority opinion. There were clearly quite variable views in the profession on this.

As well as concern surrounding the amount of participation, there was concern regarding the ease of actually being involved with participation. As Figure 6.5 illustrates, there was strong disagreement with the statement 'being involved with public participation exercise is easy' in the survey, with 72.8 per cent of respondents either disagreeing

Figure 6.4: Opinion on whether 'more public participation is needed to improve planning' (*n* = 599)

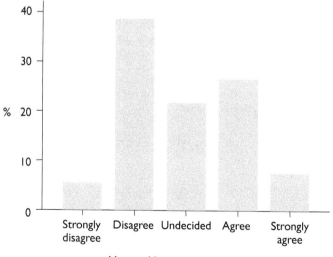

More public participation needed

Figure 6.5: Opinion on whether 'being involved with public participation exercises is easy' (*n* = 600)

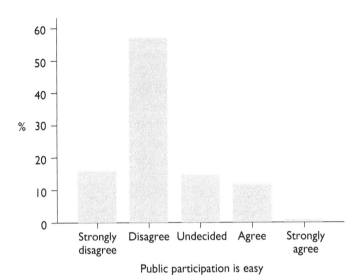

Public participation is easy

or strongly disagreeing. This suggests that planners tend to find participation difficult. Interview data suggest several reasons why. One possibility is that planners lack relevant skills, since consultation is not the focus of their technical skill:

"All planners think they're really good at consultation, [but] most of us are rubbish at it. And it's only when you come into contact with consultation professionals you realise how rubbish we are." (David)

Nonetheless, this is not a view with wide currency in the profession; no other planner made similar comments. More often they seemed to feel they lacked the time or necessary resources to do participation well.

In interviews, there were numerous tales of how hard participation could be due to the nature of certain participants focusing their anger and resentment at proposals on to the planning officer. Quite typical was Paul, who talked of the abuse sometimes directed at him during participation exercises:

"The other thing about public participation, and it's very difficult from a professional point of view, is that whereas a planning officer always has to have a calm, measured response, that's not true of the public. They can say the most outrageous things, the public, they can be very rude to planning officers and so forth and you can't really do anything about it.... Barely a week goes by without being accused of taking backhanders. That's fairly standard. I've been accused of being, well, all sorts of things."

Several respondents suggested that such abuse was common and may be symptomatic of a society with lower levels of respect for those in public service and a higher level of atomistic individualism, with the accompanying feeling that someone must be to blame for things running counter to the interests of the individual (see Campbell and Marshall, 2000).

Ray gave a more extreme example of a difficult participation event:

"I was involved in, helped with, the LDF consultation recently. I was given a schedule with a Wetherspoon's visit exercise, part of the move to hold these events in more accessible places. And I thought, great, I can pop in on my way home and have a bit of a chat in the pub, nice one. Well, what we have had is a proposed building on part of [Name] Park. And this is a building proposed on just one little tiny part of that but it has been hugely controversial. So anyway, the day before my consultation exercise, a colleague had had one in another part of the city and he had had a hell of a time of it. The press were there, people got angry, it all got a little out of hand and in the end the police were called. So I turn up to the pub, right, and there's the police.... I had a uniformed copper there when I did my meeting, standing beside me for the whole meeting."

While police attendance may be an extreme example, there is no doubt participation exercises that take such a confrontational form may well make planners find the process difficult. There is also the danger of a negative cycle occurring, whereby a bad experience of participation then poisons future interactions.

Finally, at a deeper level, planners may well find participation exercises difficult because by their nature they question the planner's professional judgement and technical expertise. Participation suggests the planner cannot know fully what is going on in an area or local preferences, which runs counter to the origins of a welfare state technocracy as one staffed by professional experts who knew what was best for the public without having to ask them. By questioning the planner's expertise, participation forces planners to think through proposals in different ways (indeed, this is the whole point). Tony told me that you could not get away with 'sloppy arguments' when involved in participation:

"However good you are as a professional I think you are bound to question and examine your own reasoning and work out your defence of your professional position much more thoroughly when the public is that active in the process and that is very frustrating in some ways but it also very good for you ... in that situation you can't get away with sloppy arguments."

We therefore have an image of an 'active public' constructing a 'defensive professional' which helps to explain why so many planners found participation difficult. This is not to say they dismiss its value – Tony, for example, was actually supportive of participation when saying it forced him to think things through more thoroughly – but rather that as 'reflexive professionals' they accept it as a necessary part of their thought process. There are, however, further reasons why participation may be difficult in practice, and these can be found in regard to who got involved and what they talked about during participation exercises.

The most commonly cited area of concern among planners was around who got involved in participation exercises in practice. A common framing here involved the use of the term 'the usual suspects'. The impression was of domination by certain individuals and organisations so that planners needed to engage other sections of the community. Gerard spoke of the 'middle-class voice' of participation, and how residents of more disadvantaged neighbourhoods usually felt disenfranchised, so were less likely to participate. Mike went further and suggested you could not reach beyond the 'usual suspects' no matter how hard you tried:

"I think the trouble with public participation is that it doesn't actually reach the majority of public no matter how hard you try. Basically you get a small number of the same people turning up time and time again and they're the ones who will make their views known. It's largely, not exclusively but largely, the middle-class vociferous and articulate sorts who make the noise."

Although others highlighted the stringent efforts being made to engage the 'hard to reach groups', there seems to have been a feeling among many of the interviewees that not only was it was the 'same old faces', but that these 'usual suspects' could be characterised as 'vocal activists' who dominated the processes. Bill, for example, mentioned that:

> "It's very difficult, when you're dealing with activist objectors, it's very hard to determine whether these objections are representative of the community ... or whether they actually represent the feelings of a very vocal minority."

Bill seemed to have some difficultly determining the legitimacy of complaints. Other planners did not share this difficulty; David had no doubt that certain lobby groups did not represent the wider public interest:

> "It tends to be dominated by pressure groups and individuals who are, are personally very vocal and represent a very sectionable interest within the community."

This evocation of a threatening imagery of vocal minorities dominating the process was used by many in defence of their own professional importance. Representativeness is a commonly cited problem with participation in academic debate (see, for example, Thomas, 1996).

An image of such pressure groups brings to mind the classic figure of 'NIMBY' (Warburton, 2002; Portney, 2003). This may well be a pejorative term, but the term was raised during the initial interviews so the survey included the statement 'In practice, public participation is dominated by NIMBYs'. Some 70.1 per cent of respondents agreed or strongly agreed with the statement (see Figure 6.6). It was striking that not one of over 600 respondents strongly disagreed with this statement.

It was therefore of little surprise that the term NIMBY appeared in the in-depth interviews. For example, Patrick commented that:

> "I'm afraid I think that the system is monopolised by a very small number of people, call them NIMBYs if you want. I think planning gets a bad name from people who do monopolise the system in a negative way and do stifle development taking place."

A couple of planners, notably Margaret, did say they felt that NIMBYism was a perfectly understandable position to hold. Indeed, through having public participation, the public are encouraged to

Figure 6.6: Opinion on the statement 'In practice, public participation is dominated by NIMBYs' (*n* = 601)

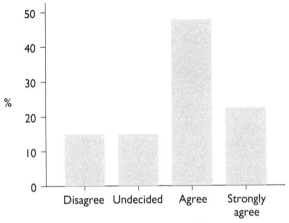

Public participation is NIMBY dominated

express their opinions about the impacts on their property and local environment. Nevertheless, the overall impression was that planners tended to find difficulties with participation exercises because they were 'dominated by NIMBYs'.

Clearly the NIMBY represents a particular type of person, a 'vocal minority' (linking to the issue of representativeness of participants), but also someone who raises a particular subject matter during participation: opposition to development. Andrew felt that people got involved in planning just to object because "they don't want to see any change". Simon even suggested the public had become increasingly opposed to development during his career.

There was clear evidence of NIMBY-type attitudes making participation difficult for planners across Britain.[3] The reason why this should be so is evident from Derek's comment:

> "I think people have to realise that development is happening, and will happen, and the key to doing it is to influence it at the start, not trying to fight a rearguard action."

The key to this is that 'development is happening, and will happen', and simple opposition to that is not, for the professional public sector planner at least, an option, particularly given the strong pro-development (particularly housing development) push which was then (and to a large extent still is) coming from central government. It is therefore planners at the coalface who are left mediating the tension between such government pressures and the opposition of NIMBYs.

A further area of concern was that participants frequently wanted to talk about matters which planners considered outside their remit. Sometimes it was emotional factors, as Lisa outlined:

> "I think it's difficult for people to grasp sometimes what are planning issues and what aren't, and people tend to talk about, well I've been there since I was five, it's always been lovely … the fact you've lived there all your life and you love it how it is, that isn't a consideration."

John stated that in some cases, people tried to bring in civil disputes and other matters to planning:

> "I'm not going to sit and listen to crap, people talking about civil issues attached to their site – I will tell them straight, 'this isn't a planning issue, I can't talk to you any more about this here'…when you have people continually coming back using the planning department as a vent for their frustration or neighbour disputes, I won't take it."

On other occasions it was that the issue was something over which there was very little local discretion:

> "It makes it very difficult when you say to people, 'actually our room for manoeuvre on it is very limited because we've got to have 11,000 dwellings here because the Regional Spatial Strategy says so'. 'We don't want them.' 'Well sorry but you're going to.' What's the point of the consultation? So people are concerned, if they do get involved, their ability really to change things….There's not a great range of freedom to act. And that breeds a bit of cynicism." (George)

In other cases, Mike said it was simply nothing to do at all with the topic of the participation exercise:

> "'It would be worthwhile', usually written in capital letters and green ink, 'if you would do something about the bloody dog crap in the park'. That's what it really came down to. That's public participation. There was nothing that actually contributed directly to the topic we were consulting on."

The image of "dog crap in the park" is striking. This is not to say that neighbour disputes or dog faeces are not things about which people feel strongly, it is just that the individual planner has no authority to deal with them and this, perhaps, may make participation processes difficult for them.

Such concerns being unmet may be difficult for participants as well, an idea prevalent in the interviews. People may express their opinion and then feel somehow let down when the LPA, for whatever reason, acts contrary to it. Daniel called this "sowing disappointment", and Jane felt this could make future participation more difficult:

> "It's, it's sad really that people in communities put so much energy into this sort of thing, and they do. They spend hours and they have public meetings, people go along, they say what they think and they feel that they've done their civic duty. And nothing comes of it. I think my fear is that then just brings forward a mood of cynicism and refusal to participate."

Indeed, this was actually presented as a 'danger' by Vic:

> "There is also a danger of consultation, consultation, consultation and nothing actually changes."

Such concern speaks of a desire for participation to work effectively, although there were very few suggestions during the interviews for how participation could work better.

The planner's place in participation

Beyond the data highlighting both support for, and concerns about, participation in practice, a further clear trend emerging from the data was that planners often implicitly or explicitly positioned themselves as a professional self in relation to public participation. So, for example, whether participation was a good thing or not, it was something that needed careful management by professional planners. Mark was clear in suggesting there was a need for management of participation:

> "By their very nature, participatory mechanisms are often quite uncontrollable, and that does set off a tension. So, it, it needs a lot of managing and, I think, as the nature of local government politics is changing, there's more and

more focus on, on officers to manage that, rather than local members to manage that."

We can only speculate about why it should be so uncontrollable; perhaps it is because issues may be raised that are not relevant to planning, or concern about certain opinions dominating the entire event, or because of experiences such as that of having to have police protection during a participation event. Martin offered an interesting anecdote about the technique he had developed to manage participation events, which involved having people sit at round tables, six or so members of the public and one professional planner at each table acting as a mediator. He explained:

> "We developed a technique for public meetings because it was fatally easy with a public meeting to have the council on the stage at one end and 200 people in the hall being taken over by activists, if you like ... who would set up a sort of anti-dialogue and it would turn the whole thing into a completely negative experience."

The result was apparently that:

> "At the end of that process people had had a dialogue. People who wouldn't be seen dead standing up in a public meeting and being able to talk to somebody, and at the end of that process the officer stood up reported back so that people could hear these concerns being expressed around the room. You could hear the consensus of the areas of concern emerging, if you like, and everybody knew that their concerns had been put fairly and they were then responded to by senior officers. It really was effective because it took all the steam out of the meeting."

This technique could be seen in a negative light as a tool of control and manipulation, of planners trying to stifle what was said by participants and of evading difficult topics. But it could also be seen more positively as a method for promoting consensus and even 'communicative rationality' by helping to ensure a more productive dialogue between all participants and planners rather than just a shouting match between professionals and a vocal minority. That said, the mediator role promoted here appears to be one very much where the planner was in control, so there could be a degree of professional self-interest driving such techniques.

A second way in which planners seemed to be maintaining a central role for themselves in participation was with the suggestion 'ultimately decisions have to be made'; John succinctly commented that:

> "There's a balance to be found, you need people to make decisions. But also we need some public participation."

This suggests that decisions could not be made by public discussion alone. Instead there was a need for a professional, a point Barry was quite clear on when he suggested planners still needed to be in the 'driving seat':

> "If you think planning is basically about conflict resolution someone is going to lose out and again I think there's a naivety that actually if you sit and talk about it everyone will be happy."

It is therefore apparently vital that the planner retains the ability to frame the debate through writing development plans, to recommend a decision to elected members or to determine planning applications under delegated powers.

Finally, planners also tended to identify themselves as the ultimate judges of legitimacy in the participation process. Michael was actively judging the legitimacy of some concerns expressed during participation:

> "Obviously sometimes you, you get some very silly remarks from people. It's inevitable."

Bill even more explicitly suggested that some concerns can be "legitimate":

> "I think there are many legitimate concerns for communities, and many of these that do come back can be very legitimate, and all lead to changes in the plan."

While some may be reassured to hear that 'legitimate' concerns are taken into account, this does beg the question of what happens to 'non-legitimate' concerns. Presumably these are discounted or ignored, and the planners themselves decide legitimacy. This is indicative of planners placing themselves in a privileged position with respect to participation.

The argument made by many planners during the interviews was that there was a need for planners to ensure that those who shouted the loudest did not come to dominate the planning process, to the detriment of the "greater good":

> "It must be a democratic decision and process to a certain extent. What they say is important but it's obviously a question of balancing what are in effect kind of private, personal interests against the greater good." (Toby)

Indeed, the planner is seen as a champion of the values and interests of the 'silent majority', the polar opposite of the 'vocal minority'. It is easy to be critical of such ideas. One could question how exactly planners are in a privileged position to know the wishes of the silent majority. Indeed, there are longstanding arguments against the idea that planners can decide what is best for an area, with a strong critique emerging in the 1970s (Giddings and Hopwood, 2006). Further, there is evidence in other studies which suggest that opinions which do not agree with those of the planner are the ones most likely to be dismissed as coming from a NIMBY or vocal minority, whatever the true balance of opinion on the matter (Tait and Campbell, 2000; Ellis, 2004; Harrison et al, 2004; Barnes et al, 2007). And as Taylor suggests, there is a tendency for officials to want participants who could think strategically and 'play the game', but not 'the usual suspects': 'under these circumstances it was difficult to see who would be constructed as a valid community player' (2007, p 307). Nevertheless, this Benthamite 'greater good' construction appears very important to how planners justify their actions, as we explore in Chapter Seven. Overall, there is clear evidence that planners place themselves very much in control of participation processes, as actively needing to manage them and as judges of legitimacy. These themes resonate if we turn our attention from the specific public participation in planning arena to the wider public sector to be more 'customer' responsive.

Applying the 'customer' concept to planning

A term in use

When asked whether they used the term 'customers' in their work, 60.4 per cent of survey respondents answered 'yes', leaving a fairly significant minority of 39.4 per cent who did not use the term. Gerard stated that it was a corporate priority:

"We don't use the term day to day but I guess if you looked in a corporate document it would say 'customers' because the authority has this customer contact centre approach."

Those using the term highlighted its use in local authorities since the 1990s, particularly with initiatives such as the Major government's 'Citizen's Charter' leading to a growing awareness across local authorities about issues of customer care:

"Yes I use the term, although it's a bit dated these days. I suppose stakeholder has come more to the fore, customers having a John Major feel. Citizens Charter, you know. It was a legitimate thing the Tories did in changing public management to actually look at people who use the services." (Les)

There appeared to be widespread support within the profession for the ideas of improved 'customer service' that go along with the customer ideal. A number of the Likert agreements addressed customer service issues, and Table 6.3 summarises the results. It is noticeable that a strong majority of 88.9 per cent of respondents agreed or strongly agreed that customer satisfaction was important to them, as Figure 6.7 illustrates. This is perhaps unsurprising, given that there has been this corporate

Table 6.3: Summary of responses for Likert agreement measuring how much respondents agreed or disagreed with various statements relating to 'customers' and planning on a scale of 1 (strongly disagree to 5 (strongly agree)

Likert statement	n	Median	Mode	% strongly disagree	% disagree	% undecided	% agree	% strongly agree
The planning service meets the needs of its 'customers'	598	3.00	4	2.5	26.9	24.4	44.0	2.2
'Customer satisfaction' is important to me	603	4.00	4	0.7	3.6	6.8	67.8	21.1
The term 'customers' is a useful label in planning	602	3.00	4	7.6	29.6	24.8	33.1	5.0
It is important to strike a balance between 'customers'	590	4.00	4	0.0	5.0	11.9	64.2	18.6
The applicant pays so has a right to a good service	599	4.00	4	1.5	9.3	6.2	70.8	12.2

Figure 6.7: Opinion on whether "'customer satisfaction" is important to me' (*n* = 603)

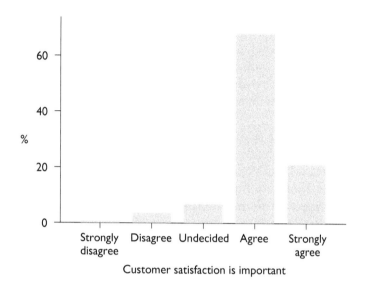

Customer satisfaction is important

drive to promote 'customer service' ideals across authorities for a number of years, although this does not tell us how those planners defined the customers or what they thought customer satisfaction meant.

Analysis of the Likert agreement statements about customers found no relationship between opinion and the age, gender, job focus or location of the respondent. There was, however, a strongly significant relationship between thinking customer satisfaction was important and job seniority, as measured on a chi-squared test ($p \leq 0.007$, df = 12). Senior planners were more likely to strongly agree that 'customer satisfaction is important to me'. Senior planners were also more likely to agree that 'the planning service meets the needs of its customers' ($p \leq 0.05$, df = 12), that 'it is important to strike a balance between customers' ($p \leq 0.000$, df = 12) and that 'the applicant pays so has a right to a good service' (senior planners more likely to agree; $p \leq 0.021$, df = 12). But again, we see a pattern of seniority within the profession appearing to be a stronger determinant of opinion than geography, even in post-devolution Britain.

A number of interviewees spoke about what customer satisfaction meant to them, and it seemed to focus on basic service levels. David commented about service standards:

"We've got all sorts of leaflets setting out service standards, what we will do, how long it will take us to meet you in reception and to contact you and all this kind of stuff. We are becoming much more, it's an over-used term, 'customer focused', but we are becoming more, more aware of that."

Similarly Alistair talked about the 'customer charter':

"We have a customer charter setting out the level of service people can expect, for example, the amount of time to answer the phone or time taken to answer letters and emails."

Andrew mentioned similar service standards, but went further in highlighting how this applied to everyone, not just applicants:

"The term came in over the last 10 years. Everybody who uses the planning system is a customer. It doesn't matter if they're an objector, an applicant, an agent. They are deemed, I think now by every local authority, as customers.... I think this authority has tried to appease customers a lot. You know, you have the complaints form, you have to reply to letters in 15 days and so on."

It is interesting that he talks about "appeasing" customers since this suggests a certain cynicism about these service standards, similar to Bolton's (2002) findings among nurses. In terms of the definition of customers offered by Andrew, Martin agreed, and said this raised a difficulty in conducting customer satisfaction surveys:

"It's everybody so it's extremely difficult identifying customers.... It's an exceptionally wide range and that makes it difficult to do the sort of conventional customer surveys."

Interestingly, one of the BVPIs for planning in England did attempt to measure customer satisfaction, but was focused on the applicant as the customer (as raised earlier). The survey data also suggested that the majority (83.0 per cent) agreed or strongly agreed that the applicant paid so had a right to a 'good service' (see Figure 6.8).

The data suggest that the majority of planners did use the term 'customers' and that the customer ideal for them came down to customer satisfaction and service standard issues. There was a belief that

Figure 6.8: Opinion on the whether 'the applicant pays so has a right to a good service' (n = 599)

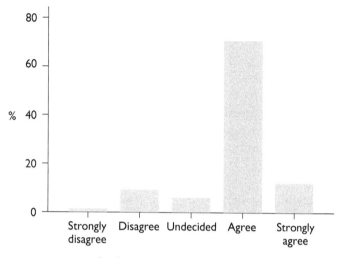

Applicant pays so deserves good service

the applicant was paying a fee and so should expect a good service. But there was also a sense that the term had become so over-used in the public service it had become anodyne; it was used as it had to be used to soothe managerial and central government impulses but meant little more than providing a good level of service.

Who is the 'customer' in planning?

Despite support for the use of the term 'customer' and agreement that customer satisfaction was important, both survey and interview data strongly suggest that planners did not define the 'customer' as just the applicant. Asked to define who they thought the 'customers' of LPAs were (in an open question in the survey), planners gave a range of responses, as illustrated by Table 6.4 and Figure 6.9.

The single largest answer here was a list of multiple customers, usually listing something along the lines of applicants, objectors, residents, community, councillors and government departments as the customers of LPAs. Other popular answers included 'everyone', 'local residents' or 'the community', 'the public' and 'anyone using the service' or 'anyone affected by planning matters'. The idea that developers were the primary customers of LPAs did not get much support; just 20 out of 612 respondents defined the customer of planning as just the applicant (or developer), compared to 59 who defined it as just the public and

Table 6.4: Who respondents thought the 'customers' of LPAs were (groups created from responses)

		Frequency	%	Valid %	Cumulative %
Valid	Everyone	76	12.4	13.0	13.0
	Taxpayers	2	0.3	0.3	13.3
	Local residents/community	73	11.9	12.5	25.8
	Applicant + Objector + Residents + Community + Government etc	257	42.0	43.9	69.6
	The public	59	9.6	10.1	79.7
	Anyone using service	88	14.4	15.0	94.7
	Society	2	0.3	0.3	95.1
	Developers/applicants	20	3.3	3.4	98.5
	Stakeholders	4	0.7	0.7	99.1
	The environment	5	0.8	0.9	100.0
	Total	586	95.8	100.0	
Missing		26	4.2		
Total		612	100.0		

Figure 6.9: Who respondents thought the 'customers' of LPAs were (groups created from responses)

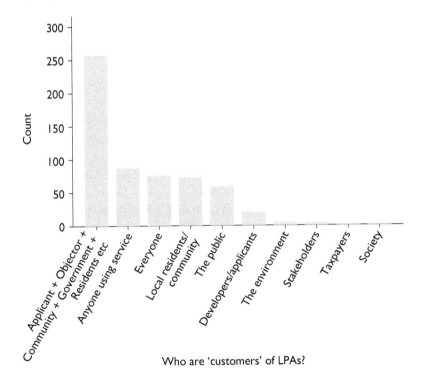

Who are 'customers' of LPAs?

73 who defined it as just the local residents or the community (not the applicant or developer).

There was support for this prevailing idea of the customer being everyone who came into contact with the planning department, both from those who seemed more supportive of the concept and those who did not:

> "I very often use the term customers, which means anybody that we deal with." (Patrick)

> "I don't often use the word customers. I usually use the word applicant or member of the public but in effect they're all customers as is the greater public good which is the most important customer of all." (Toby)

It is worth noting that Toby, who did not like the term customer, made an explicit link to the "greater public good" as "the most important customer". Such a concept is, perhaps, difficult to perceive of through a traditional understanding of the idea of customers, and is similar language as was used by some interviewees when discussing managing public participation. It was similar to a comment by Sarah, who spoke of a duty to the wider public:

> "The public are my customers, not necessarily the applicant. The wider public is who I serve and I have a duty to them and to the profession."

The most usual comment in interview, however, was to provide a list of people who the planner thought were their customers (including applicant and community), as Michael did:

> "I don't particularly like the term customers, but at the end of the day, we are public servants. And so we need to serve the customers or clients or whoever they may be and they can be the developer, the advocate, neighbours, everyone basically, consultees, objectors."

Interestingly, Michael and Daniel even added non-human objects:

> "The environment could be considered a key customer too." (Michael)

> "The interesting thing about planning is we have inanimate customers, things like listed buildings and major conservation sites. We have a job to do that, whose interests we have to champion regardless of whether people want us to or not. I regard my customers as the people of the district, the district's natural environment and business interests, in that order." (Daniel)

The idea of buildings or the environment being customers clearly goes well beyond any usual definition of the concept, yet seems to capture the spirit motivating the work of planners with the natural and built environment. It highlights that for most planners, their job was not just about processing applications but also about considering developments against the wider needs of society and the environment. Many planners clearly felt strongly about providing a good service to community groups and objectors as well as applicants. In a sense this in itself somewhat undermines the concept since it is normally defined in terms of individuals and conceptualised around a direct transactional relationship between service provider and service consumer.

Some of the wider issues were highlighted directly by Sam:

> "Customers, oh God!... Ultimately, the community as a whole is the customer of the planning service, and there's still that bit of old welfare state ideology, I think. A lot of tensions I've been talking about is because we've got a welfare state legislation based professional outlook, if you like, that's sort of, come up hard against, you know the individual, it's me, me, me."

Customers in action

The wide range of customers defined by planners thus suggests a need to somehow strike a balance between the different groups of customers. A total of 82.8 per cent of survey respondents agreed or strongly agreed (and no single respondent strongly disagreed) that it was important to 'strike a balance between customers' (see Figure 6.10). This is quite different from a typical perception of a service provider–customer relationship, even elsewhere in the public sector. The idea of balancing between customers came up numerous times during the interviews, where it was explained what this meant in practice and why it was necessary.

Figure 6.10: Opinion on whether 'it is important to strike a balance between "customers"' (*n* = 590)

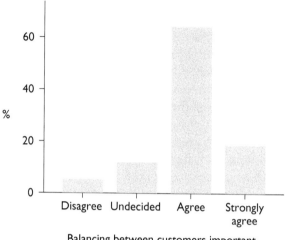

Balancing between customers important

At a base level, it was suggested that there was a need to balance between customers because all users of planning services were customers, but they had different interests and expectations. Simon, Steve and Jonathan outlined the complex dynamics of the relationship in their joint interview:

> Simon: "The customer model is very prevalent in areas like street sweeping, you know, services where, if you put more resources into them, they get better and better. And people get more and more satisfied. But planning, you're, you've got conflicting views and, you know, conflicting interests ... so you're never going to satisfy everyone."

> Steve: "Indeed, yes, yes that's right, yes.... You've got different customers. The applicant is a customer but also the residents out there on the street are customers and sometimes there is that conflict if you're satisfying one, you're not satisfying another."

> Jonathan: "Yes, and unlike other transactions, it's not a two-way process, it's not a case of the provider and the user, because in planning you've got third parties. And normally in a transaction, you know, you don't have that kind of dynamic, the three-way split."

The difficulty of planning decisions inevitably pleasing some customers but not others likewise arose in several interviews, and such ideas of ultimate 'winners' and 'losers' from planning decisions inevitably suggests a certain complexity and difficulty for planners in the use of customer ideals.

While most planners spoke of a need to balance the different customers, some felt there needed to be an overall 'principal customer'. Nigel was clear that the community was the "ultimate customer". Sam felt that there would inevitably be a perception that one customer had the "upper hand" and that everyone's expectations needed managing:

> "It's the question of which customer has the upper hand. I mean everyone's entitled to expect that the planning service will deliver something for them. I suppose it's a matter of expectation. A neighbour should expect the planning service will deliver the best designed and most suitable form of development. I don't think they can necessarily expect it will just stop the development, even if that is what they would like."

One particular take on the balancing act was presented by Mark, who mobilised notions of 'society' in his explanation of how to manage competing customer interests:

> "I think planning is about society ... there is this notion that if you act in the best interests of society, in the long run, everyone will benefit. Now, that's what I think planning's about. So you know, I could probably list a whole series of customers but all these customers have conflicting requirements from the planning system. And therefore, the best way is to try, and whatever way possible, to act in the best interests of this notion of society."

This discussion of serving society takes us well beyond traditional notions of the customer, but seemed a fairly common idea that planners used to justify their professional actions. The basic idea of 'balancing customers' was widespread, even among ardent supporters of the language of customers (see also Kitchen, 2006, a former frontline planner who himself made this very argument).

Such ideas of customers as everyone and of competing customer interests needing balancing represents a marked departure from traditional conceptions of the customer. This therefore raises the issue of whether 'customers' is a useful label in the planning context. Opinion was markedly divided between survey respondents, with 38.1 per cent agreeing or strongly agreeing that it was a useful label, 37.2 per cent disagreeing or strongly disagreeing and 24.8 per cent undecided (see Figure 6.11). Opponents of the label tended to be much more vocal in interview than supporters, although some of the factors cited by supporters have already been mentioned.

Many opponents were concerned that using the language of the customer and associated ideas would inevitably lead to some sort of privileging of the applicant (particularly as they paid directly for the service, as opposed to local residents who paid indirectly through taxation). Tony said that he was "suspicious" of the term 'customers':

> "It's not a term I use. I suppose it's a term that I'm slightly suspicious of ... I suppose one of my fears about the use of the term customers with respect to development control is that it's quite easy to see the people who make planning applications as customers and it's rather more difficult to assesses how other people who are affected by it are being served."

There was concern that, while applicants deserved a good service, they could not be *the* customer, and this was explicitly talked of as a 'danger' by two interviewees.

Figure 6.11: Opinion on whether 'the term "customers" is a useful label in planning' (*n* = 602)

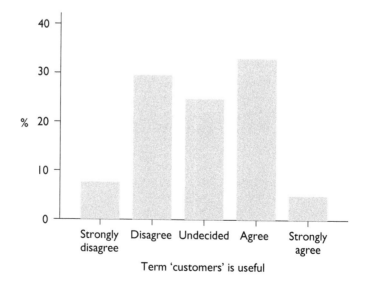

Term 'customers' is useful

More broadly, some planners opposed the label for more ideological reasons. They felt the notion of customers was inappropriate in the public sector planning context:

"No I don't use the term customers, not unless I am out shopping. I don't think planning does have customers, I think it is service in the public interest." (Lucy)

Roger provided more detail:

"Customers is a concept which clearly has validity in a market economy, where customers have a choice. But in the planning system, which is sort of a regulatory system, people don't have any choice, unlike a customer going into a shop … you deal with a developer, but have to also think of your other customer all of the time, which is the community, and I just don't think that the term customer helps at all. It just absolutely gets in the way, and you get a totally false picture of the nature of the relationship that you have with the people who are trapped with the planning system."

Such ideological concern was strongly expressed, but it seemed that it was more common for opponents of the customer label to be concerned about the practical danger that it might overly privilege the applicant over other groups.

There was therefore mixed feeling about the use of the label customers in planning. While there was a feeling that the customer service provision was important (perhaps partly driven by such ideas becoming corporate priorities for many local authorities), there was also a feeling that all users of planning services were customers. A significant number of planners seemed to suggest that the community, the 'public good' or society were more important customers than the applicant, even if most also thought the applicant should have a good quality service in exchange for their fee. It is easy to suggest that such ideas again privilege the role of the professional planner as the one to do this balancing of interests and to respond to the 'public good' – just as seemed to be the case with respect to public participation – without much evidence of how they were equipped to do this. But we would suggest that these ideals stem from the very motivations and ideals of the profession. They are the reasons most people entered planning, and what they believed it meant to be a planner, as we explore further in the next chapter.

Localism and neighbourhood planning

The broad approach to public participation in planning pursued under New Labour in the first decade of the 21st century remains the current situation in Scotland and Wales. However, since the election of the Coalition government in 2010, the prospect of radical reform in this arena has emerged, with the headline-grabbing adoption of neighbourhood planning. Neighbourhood planning:

> ... empowers communities to shape the development and growth of a local area through the production of a neighbourhood development plan, a neighbourhood development order or a Community Right to Build Order. Neighbourhood development plans will become part of the local statutory development plan and will form the basis for determining planning applications in that area. A neighbourhood development order enables the community to grant planning permission for the development it wishes to see. (DCLG, 2012b)

The introduction of Neighbourhood Plans follows the rhetoric of *Open source planning* (The Conservative Party, 2010) which promised local planning rooted in civic engagement and collaborative democracy, playing a major role in decentralising power and strengthening society. Where parish and town councils are in existence (mainly rural areas), they will lead the production of Neighbourhood Plans. Elsewhere, groups of at least 21 local residents and stakeholders will need to come together to form a Neighbourhood Forum, defining the area covered by their neighbourhood and get approval from the relevant LPA that they are a representative forum covering a coherent neighbourhood area. Once a plan has been prepared, an independent examiner will check the plan is in conformity with local and national policies, and there will need to be support from the majority of local electors voting in a referendum before it becomes part of the statutory development plan (DCLG, 2011b). The bar is thus set quite high.

It is also interesting to note that, contrary to many expectations when the policy was first mooted, DCLG stated that:

> If the local planning authority says that an area needs to grow, then communities cannot use neighbourhood planning to block the building of new homes and businesses. They can, however, use neighbourhood planning to influence

the type, design, location and mix of new development. (DCLG, 2011b, p 3)

This is interesting because of the relationship between the localism/ participation agenda and the efficiency agenda discussed in the previous chapter. Virtually none of the planning element of the Budget statement 2011 had featured in the Conservatives' *Open source planning* Green Paper of March 2010 (The Conservative Party, 2010). And very little of it was originally intended for inclusion in the Localism Bill. So what accounts for the apparent contradictory commitments between more local participation and more top-down policies in favour of economic growth?

Perhaps the reason could have been that, as some commentators had been speculating (Tewdwr-Jones, 2011), the Localism Act and the switch to neighbourhood planning and decision making at a very localised level may have caused the opposite to the intention. Communities would not perhaps decide whether they wanted development and what sort of community facilities proactively. Rather, in the Home Counties especially, they would use the new powers to say 'no' to any form of development or change. It is little wonder that the Localism Bill was labelled a 'NIMBY-ist charter'. The government acted quickly to stop this scenario during the progression of the Bill through Parliament by stipulating that neighbourhoods could not unilaterally say 'no' to new development, and only allow further development above and beyond existing commitments contained within the LDF. But the balance between countryside protection and economic growth remains a fragile issue for planning, and even more so for the Conservative Party.

South East England, where a great deal of opposition to new development occurs locally, not only has 25 per cent of the UK population, but it is also the second largest economic contributor to the UK after London (Government Office for Science, 2010). According to the Government Office for Science in 2010, one third of the UK's economic output was generated by Berkshire, Buckinghamshire and Oxfordshire alone. So successive governments have a quandary: the government needs London and the South East as the economic heart of the nation, and where market demand for development sites remains high. Many sections of the public, on the other hand, are resistant to new planning projects, housing growth, economic development and infrastructure renewal, particularly where they have an impact on local communities in the Home Counties, and where a considerable number of Conservative politicians have their constituencies.

Under the Localism Act, if neighbourhoods in the South East attempt to say 'no' to pro-growth projects (to a greater extent than local planners have been accused of up until that time), then this will affect the economy nationally. The economic growth stance, Enterprise Zones initiatives (Townsend, 2011) and business-leaning initiatives announced by the Coalition government are therefore partly about regenerating all cities and regions of the UK post-recession. But they are also a knee-jerk reaction to the possible on-the-ground use of the provisions of the Localism Act, and very much reflect national concerns. The result in some parts of England will be interesting. Expect local planning projects to become bogged down in policy argumentations and contentions between national, local and neighbourhood interests. That is not the fault of the planning system. That is healthy democracy. But the delivery of projects may well be slowed down and when that happens, expect ministers to be eager to point the finger of blame at the planning system.

Whatever tensions emerge, the data from the reaction to the earlier participation agendas suggest a continuing role for the professional planner is likely to emerge in relation to neighbourhood planning. A degree of that 'managing participation' role is likely to emerge through the ability for LPAs to designate Neighbourhood Forums and agree the coverage of plans outside parished areas. Furthermore, LPAs are required to provide 'support' (loosely defined by government) to the production of Neighbourhood Plans. While this may present further resource issues, it will also provide further opportunities for local authority planners to place themselves in a mediating role. They will be able to draw on the vast data sets about local places amassed as part of the evidence base for Development Plan Documents, and thus to take on an 'informing' role. We may also see planners taking on roles in helping communities make sense of the options and their implications and mediating between neighbourhoods, local authorities, developers and other stakeholders (Tewdwr-Jones, 2011). This may be a slightly different role for planners, but they may react by drawing on their existing understandings and their ability to influence implementation may see the emergence of a role for professional planners not vastly different from anything seen before.

Participation and customers as seen from the coalface

We have seen, then, how New Labour tried to promote increased public participation in planning and how, over recent years, there has been a move more generally to make public services more responsive to their customers across Britain. This agenda, and some of the tensions with other government policy imperatives, has largely continued under the current Coalition government in England and the Scottish and Welsh devolved governments, particularly the emphasis on public participation. The reaction of planners to both the participation and customer initiatives shows a number of common themes.

Overall, while the exact position of any individual 'active agent' planner towards participation is likely to depend on a number of different factors (for example, individual preferences, experiences and the culture of their own local authority), the data suggest that the broad response of planners to the participation agenda seems to have been one of lukewarm support. There was some evidence that planners might want to appear more pro-participation than they actually were, perhaps because it was seen as professionally important to be on board with the reform agenda. So, for example, when asked if public participation was important to them personally, Jo and Andrew both responded, "I should say yes." Nevertheless, the support for a process which could yield information on local knowledge and preferences and was seen a democratic right seemed quite genuine, in contrast to the cartoon sketch of planners being merely anti-participation, seen in some of the existing literature.

There was, however, apparent resistance to anything that might seriously lead to a loss of the planning profession's privileged position. The data suggest that the participation that planners wanted was participation on their terms, a one-way dialogue with professionals setting themes and framing questions and the public responding, and planners then deciding what was a legitimate response. A few planners recognised that participation was precisely about questioning that professional privilege, but there was a sense that most had a vision of 'ideal' participation that would be pretty low on the Arnstein ladder. Therefore participation was seen as something that must be actively managed by the planner who was there to represent the 'greater good'. This is far removed from the model of true collaborative planning. The idea that participation needs professional management serves to reinscribe a professional authority seemingly undermined by the call for greater public input. In other words, what authority is ceded to the public through participation, planners simply take back with the idea that participation is difficult, needs managing to ensure all voices are heard and is different from actually making decisions.

Such a view, however, becomes more understandable in light of the practical problems raised by planners about the actual experience of participation. NIMBYism and the dominant 'middle-class voice' of participation in fact go to the heart of participatory democratic theory and to the fundamental tensions with representative democracy. Ellis (2004) argues that narrow individualism in participation is somewhat inevitable, and perhaps creates a space for the planner professional to occupy, albeit as a more listening, and reflexive, professional (as Campbell, 2002, cogently argues). Interestingly, as we saw in Figure 6.4, there was a fairly even split in opinion over whether there needed to be more participation or not. Perhaps this is evidence of a growing number of planners responding to culture change and promoting a more collaborative agenda, as Healey (1997) suggests.

Similarly with the pressures of participation, so the concept of the customer may at face value be seen to be about removing power from the professional planner. The customer concept and the ideal of the 'sovereign customer' are central to new public management, but there is widespread concern about the applicability of the concept to the public sector. Since elements of new public management such as the customer concept are about a power shift from bureaucracies to service users, a total rejection of the concept might have been expected, and is suggested by some previous work (see, for example, Sturdy, 1998). This was not what the data revealed, however: the reaction of frontline planners was more subtle than that.

Certainly, the majority of survey respondents said they used the term 'customer', and that customer satisfaction was important to them, with over 83 per cent feeling that the applicant paid and so had a right to a good service. There was a sense evident in the interviews that customer service was genuinely felt to be important to planners, and there are certainly examples of what Peccei and Rosenthal (2001) would term 'customer-oriented behaviour'. Nevertheless, there was mixed opinion as to whether the term 'customers' was useful in planning. Asked to define who the customers of planning were, the usual response was a long list of all possible users of the planning service, even including such notions as the community or non-human objects such as the environment. The customer was certainly not simply the applicant alone. This takes us far beyond the normal definition of the customer as an individual, and the planners' all-encompassing definition arguably renders the very term meaningless. Some 83 per cent of respondents said that there was a need to balance between customers, and interviewees suggested that some of their customers were in direct conflict with each other. While this reflects the reality of much planning practice, again this renders the notion of a 'sovereign customer' decidedly impotent.

Some planners were clearly more supportive of the customer ideal than others, but overall there was a sense that, while providing a good quality service to all users was important, ultimately planning was not there to simply fulfil the wishes of the applicant but instead was about serving society. That there was confusion over exactly who the customer of planning was reflects wider debates about the interests of planning services (see Rydin, 2003). Du Gay (1996) argues that new public management is essentially an 'identity project', and it seems the identity of planners is built firmly on collective societal concerns, rather than serving individual interests such as those of the applicant, which helps explain the somewhat lukewarm adoption of the customer concept. We comment further on the identity of planners in the next chapter.

It is easy to criticise such notions of planners serving 'the public interest', and this has been a persistent source of negative comment (see also Chapter Three). As Campbell and Marshall highlight, planning may be 'built firmly on the foundations of altruism and a public service ethic', but:

> ... in practice the commitment to altruism is not easily discharged ... the concept of the public interest is, of course, highly contested, yet this often is the case precisely because in most situations there is no clearly identifiable client except in the vague shape of society at large or the local community. (2005, p 204)

The lack of an easily identifiable client thus opens up a space for professional planners to justify their own role, but it is questionable to what extent planners actually respond to the 'greater good' and to what extent they simply respond according to their own interests and prejudices.

The extent to which planning actually serves the public interest is not, however, the key issue. As Kelly highlights when writing about professional values, 'whether or not individuals' interpretations of their experiences are accurate is beside the point, since their beliefs are real in their consequences' (1991, p 867). Planners clearly draw on a discourse of public service, of collective customers with competing interests that need balancing and of appeals to the 'greater good'. These ideals are essential to understanding their reaction to the 'customer concept'.

Whatever the arguments for or against a more participatory planning and for or against the use of the customer concept in public services, we have seen in this chapter how local authority planners are able to influence the implementation of these agendas. With regard to participation, this influence is exerted through their role mediating tensions in the overall reform agenda and through their discretion. Therefore participation becomes something in need of management by the professional planner. Just as the debate has often treated participation as an all or nothing, all good or all bad, and failed to identify carefully enough contexts where more participation might be needed and those where less might actually be preferable, so we must appreciate that it is not just a dialectic relationship of government and community. Rather, there is a planning profession between central government and the public with a tendency for a lukewarm view of participation. Indeed, frontline planners embody and, in so far as they are the public face of participation, crystallise, the contradictions that run through planning reform.

With regard to customers, as they put the customer ideal into practice, so planners have the ability to:

> Exploit the spaces, weaknesses and gaps within NPM in order to assert alternative subject positions.... Individuals confront and reflect on their own identity performance and in doing so pervert and subtly shift meanings and understandings. (Davies and Thomas, 2003, p 695)

Therefore we see that the language of the customer is put into use, and concepts such as providing a high quality service widely adopted, but at the same time the very concept is undermined and subverted by planners broadening the definition of customers and appealing to a public sector ethos.

This accords with findings from McDonough (2006), looking at local government employees in Canada, and Davies and Thomas (2003), looking at police officers in England. McDonough suggests that 'new discourses are not unproblematically mapped onto the minds of docile workers' (2006, p 643), but that a 'public service habitus' sets the structural limits for action (McDonough, 2006). With respect to the implementation of customer service ideals in Jobcentre Plus, Rosenthal and Peccei (2006c) argue that the structures of reform frame sense making by frontline staff but cannot fully account for them, hence the SLB notion is useful in considering how the customer ideal is negotiated into reality. This appears to apply here, too, and also fits within our broader institutionalist frame: the response to attempts to make planning more participatory is influenced by the various 'rule sets' (Lowndes, 2005) that the professional planner is guided by. That participation is seen as so important may reflect the strong public service identity that we found in many frontline planners, reflecting their status as local government officers and public servants, but equally participation is also understood as a threat to a privileged role and expert identity, reflecting their status as professionals. The result of this interplay is a framing of participation as vital, but in need of managing by the professional planner. This is likely to influence the implementation of neighbourhood planning, and familiar discourse can already be seen in the reaction of much of the profession to the localism policies.

In the case of both participation and customer services, a key discourse justifying the role of the planner appears to be that of public service and appeals to the 'greater good'. In this, new public management-style reforms are clearly interacting with much older identities of planners. We explore the 'planning ethos' in the next chapter.

SEVEN

Culture: the planning 'ethos'

In a series of articles spanning the 1970s into the 1990s and 2000s, Wildavsky (1972), Reade (1983), Wadley and Smith (1998), Huxley (1999) and Phelps and Tewdwr-Jones (2008) have considered the questions of what is planning and whether it can be distinguished as a discipline. Aaron Wildavsky set this series in train with perhaps the most critical perspectives of the discipline of planning, whose reputation was restored to some extent in subsequent articles by Reade (1983), Huxley (1999) and Phelps and Tewdwr-Jones (2008). Nevertheless, Reade came to the conclusion that 'we should regard with considerable scepticism the idea that there can exist a specific way of informing or making public decisions called "planning"' (1983, p 168). The debate here, and one that academic planners and politicians constantly concern themselves with even today, relates to the merits, purpose and ethics of state intervention in regulating private property interests, contention over individual rights versus public protection, notions of planning versus pragmatism, long-term sustainable visions and short-term economic gains, utopian ideals and the practical realism of economic and political agendas, and finally – and put simply – fundamental objection to the very concept of planning. Underlying these contentions is a concern – still apparent today – of how decisions are made, in whose interests they lie, and whether planners (predominantly in the modern era) were supposedly rational unbiased creatures (cf Faludi, 1973; Cooke, 1983; Allmendinger and Tewdwr-Jones, 2002).

Planning today has undergone a metamorphosis into a very different activity than in 1945, 1960 or even 1980 as it has ebbed and flowed within a political arena. It survived the New Right period, the Blair period, and if anything, has been strengthened since 2004. Presently, it has been suggested that planning now lacks a central paradigm or guiding principle, particularly since the demise of comprehensive planning (Beauregard, 1990). Instead, Phelps and Tewdwr-Jones (2008) suggest that it is suspended between modernism and postmodernism (Wadley and Smith, 1998; Allmendinger, 2002a). For others, the evolution of planning thought and practice may have become at least partly detached from its role within capitalist economic systems. As Reade notes, 'planners appear to abandon particular ways of working, and to adopt new ones, not on the basis of empirical evidence, but in accordance with changes in professional fashion' (1983, p 160).

Recent discussions of the nature of planning have gone as far as to explicitly define it as 'a support of capitalism – as a branch of economics' (Wadley and Smith, 1998, p 1025). One need not agree with this to recognise that planning (both practice and theory) has from the outset been deeply implicated with the policy-making process, and that it is quite appropriate to view planners as part of what Harvey (1974) some time ago termed the 'corporate state apparatus'. Planners' position as part of the corporate state apparatus is underlined in less stark definitions of what planning is. While the development of the planning profession in the UK in particular is intimately associated with the development of central and local state capacities and activities (Healey, 1985), planners take their position alongside other professions and occupations drawing on various disciplinary backgrounds, a cadre of what Majone (1989) has termed 'rule intermediaries'. Majone argues that the increasing complexity of society means that, rather like the host of intermediate industries that have grown up as a result of the increasing 'roundaboutness' of, or division of labour in, the economy, a cadre of such intermediaries has grown to be involved in the policy-making process. One key characteristic of the actions of such intermediaries is that the policy-making process is less about the elegance or veracity of particular theories than about the art of persuasion.

One important by-product of planning and planners' incorporation into the state apparatus has been that since the 1960s, if not before, practising planners and the planning discipline have been acutely aware that their art – alongside that of politicians – is the art of what may be possible (Phelps and Tewdwr-Jones, 2008). As Bruton (1984) noted, the planning profession has been torn between the comprehensive ideal of grappling with the complex interrelations between economic, social, environmental/physical issues on the one hand, and the practical expediencies of its centrality to the policy-making process and the political and administrative machinery of the state on the other. As such, 'it is not always easy to distinguish between professional input and political outcomes, and this is one reason why "the planners" are a group that are blamed when things go wrong' (Grant, 1999, p 5). The actions of planners have had paradoxical or unintended consequences, according to Beauregard (1989). This is not the same thing as saying that there is no meaningful role for planning. Rather, the sorts of solutions provided by planning must necessarily be seen as partial, piecemeal and temporary fixes to problems, and both fixes and problems evolve and change over time.

Decline of the public sector ethos?

In order to fully understand the ethos of local authority planning, however, it is necessary not just to consider the perspective of planning as a specific field of activity, but also to consider the culture of the public sector context in which it sits. In attempting to change the orientation of the public sector, the customer ideal discussed in Chapter Six is seen by some scholars as leading to a decline in the concept of 'public good' (von Bockel and Noordegraaf, 2006). There are therefore links to wider questions about attempts to change the ethos of the public sector. These issues are examined in this chapter. Alongside debate about the nature and applicability of the 'customer ideal' to the public sector, there has also been a great deal of concern about its impacts on the so-called 'public sector ethos'. A number of authors argue that new public management-style reforms and its 'sovereign customer' have weakened the public sector ethos (O'Toole, 1993, quoted in Hebson et al, 2003; Brereton and Temple, 1999; Horton, 2006) by challenging the traditional definition of the public good (McDonough, 2006), and encouraging a 'high output/low commitment' public sector workforce (Hoggett, 1996) that values efficiency over integrity. It is suggested that an increasing emphasis on the 'logics' of the market (Freidson, 2001) and working towards 'customer needs' does not fit neatly alongside working for the 'public interest', and even that 'a new moral and political order built on individual rights and public accountability of government to consumer choice in the market place is fundamentally flawed' (Ranson, 1990, quoted in Brereton and Temple, 1999, p 467). Du Gay (2000) provocatively defends the distinctiveness of worker motivation and norms in the public sector. In a more empirical study, Hebson et al (2003) find transformations to the traditional public sector ethos, with a clear weakening of traditional notions of managerial accountability and bureaucratic behaviour but a strong concern for working in the public interest. They conclude that there was short-term resilience of values of public interest and altruistic motivation, but these could be threatened in the longer term by efficiency pressures.

Defenders of the distinctiveness of the public sector draw on a common set of frames to define what they mean by the 'public sector ethos', with some consensus over the constituent values despite the 'nebulous status' of the term (Corby, 2000; Hebson et al, 2003, p 485). Tables 7.1 and 7.2 give examples of how the 'public sector ethos' is commonly defined in academic literature. Hugman (2003) argues that an actually existing sense of public sector ethos characterised the postwar growth of the welfare state, and McDonough notes that

Table 7.1: A range of definitions of the 'public sector ethos'

Source	Definition of 'public sector ethos'
Farnham and Horton (1996, in Hebson et al, 2003)	The principles of political neutrality, loyalty, probity, honesty, trustworthiness, fairness, incorruptibility and serving the public interest
Rouse (1999, in Hebson et al, 2003)	Equity, fairness, community, citizenship, justice and democracy (as distinctive to the public sector)
O'Toole (1993, in Brereton and Temple, 1999)	First and foremost about setting aside personal interests and working altruistically for the public good; second, about working collegially and anonymously with others to promote the public good; third, about integrity in dealing with the many problems that will need solving if the public good is to be promoted
Pratchett and Wingfield (1994, in Brereton and Temple, 1999)	Core values of accountability, honesty and impartiality, serving the community, altruistic motivation, and a sense of loyalty to community, profession and organisation
Connolly (1995, in Allmendinger et al, 2003b)	The principles of altruism rather than being a 'grubby and selfish' market-based activity

Table 7.2: Pratchett and Wingfield's (1996) five principles associated with the 'public sector ethos'

Five principles	Public sector workers are expected to:
Accountability	Accept legitimacy of political structure and be committed to implementing political policy without reference to their own views
Bureaucratic behaviour	Demonstrate characteristics of honesty, integrity, impartiality and objectivity
Public interest	Display an interest beyond the boundaries of their particular organisation, and to serve the 'public good'
Motivation	Identify with an altruistic purpose of motivation (rewarding work that has a value for the community) rather than self-interest or a profit motive
Loyalty	Operate within a complex set of loyalties (including to the department, organisation, profession, institution and community)

Source: From Hebson et al (2003)

there are struggles over the definition of the 'public good', yet there is clearly a 'traditional' conception that this is about 'maintaining and implementing the democratic principles that protect the interests of every citizen' (2006, p 631). There is also an apparently defining altruistic element of public service work, rather than profit motives, which is reflected in many public sector officials apparently believing that the private sector would operate public services worse (O'Toole, 2000; Hebson et al, 2003; McDonough, 2006).

Nevertheless, there is not universal agreement that the 'public sector ethos' even exists, let alone that it is under threat. Pratchett and Wingfield suggest that this has helped foster 'a myth' that there has always been a set of values and beliefs characterising those employed in the public sector (1994, quoted in Brereton and Temple, 1999). Brereton and Temple (1999) argue that the success of New Right reforms exposes the fragility of the myth of public sector values, although this seems questionable given that others suggest it is those very reforms that have led to a decline in values (see, for example, Craig, 2006). An alternative criticism is not that the public sector ethos per se is a myth, but the idea that there was a 'golden age' of professional discretion and higher values (Taylor and Kelly, 2006).

Alongside this are those who do not subscribe to the view that the public sector ethos is under threat by the rise of 'the customer'. Brereton and Temple (1999) argue this point, and suggest that there is a productive exchange of values between the private and public sectors, and that it is a 'public service' rather than a 'public sector' ethos that matters. Taylor and Kelly similarly report that 'there is no evidence to suggest that public service professionals are less concerned about questions relating to social justice than under the traditional welfare state' (2006, p 640). A different argument is made by Allmendinger et al, who also argue that there is slim evidence for any 'creeping deterioration of public standards' thesis, but this is because 'part of the basis for the deterioration thesis is a mythical image of probity. Such visions hark back to a golden age of integrity that often masked a sordid reality' (2003b, p 777).

Despite such suggestions that the public sector ethos is somewhat mythical, a host of empirical evidence shows that people do subscribe to such values. Fagermoen (1997) suggests such values, norms and ethical standards form a professional culture that is internalised through socialisation during university training. Taylor and Kelly similarly comment that professional training and education provide the wider societal and organisational context, so that:

> Decisions were often based on perceptions of social justice, social duty and codes of ethics of professional codes on conduct, although critics of the old system would argue that professionals also prioritised their own interests. (2006, p 635)

Such processes can be seen in conceptualisations of planning as a profession, something with both supporters and critics, as seen in

Chapter Three. Other scholars use a Foucauldian approach, drawing on conceptions of 'the ethics of the self' and 'the technologies of the self' and plurality of perspectives about the 'good life' to understand public sector values (Hugman, 2003). McDonough (2006) convincingly suggests that Bourdieu's theory of practice and habitus are a way of understanding the public sector ethos, highlighting that just as public service makes public servants, so public servants make public service. We now consider the evidence from some of our empirical data as to planning's culture.

Planning biographies: an empirical picture

Reasons for entering the profession

A first source of evidence about the planning ethos concerns the very reason planners entered the profession. The question of why people had become planners was not one that was asked in either the initial interviews or the survey, but an emerging sense of 'planning as a vocation' (cf Weber, 2004) meant a question about it was included in the in-depth interview schedule (those carried out during 2007–08). Fifty of the 53 in-depth interviewees were asked why they had become planners (the semi-structured format of the interviews meaning that not every person was asked every question). Table 7.3 and Figure 7.1, below, illustrate a quantification of this data.

The single largest route into planning for the interviewees was through a geography degree, which some 39.6 per cent of interviewees

Table 7.3: Why interviewees had become planners (open interview question, groups created from responses)

		Frequency	%	Valid %
Valid	Geography interest/degree	21	39.6	42.0
	Environment interest	12	22.6	24.0
	Make world a better place	4	7.5	8.0
	Architecture interest	3	5.7	6.0
	Knew a planner	3	5.7	6.0
	By accident	2	3.8	4.0
	Through surveying/construction	2	3.8	4.0
	Through other local authority work	2	3.8	4.0
	Through archaeology	1	1.9	2.0
	Total	50	94.3	100.0
Missing		3	5.7	
Total		53	100.0	

Figure 7.1: Why interviewees had become planners (groups created from responses)

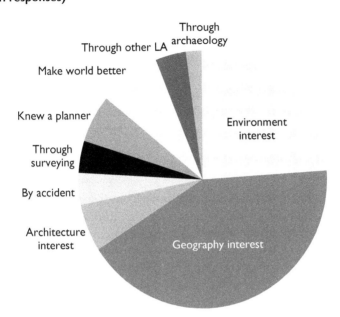

spoke about. This included those who clearly wanted to be planners as they saw it as applied geography, for example, James and Martin. There were also those who spoke about 'falling into planning' as they wondered what to do after a geography degree, like Shaun. The second largest group (22.6 per cent of interviewees) spoke about entering planning because of a specific interest in environmental issues. Mandy was fairly typical of this group:

> "When I did my planning qualifications I wanted to work in improving the environment and that is what motivated me, I wanted to have a positive effect on the world I'm in, but I also wanted to do something where you had interaction with the public."

Beyond these two groups were a diverse range of other reasons for becoming planners, such as the recommendation of someone they knew who was already a planner or an interest in architecture. The most interesting of these remaining groups was those who said they entered the profession specifically to 'make the world a better place'. These four interviewees were all older. Michael explained this in terms of planning being the "bright new profession" in the 1970s:

"What made me become a planner? Actually it goes back to 1974 when I was at school. Planning was the bright new profession at the time."

Lucy felt such desires were fairly typical among older planners:

"What made me become a planner originally?... Because I wanted to make the world a better place. Lots of planners of my generation were motivated by that desire."

Jane cited the apparent labelling of planners as "evangelistic bureaucrats":

"I went into public sector planning on purpose. I had all these ideals, of wanting to serve the community. Was it Prince Philip who called us evangelistic bureaucrats?"

In fact, this line comes not from Prince Philip but from John Davies in a 1970 paper and 1972 book, more of which later (Davies, 1970, 1972).

The trends in the interview data broadly reflect the survey of planners conducted by the Idox Group. This identified five general reasons for entering the profession. The most common reason was coming from a geography degree background, followed by the 'wish to make a difference' and influence the environment that people live in (Idox Group, 2007).[1] People entered the profession through interests in geography (which we might characterise as people and places), the environment and in trying to improve places for communities. While some interviewees spoke about wanting to facilitate the right development in the right places, none spoke of having entered the profession because they wanted to help developers or process planning applications more quickly.

Motivations of a planner

Further data about the ethos of planning comes from considering what motivates frontline planners, and what achievements they are proud of. A Likert agreement on the survey (sent out in 2006) asked planners to consider a number of descriptions of local authority planners as a group. One of the statements with the strongest support was 'planners are motivated by their work', with 76.6 per cent of respondents agreeing or strongly agreeing (compared to just 14.3 per cent disagreeing or strongly disagreeing; see Figure 7.2). Such a statement suggests a motivated profession and such a response is by no means automatic

Figure 7.2: Opinion on whether planners as a group are 'motivated by their work' (*n* = 607)

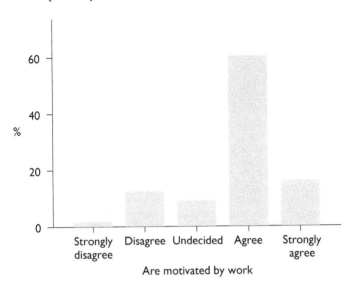

(recall Figure 4.7, in Chapter Four, showing a strong feeling that planners were stressed by the LDF reforms).

This raises the question of what it is about their work that motivates planners. The survey respondents were also asked to rate a series of statements on a scale of 1 to 5 ('not at all important' to 'very important') according to how important they thought those factors were to their sense of being a professional planner. The statement that gained the strongest support out of all 12 possibilities was 'a sense of making a difference to people and places'. Some 68.9 per cent of respondents rated this as 'very important' and a further 29.4 per cent as 'important' (a strong 98.3 per cent of respondents in total; see Figure 7.3). This suggests ideals of helping 'place making' (to use contemporary government parlance) and creating better communities were the key motivators for planners.

Most in-depth interviewees were asked what motivated them and what particular professional achievements they were proud of. The most frequent response with regards to motivational factors was that planners were motivated by a public service element, as Boyd and James highlighted:

"I guess there's an element of that naive public do-gooder kind of thing which first attracted me to it." (Boyd)

Figure 7.3: Opinion on how important respondents thought 'a sense of making a difference to people and places' was to being a professional planner (*n* = 608)

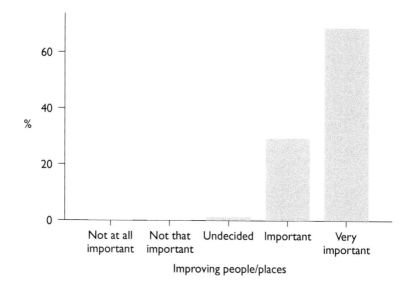

"It sounds a bit trite, but it's about serving society, for, hopefully, its benefit." (James)

Vic spoke similarly about job satisfaction from working 'with and for' the local community, and David was motivated by the 'buzz and challenge' of being held accountable to the public. Mark went further and said that he was motivated by:

"Screwing as best a deal as you possibly can for the public good."

There were also a number of planners who were motivated by particular elements of their role; environmental protection was mentioned several times.

"I kind of feel I've contributed my bit to the environment.... It just means an awful lot really, just being there to sort of protect what's valuable." (Paul)

"You're trying to, to conserve the natural and built environment assets that you have, while also promoting economic development and the interests of the social and economic needs of the area." (Emma)

Emma also spoke about the "needs of the area" and there seemed to be place-specific motivations at work too. Michael put this in terms of what we might call flippantly RTPI professional planning institute jargon, when he said that he was motivated "very much by place shaping". Jenny put this in terms of being proud of a particular location, and Gerard spoke about seeing the results of the planning process on the ground:

> "The more you see the fruits of the stuff you were involved in a few years ago coming through, the actual physical results of policy, the more it motivates you."

A final motivational factor for some more senior planners seemed to be through managerial success. Patrick explained how he was motivated by trying to have a good planning department:

> "There was a real cultural change that we had to go through there with staff and members to get to a point that actually got us to a level of performance and standard that we could be proud of really and that's very, very important to me and this very much motivates me as well: to be good, to be good at what we do, to have a good reputation."

Here we have a planning manager motivated by trying to make his staff change their culture and embrace reforms, such as the customer rhetoric. Nevertheless, such managerial motivations were much less common than factors such as public service, environmental protection or place shaping, even among planning managers (Lucy, a manager, spoke about being motivated "by the love of planning", for example).

Alongside this, the achievements that interviewees said they were proud of also showed a distinct technical bias. In some cases, these involved achievements related to getting Local Plans adopted, or particular policies placed into Local Plans:

> "I am proud of being responsible for the team that took the local plan through to completion and adoption in 1996, which in a sense may not necessarily appear to be a huge achievement but as we had not had a comprehensive plan

in place since 1961, I thought it was quite a reasonable achievement." (Brian)

Other planners mentioned being proud of helping individuals gain planning permission. These included an example that Mandy felt was morally right to support:

> "What is my proudest achievement as a planner? I think probably I managed to persuade a very angry planning committee and my manager and his manager and his manager up to the chief exec in the end to back an application that we had for a drug rehabilitation centre in the town centre. I think it was the right thing to do morally."

Jack's example included being proud of both helping someone get planning permission and also in being recognised for providing a certain level of public service:

> "I mean, there are these things like helping an old lady get a summer house because she couldn't leave her house. And she was phoning up crying and saying it was wonderful. You know, it's a bit naff, but it's just, it feels like you're making a difference."

Finally, a number of planning elements were combined in George's proudest achievement, which was having helped an historic town centre thrive through both policy and development management techniques:

> "Proudest achievement? Well I think no single thing, but in many – I am proud of maintaining the town centre, it's a really good, active and vibrant town centre and I have been involved in some shopping revamps which have maintained its historic character."

Like the factors that planners typically said motivated them, the achievements that they were proud of tended distinctly towards what we might term technical planning matters rather than overtly customer service achievements (although there was a hint at that in Jack's comments) or the efficient processing of applications. This is not to say that a sense of providing a good customer service did not matter to planners; it clearly did (as survey data in Chapter Six shows), but planners seemed more focused on other elements of their work. It is interesting that reference was frequently made back to being motivated by a sense of public service. We further explored this issue in the interviews by asking what it meant to the planners to work in the public sector.

A 'public sector ethos' in planning?

Strong reference was made by a number of planners to ideals of serving the public in justifying their professional positions in a number of areas, most particularly in relation to defining the 'customers' of planning and with respect to public participation. The majority of the in-depth interviewees were asked what working in the public sector meant to them. All but two of the interviewees commented in a positive way about working in the public sector, and there seemed a very strong feeling that a sense of public service was important to the professional identity of the planners interviewed. Brian made reference to what he termed the "old concept" of public service:

> "I've always been, I've always enjoyed working in the public sector. I believe in the old concept of public service, I believe that planning is something that is rooted in public service and it's the area in which I feel I can achieve most of what I would want to achieve…. Working in the public sector is about that public service and valuing in a sense public goodness that we're there to deliver through people's quality of life."

But reference to ideas of public service contribution occurred just as strongly by younger planners as by more experienced ones, such as Brian.

While there was very strong agreement that working in the public sector meant something to the interviewees, there were a number of differing accounts of quite what it meant. At the most general level, there were those for whom it meant 'making a difference', such as Mike:

> "Working in the public sector means to me, above all it means the ability to provide, it means public service, it means the ability to make a difference, albeit I have no illusions that the difference I make is pretty small."

The way that planners seemed to think they could make a difference was frequently through appealing to ideals of serving the 'public interest' or the 'greater good'. 'The public interest' as a 'primary driver' was raised by a number of interviewees, while some others referred, similarly, to the ideas of 'acting for the greater good'. This notion of the 'greater good' echoes some of the comments made in relation to public participation.

It is easy, as highlighted in Chapter Six, to be critical of such commentary. O'Toole (2000) writes about the public interest as a 'political and administrative convenience', while in the planning context, Kitchen (2006) gives the example of Burns (1967), a Newcastle-upon-Tyne city planner who wrote an account of his team's efforts, convinced they were working for the greater good of the city. This prompted Davies (1972), a community-based researcher, to write a counter-argument highlighting how the planning process was not operating in the interests of the poorest in the city. Davies coined the term 'evangelical bureaucrats' to describe planners, and argued that well-meaning experts were very dangerous as they were unable to take anyone else seriously, constantly depicting themselves as far-sighted, imaginative professionals 'beset by the criticisms of narrow-minded rate payers, greedy speculators, parochial councillors, apathetic citizenry, calculating vested interests …' (1970, p 25). Such critique might still be made today, but it is too easy to just dismiss outright a sense of working for the 'greater good' as empty rhetoric when it appears to hold very real value to planners at the coalface.

The idea of working for a particular place was linked by a number of interviewees to their sense of what public service meant. Toby reinforced the idea that working in the public sector meant a lot, and defined it in terms of a sense of service to the city where he worked:

> "It means a lot actually [working in the public sector]. The more I work in the public sector, the more I feel a certain pride in the public service that I provide really. For me, that basically means trying to make the city, the developments coming forward, a successful urban environment for the people that live and work in it."

Michael made similar geographical links:

> "One of the, one of the key things about the public sector, is you work in a geographic area. So there's very much the opportunity to see the fruits of your labour … rather than flitting round the country."

Notice that in the last quotation, Michael made a 'rather than' comment. This was a reference to the practice of private sector planning consultants, and it is noticeable that for a number of planners, the definition of what working in the public sector meant to them was made by referencing what it was not: the private sector. We will return to this momentarily. Before that, however, it is worth noting that there was one planner who mentioned a downside to working in the public sector. Mandy said that working in the public sector meant:

> "… a lot of the local government constraints of not having any biros, you're working in an awful building, the computers don't work, the photocopier is broken, those kinds of constraints which are very wearying."

Justin also made a negative comment, although his feelings were more mixed, starting with the positive:

> "Working for the public sector, you're working for a particular area which you represent and is obviously close to your heart and is your patch. So that's, that's the good thing about working for the public sector, I guess. You feel that you're working for the benefit of the community. The downsides, as I say, it's an incredibly bureaucratic organisation and it can be frustrating sometimes when you want to get something done."

It is thus worth noting that there was not universal praise for all aspects of a public sector career among those planners already in one.

Two of the 53 in-depth interviewees were about to leave the public sector to pursue careers in the private sector, while another was considering the move, but five others had previously worked in the private sector and had no plans to return. The rest had always worked in the public sector, and in many cases stated they always wanted to. Planners Derek and George are both typical of this group, explaining they somehow felt more comfortable working in the public sector:

> "I don't have a problem with people working in the private sector. But I personally feel more comfortable working the public sector because your end result is, if you like, more community-based than shareholder-based." (Derek)

> "I've always seen planning as a kind of public service and
> have always been more inclined to provide a service for the
> public than to make a lot of money in the private sector."
> (George)

It is noticeable that George spoke of 'public service' rather than 'the
public sector'; while the two usually go together, this is not inevitably
so. Most people, however, spoke specifically of the public sector as
they defined what being a public sector planner meant by contrasting
it to what working as a private sector planner was like (in a few cases,
this was drawing on direct experience, but more often, it seemed to
be an imagined professional landscape). None of the planners thought
that working in public sector planning was identical to working in
private sector planning, and none thought it should be. Vic suggested
there were similarities but that there needed to be some fundamental
differences as well:

> "People have this assumption that local authority workers
> are paid a lot of money for doing very little. I've never sat
> round doing very little for 10 years. Yes there are elements of
> private practice that can be brought into local government
> and applied extremely well, but as I say, there are elements
> of private practice which are just not right or workable for
> local government."

On the whole, there were two slightly different perspectives here. On
the one side were those like David, who just thought that working in
the private sector was different:

> "Those working in the private sector have a different
> ultimate motivation, that's not to say you're any less
> professional, certainly not."

The second type of perspective were those, represented by Michael,
who thought professional standards might somehow be compromised
by working in the private sector:

> "Working in the private sector would compromise, well, not
> so much standards, it would compromise my professional
> views."

Looking across the interview data, it seemed that the sentiments of David dominated. There was certainly a sense that the type of work undertaken in the public sector was somehow different:

> "I know people that worked in the private sector and, although the early potential was much greater, the pressure was much greater and you would often be doing things you may not agree with … I couldn't see myself drawing up plans for a Lidl and screaming at some DC officer about why I should be allowed a 12 foot by 24 foot illuminated sign in a Conservation Area."(Mandy)

But Mandy seems to be suggesting that not only was it different in the public sector, it was somehow morally better. Lucy added that she believed that there was much less discretion in the private sector, and clearly thought that was a bad thing:

> "I just think if you're working directly for a big consultancy, there probably isn't much freedom. You are very much tied to the specific wishes of your client."

This feeling of difference between the sectors was made much more explicitly by some of the other interviewees. Patrick argued that private sector planners were less objective:

> "I just don't think working for a client you could be as objective as I'm able to be here. It may not be so easy because ultimately you rely on the client, and that drives consultancies, and your survival."

This was presented as if it was almost inevitable, due to the need for business from clients. Gareth made a similar point:

> "You know I can understand the attraction of private sector wages.… I think if you're in the private sector, you're just looking to deliver that outcome for an interested individual, and once you're at that point I don't think you're necessarily looking at the planning merits of the case."

Ray starkly called this "selling your soul to the devil". This seems similar to Brereton and Temple's finding that, while ethical objectives do exist in the private sector, 'local bureaucrats often have negative views about business and business people, believing that public sector workers behaved with more honesty and integrity' (1999, p 465).

It is important to note that not all planners used such emotive language as Ray, but there was clearly a majority feeling among the interviewees of a need to balance developer and community interests, something that could only be achieved in the public sector:

> "You know, it's necessary for there to be a balance between private sector interest and forces for development and looking after the environment. As the planner, unless you're in the public service, at the end of the day, the dollar always wins." (Austin)

Such opinions were neatly synthesised by Brian, who spoke about there being a particular value to working as a local authority planner:

> "I genuinely don't believe it's like working in the private sector where you are a bit like a hired gun and you're paid or you will do what you're paid to do or say what you're paid to say ... whereas I think a lot of people that work in local authorities feel they work in a way that is consistent with their own ambitions or values and it's that it tends to be, it's a value-driven thing."

Brian's values coincide with the traditional definitions of the 'public sector ethos' discussed above. Clearly many planners believed that working in the public sector was rightly different from the private sector; that somehow one could be more objective and even more professional in the public sector; and that ideals of service and the greater good were key to public sector planning. This is important because it helps us understand how public sector planners conceptualise their role and legitimate their actions, and also because managerial ideas such as the customer service rhetoric are often imported straight to the public sector from the private sector. But planners are highlighting differences between the sectors, therefore questioning the suitability of such imports, or at least showing that despite them, planners continue to define their role differently. The motivations of planners are worth considering further.

The personal dynamic in collaborative arenas

Planning has always been concerned with the nature of decision making involving a variety of actors communicating, negotiating, bargaining and arguing over an appropriate course of action. The communicative school is the most recent body of theory that has sought to analyse the interpersonal relationships between actors in the planning arena (see, for example, Forester, 1989, 1993, 1999a; Sager, 1994; Healey, 1997). The literature has opened up some reflective debate about the very purpose of planning theory, its tributary and cadet branches and ways forward. Tewdwr-Jones (2002) examined the relationship between politics, professionalism and public participation, and assessed – in the context of the communicative debate – the planner's personal behaviour, motivations and dilemmas. The 'personal dynamic' (Allmendinger and Tewdwr-Jones, 1997; Tewdwr-Jones and Allmendinger, 1998; Tewdwr-Jones, 2002) or individualistic dimension of planning has not been developed in more recent planning theorising, but is very relevant in looking at the extent to which new processes are acted on or are judged to be successfully implemented. The personal dynamic, thoroughly debated by the likes of such respected theorists as Friedmann (1973, 1987), Faludi (1987), Schön (1983) and Hoch (1994), remains just as relevant today as it seemed 40 years ago. Within the context of a reformed planning process that is, arguably, becoming more communicative and neighbourhood-centred, the position of the individual planner, with his or her motivations, ways of thinking and styles of acting and communicating, employing personal and professional goals, seems to be pivotal in the adoption of more interpersonal relations between different planning actors. Forester's (1999b, 1999c) call for planners to supplement their reflection-in-action role with a more social and political work of deliberation must be seen within a new untapped challenge: convincing the individual planner that a particular ethical position in the way they approach decisions, reconcile different thoughts and then decide to act is warranted and can be justified. If this ethos is one that planning academe aspires to, more work needs to be undertaken in the world of planning practice concerning the behaviour of individual planners.

Forester contends that it is simply not sufficient for planners to identify or rediscover power in practice (Forester, 1999a). But are planners that interested and motivated to undertake their roles while imbued with liberal notions of democracy (cf Allmendinger, 1996; Tewdwr-Jones, 1996; Allmendinger and Tewdwr-Jones, 1997)? There are both institutional and territorial dependencies to 'acting on', let alone varying personal capacities of thinking whether and how to act, that as educators we need to consider further. There is also an alternative view why planners tell each other stories, learn from each other and act in a reflective way and, at times, deliberatively. To put it in the starkest terms, they reflect as autonomous individuals and learn 'how not to get caught out', either in adversarial settings, in politically charged debates or at public meetings. Here, under this scenario, it is self-interest, career development and professional esteem that are the goals at the forefront of planners' minds. The difference is actually one of presentation (Goffman, 1959), or rather between backstage and frontstage deliberations so that there occurs a dressing up dramaturgically in the language of participation generation, fostering open and inclusive dialogues and mutual learning. This is obviously a less receptive view in planning academe than that propounded by Forester and Healey, and might even be called 'cynical'. But there is nothing anti-community about this view, nor is it necessarily a weak view in the face of a political challenge within planning 'to act'. What is more important for planning theorists and educators is to highlight the possibility for these individual types of thought processes to exist or, rather coexist, and to dissect the notion that encouraging collective open action in planning necessarily equates to the correct moral stand of the planner.

Healey (1999) has discussed, after Latour (1987) and Bourdieu (1990), how webs of relationships are important in the development of intellectual, social and political capital, citing Hwang's (1996) discussion of the relationship between knowledge and action and Shotter's (1993) view that social life is 'an active process of continual creating and transforming of identities and social bonds in interaction with others' (Healey, 1999, p 114). Webs develop some meaning and coherence as they become relational worlds in which people construct their being, and some sense of themselves, although these webs tend to differ in different places, spaces and at different levels without, perhaps, interacting (Healey, 1999, p 115). Individuals do develop their own sense of identity and mature their opinions as they become involved, or are affected by, relational webs. And these relational webs do need some coordinating to ensure some element of compatibility or coherence is provided strategically in order to develop shared understandings. But what are individuals' thought processes as they exist – perhaps subconsciously – prior to interaction in or with their relational webs (that is, before individuals are subjected to interaction with other planning actors)? Or, to place it in the context of webs and planning, how do planners resolve their existing relational webs (developed prior to or outside education and professional practice) with new or emerging relational webs (developed once their education commences or once graduates are employed within particular planning organisations)?

As we have heard in this chapter, individuals can hold personal preferences, gathered independently from experiences and influences, not only from relations with other contacts but through varying sources, including media, culture, education and environment, and bring these to bear on their professional planning activities. Alexander, discussing the relationship between the self as a strategic actor, and the need to foster open inclusionary participation in the style of communicative planning, has stressed that 'Planning never really involves independent, autonomous action' (2001, p 320). We would agree with the sentiments of both Healey and Alexander with regard to *action*, but both seem to miss the point that the individual planner will possess autonomous *thought* prior to his or her interactions with others in the planning arena. It is possible that the individual planner will possess dilemmas of how to resolve the pre-professional relational webs with post-education relational webs. These pre-professional webs may yield a particular thinking style or belief that becomes stamped on the heart of the individual; they may even relate to beliefs, values, trust, sincerity and legitimacy, some of which are features of communicative action. They may, alternatively, possess beliefs that are strategic, competitive or political. The question for the individual planner once he or she graduates into employment, is 'How do I resolve my possibly conflicting values developed from my different relational webs?' or 'For the purpose of my personal thought processes – rather than of the institutions I work within – who is going to advise me on how I should resolve my thoughts?'.

Personal preferences are pivotal to the delivery of both communicative planning ideals and culture change. Some of what we know is generated 'implicitly', that is, without our conscious awareness (Underwood and Bright, 1996), and it would be correct to believe that parts of us, and what we believe, are determined by other people, our contacts with them and the way we react to these representations. But that is only part of the picture. Planners, as professionally trained individuals, are influenced by a whole series of codes and experiences, some explicit and some implicit. It is notoriously difficult, even for cognitive psychologists (Wilson and Stone, 1985), to identify the way people perceive and remember objects and events, store and retrieve knowledge, think, reason and solve problems (Dorfman et al, 1996). But the pre-packaging that is inherent within individuals does not necessarily cancel out other interests or opportunities when they need to be confronted, as Healey (1996) suggests, and certainly it seems inappropriate to generalise that all individuals think in the same way. This broader argument, that attempts to distinguish between implicit and explicit cognition within individuals and their perceptions towards situations, merely *acknowledges* that the psyche of individuals is a relevant factor in establishing interpersonal relations. If anything, it legitimises the planner and his or her background (and thought processes) even before discussions take place on fostering open communicative action (through the ability to act). Why is this relevant? Put simply, analysis of the thought processes of the planner before considering whether and how to act is one of the fundamental determinants in whether communicative processes are able to be delivered.

With particular regard to planning, there are two problems with a more participatory role if, in the style of Forester (1999a), planners are to be persuaded to take a more proactive role. First, how do and why should planners think that acting communicatively to counteract incidences of distorted communication within a public arena is an ethically correct position? The public are only one part of a multifarious, conflicting and confusing number of clients in urban planning. Campbell and Marshall (1998, p 117), in discussion of the various roles expected of planners, rhetorically ask:

> Are planners obliged to secure the interests of their political employers, the organisation, personal values, clients, the wider community, future generations or the profession?

As we saw in Chapter Six, there is some evidence to suggest that some – but certainly not all – planners do not hold thought processes to suggest that they should act in a more open and democratic way (Kaufman and Escuin, 1996). The very notion of 'professional' is premised on the idea of specialist knowledge, something that separates the professional as an elite (rightly or wrongly) from the rest of society. Planners are consequently caught in a trap: to be a professional requires possessing a specialised area of knowledge for which they are rewarded, and this fact rests heavily in their mind. But the culture change argues for a more pluralistic and equal relationship between 'the planner' and 'the planned'; it is hardly surprising, therefore, that some planners are reluctant to question their supposed professional status even if they share the values that underpin enhanced participation in planning for fear of losing status or rewards. This provides a good example of the problem of attempting to marry up the personal dynamic with the will to act, and to act in a particular way.

If planners are required to ditch their pre-packaged attributes before entering into an arena of debate, one assumes that this includes their education, training, professional status and even personal views. Disarming planners of their professionalism would seem an obvious move to rid the system of some of the pre-packaging. This is something that has not been discussed in the literature to date, but something that certainly could be expected if the theorists advance their theses to their logical conclusions. The outcome of this, however, might prove to be a weakening of planning. Overall, then, the personal dynamic or individualistic dimension of planning will prove to be a contributory, although imprecise, factor in determining whether and how the planner acts in the first place and then acts in a particular way.

Imagining the profession and public service

In this chapter, we have discussed why planners report they entered the profession and what motivates them, and how they draw on discourses of serving the public good to explain their role. While the idealism Healey and Underwood (1978) found in their work on planners may have been somewhat diluted, there was still a sense that planners were strongly motivated by the desire to make a real difference to society and to places. Planners seem to have entered the profession through an interest in people and the environment, and are proud of technical planning achievements. There was a strong sense of a public sector ethos, and that working in the public service meant something to planners on the ground. Working in the public sector was seen as different from working in the private sector in planning.

The role of any discourse on planning theory–practice – particularly in planning education – is to assist students and practitioners to understand how the world exists and what theory might offer to our understanding of the world. Equally, we can learn from practice for the benefit of improving our theorising, and theory teaching, to students. Educators need to identify the dilemmas and uncertainties, the problems and complexities within the translation from planning theory (implicit thinking) to planning practice (explicit thinking). In many ways, the translation process for individuals between preconceived knowledge and problem solving (or action) necessarily involves planners recognising the impact of political, professional and community thoughts, on the individual's thoughts in their problem-solving process. The translation process between implicit and explicit cognition in the individual is the power player: it is both the strength of the translation from planning theory to planning practice and its hindrance. Making sense of the translation between theory and practice is an attempt to understand the dilemmas associated with the conflicts in implicit and explicit thought processes, not to remove it. Making sense of the translation between theory and practice is an attempt to understand the dilemmas associated with an individual's thought processes. Forming a judgement about issues and going on to make a decision involves both implicit and explicit factors. These factors, in turn, comprise cognitive determinants that influence, amend or sway the individual's thought processes. Such determinants involve access to knowledge, the use of language, the discourse surrounding the decision, and the form of communication used.

Cognitive and experiential processes within individual planners are formed through individual frames (Rein and Schön, 1993; Schön and Rein, 1994), and are important in the formulation of strategies to enable particular tactics, which may take on some relevance within organisational settings. Planners possess personal thoughts, knowledge and facts before entering into the translation process; they possess both implicit and explicit thinking and learning. Implicit thinking stems from beliefs and values derived from life and education. Explicit thinking stems from reaction to influences while one is making sense of the implicit. Divorcing the explicit thoughts from the implicit cognition during the translation of theory to practice is a theorising process in itself (Underwood, 1996). Different planners can react very differently within the process of translation from implicit thinking to explicit thinking and action, according to how 'passive', 'principled', 'vulnerable' or 'strategic' they are.

Communicative planning theory could benefit from this analysis: the theory is concerned with generating communities' desires and forming policy from a collective voice. Healey (1999) has made a useful start by highlighting the importance of relational webs around actors, but this style of thinking needs to be transferred from the institutional scale to the level of the individual. Little has been stated by communicative planning theory proponents about the translation process, how planners take communities' desires and translate them into practical policy responses. It seems that a focus on the translation, on the motives, values and beliefs of the planner in this process, is a natural step in discussing how planners can be persuaded to both think and act more deliberately. If we view planning discourse and implementation as a transpersonal activity constituted out of both socio-political reality and psychic reality (Samuels, 1993), we might better understand the translation or gap between planning theory and practice that planners find difficult to reconcile.

We are not advancing political cognition as a theory to enable us to understand planning practice; rather, we are striving to identify the factors that lead to dilemmas and uncertainties within the translation process between ways of thinking (which are often well intentioned) and the decision to act in a particular way. These are the factors that can cause the breakdown between theory and practice, between knowledge and action and between intention and implementation.

EIGHT

Conclusion: the importance of planning's front line

Themes under fluid processes of reform

In this book, we have discussed how we can conceptualise and understand the role of frontline planners, and how those same planners experience the ongoing reforms of planning and the public sectors. As Schofield and Sausman write:

> The reality of policy initiatives is experienced by the front-line professionals and public servants who do not generally make up policy elites. If the elite system has no feedback mechanism by which to monitor and access the policy reality, the whole arena of knowledge capture based on experience is lost. (2004, p 245)

The accounts of frontline planners constitute the reality of planning practice, and rigorous data is essential if we are to properly understand it. Drawing on a large-scale, carefully administered postal survey and a detailed collection of semi-structured interviews, this book provides a significant empirical contribution. This is important because context matters. Although planning shares similarities with other public services, there are differences too. Thus, broad agendas such as the move to promote the ideal of customers lead to confused narratives and contested ideals when they are imported with little context-specific understanding into the planning arena.

Chapters Four to Seven looked, successively, at: the reaction of local authority planners to implementing spatial planning through revised local planning policy frameworks, the emphasis on targets to speed up planning, moves to make planning more participatory and the broad impulse for increasing customer sovereignty. In each case, the response has been mixed, involving apparent embrace of some elements of the reforms and rejection – in terms of conceptual rejection, at least – of others. A number of themes seemed to emerge through these chapters, which we now consider in turn.

Imagining modernisation

A first emergent theme is the question of how planners are imagining modernisation, how they appear to conceptualise the broad programme of planning and public sector reforms to which they have been subject over recent years. This reform agenda appears to be seen overwhelmingly in terms of threats and opportunities, in contrast to some texts that suggest public sector professionals reject all new public management reforms (Berg, 2006). There is a clear feeling evident in the data that planners supported the idea of some reform being necessary; in Chapter Four we saw that almost twice as many survey respondents agreed rather than disagreed with the statement 'I support the reform agenda'. In interview data, there was acknowledgement of issues such as out-of-date development plans (Chapter Four) and applications that could sometimes take too long to process (Chapter Five). This support was quite strongly felt. There really was a tangible sense that interviewees thought the ideals of the (New Labour) reforms were correct, even if the content of those reforms was, at times, strongly criticised.

Despite an acknowledgement of the need for reform, even when that reform called into question the past practices of planning, in practice it was those reform elements which seemed to most enhance the status of the individual planner or the planning profession that were most enthusiastically embraced. As a group, planners seemed quick to exploit the spaces of opportunity opened up by the impulses of modernisation. This can be seen through the widespread support for the principles of spatial planning, the idea of which was supported by the majority of respondents and called "hugely exciting" by some interviewees (Chapter Four). One could almost reply 'they would say that', given how the post-2004 spatial planning approach placed local planning policy documents at the heart of local authorities, coordinating the spatial implications of a broad sweep of local policy. But such support was by no means guaranteed, given the huge challenges involved in coordinating the simultaneous existence of land use planning and a spatial planning approach.

Furthermore, opportunities have been seen in areas that might not be expected, such as in the use of targets to justify the importance of planning and to lever in extra funding, extra prestige and resources for planners (Chapter Five). We might say that just as targets have had well-reported 'unintended' negative consequences, they have also had a series of less well-reported 'unintended' positive consequences for planners and the status of planning. Sometimes this is down to planners seeing opportunities in the reform, for example, the chance to tell local government management that a cherished standing for the council as a whole in a performance table was under threat unless more resources were allocated to planning activities. In the near future, this may also be seen in defence of the need for professional planners – in a time of austerity – to ensure an up-to-date Local Plan is adopted, or that someone is there to 'assist' with Neighbourhood Plans. This all seems to support Lowndes (2005), who argues that 'institutional entrepreneurs' can exploit ambiguities in the altered rule sets associated with reform to protect and even further their own interests.

Other elements of the reforms are seen as more threatening. It is noticeable that the qualitative impression was of planners seeing more opportunity through the changing physical structures of the system, for example, the move to local spatial planning or the existence of NIs for planning, than through the elements of the reform that involved a perceived rebalancing of power between themselves and 'the public'. Therefore, while there was certainly not the simple rejection of public participation some previous literature would have us believe, there did appear to be a greater sense of seeing participation and the customer rhetoric as a threat, and one where the opportunities were more limited. Some elements of the reforms appeared to be conceived of as threats simply because they presented the opportunity for planners to fail, for example, the LDF process which was seen as too complex and over-engineered (Chapter Four), or because they risked damaging the reputation of the profession or system. The over-emphasis on performance speed targets was seen as leading to a range of unintended consequences by which planners ended up providing a worse service overall (Chapter Five). Similarly, meaningful participation was seen as very difficult to do in practice (Chapter Six), which might thus appear a slur on the professional's skills and abilities. Such 'practical' issues frequently had far reaching concerns for the policy concerned.

Much of this accords with Gaster and Rutqvist's (2000) commentary that change is difficult to implement and can almost appear overwhelming, so there is a tendency for frontline staff to look for 'lines of least resistance'. This is human nature. But the more active embracing of some elements of the reform agenda seems to go beyond simply those that are seen as easiest, and there is more to this than merely the apparent tendency of welfare state professionals to promote their own interests (Cochrane, 2004). Partly, the embracing may be due to individual interests, for example, some planners have much stronger interests in environmental issues, others in design factors, others in economic development, and so on, and different reforms present varying opportunities to pursue these. Thus the embracing of reforms is not just a case of which are easiest, but rather, which accord with the professional's own sense of priorities. Indeed, there are some similarities here to Davies and Thomas's findings, with regard to police officers and modernisation:

> When facing the subjectivizing effects of the discourses of NPM, individuals are choosing to draw on some aspects, as a discursive resource in asserting a particular identity, while attempting to subvert and 'wriggle out' of the other ways that NPM attempts to classify, determine and categorize them. (2003, p 687)

It must also be noted that some frontline workers can get job satisfaction simply from complying with new procedures: Taylor and Kelly (2006) found this of social workers, and there were some planners who seemed to gain great satisfaction from meeting their application processing targets (Chapter Six), although they were very much in the minority. Most seemed to see more threat than opportunity in an apparent over-focus on targets.

More generally, it seemed that modernisation was conceptualised as somewhat of a 'necessary evil'. There were certainly comments during interviews that planning was about managing change, so planners could hardly object to change themselves, and there was a definite desire not to be seen as 'anti-change'. However, there was a very real feeling that there was too much change, too quickly, without time for things to 'bed down' before the next new initiative came down the pipeline (Chapter Five). This non-stop cycle of reform has been seen elsewhere and was a defining feature of Labour in power (Chapter Two); it has continued under the Coalition government, and is probably one that causes great difficulties for public sector workers across the board. Interviewees spoke of the reform experience as like being on a conveyor belt, with everyday workloads still continuing without the time needed to take stock of the reforms. Furthermore, while there was support for the ideals of the reform agenda, modernisation was overwhelmingly conceptualised by planners in terms of central government spewing out reforms, as if it were the government's reform agenda that was then given to the front line to enact. In other words, planners felt little ownership of the reform process; it was something imposed on them from above. Therefore, when things went wrong, for example, slow progress with LDFs, they blamed central government for giving them reforms that were viewed as too complex, or for not adequately resourcing planning departments. In this way, frontline planners sidestepped the question of whether it was their culture that was in need of modernisation. Instead, it was they who were the ones getting on and making the system work. This is in stark contrast to central government, which has tended to see individual planners as the problem, and in need of 'culture change' or new skills.

Questions of control

With planners tending to see the reform agenda as very much centrally driven, questions arise about how much they see themselves as in control of reform processes alongside issues of autonomy and resistance. In some of the data, there was an impression of powerlessness, as if planners were indeed being subjected to powerful reform processes far beyond their control. We can see this in the apportioning of blame for slow progress on LDF documents to late guidance being issued by central government or poor advice from the regional government officers (Chapter Four). More strikingly, the number of planners apparently stressed out by the LDF process (over 40 per cent said they felt stressed by the reforms, a significant minority) and by the targets (which over 87 per cent said increased stress for planners) create an overwhelming sense of a lack of control. This coincides with the interviewees recounting stories of colleagues going off work with stress and related health illnesses, which they frequently linked to the reforms, and even the odd person apparently resigning in protest at the overwhelming target regime (Chapter Five). Similarly, there was a tendency to see powerful impulses at work, particularly those such as the speed agenda that were blamed not just on central government, but specifically on HM Treasury. This implies an image almost of a conspiracy against the profession, but perhaps this assigning responsibility for such processes on higher levels of government actually assists planners in coping with everyday workloads in the pressurised environment of street-level bureaucracy. It may, however, be evidence of a certain fatalism and result in disengagement when central government does try to engage with the profession. This was more evident in England than in Scotland or Wales (see below).

In Chapter Five, the idea was presented that 'everyone has targets', so planning must have them too. This might be seen as a desire to maintain planning's status as an important function worthy of targets, but it might also be seen as colonisation by the imperatives of new public management. Therefore, the idea that a public service must have targets is not a conscious desire by planners for targets, but instead reflects a more subtle appropriation of their imaginations by the framing discourses of modernisation: the subjectivities of neoliberalism become such that no one can imagine an alternative. As a result, most planners report that they would not abolish targets even though they report a range of negative consequences for planners as individuals and for the planning system more generally. We do not think, however, that such analysis fully captures the dynamics of what is happening, as will become evident. For now, however, it is important to note that there were feelings of powerlessness, of being subject to large reform processes beyond their control.

Alongside feelings of powerlessness, and in stark contrast to them, there were also very real examples of reform processes actually opening up new spaces for autonomy, or at least of planners being able to defend their autonomy. Autonomy and discretion are traditionally seen as the hallmarks of professional identity, and much of the literature presents new public management in terms of restricting that autonomy and discretion, for example, through targets or the customer ideal. In practice, however, there is no simple rejection of professionalism or simple dichotomy of power either being in the hands of the public or in the hands of the bureaucrats (cf Gaster and Rutqvist, 2000). First, it is important to note that planners retained an essential element of discretion in their job, in that they could still exercise some degree of professional judgement in deciding whether or not to recommend planning permission and in deciding which policies to pursue in a plan, even if these were constrained. Beyond that, some elements of the reform agenda have actually worked to increase the ability to exercise discretion. For example, one consequence of the target regime has been a marked increase in delegation rates, so that planners are now empowered to make more decisions directly rather than simply making recommendations to elected members (Chapter Five).

Planners do not, however, just have some elements of increased discretion given to them. There has also been an active drive to create, or at least defend, professional autonomy. While participation is traditionally seen in terms of reducing, and indeed threatening, professional autonomy, planners seem to reinscribe their professional autonomy by talking about participation as something that needs professional management lest it get 'out of control' or the needs of the 'greater good' be threatened by unrepresentative NIMBYs (Chapter Six). There is a clear positioning of the frontline planner as a mediator of participation processes and as the judge of legitimacy in the knowledge produced through such processes. Very similarly, in Chapter Six, planners actively blunted the customer ideal through redefining the 'customer' as everyone (including the environment). Therefore the language of 'customerness' was used, and the importance of providing a good service internalised. But in doing so, the very idea of a 'customer' is redefined until it is rendered almost unrecognisable, in terms of the sovereign customer ideals of new public management. Instead, the professional is needed to balance the 'competing' customer interests.

Given this active agency, there is also some evidence of planners actually resisting reform. As Clarke and Newman (1997) note, managerialism is adapted and resisted on the ground, within the pattern of structural change. However, there is a strong desire of frontline staff not to be seen as anti-change, so most resistance to change is passive resistance. There is evidence of this in the reactions of planners. There appeared to be some very genuine opposition to the LDF system (Chapter Four), and while planners were getting on with producing the documents because they had to, this opposition may be being reflected in a politics of time. The slow progression on LDF documents led to the government modifying elements of those reforms so as to address the concerns of a range of stakeholders, including frontline staff. This is evidence of an active process of negotiation, even if only implicitly through the fact that government reformed its initial reforms. Likewise, planners felt they 'should say yes' to participation, but a majority said they had already had enough and there was no need for any more (Chapter Six). The speed agenda was then cited as a reason to restrict participation, and the tensions between the agendas opened up a space (albeit a limited one) for a particular element of the reforms to be contested and subverted. This situation looks likely to continue for some time, with the Coalition government emphasising speed in planning and also participation through the localism agenda. The reaction of planners seems to reflect the arguments of Clarke and Newman about people in public service organisations, which are worth quoting at length:

> We have been struck by the contradictory nature of their experience of change.... Those working in public services are having to manage not just budgets and people in the pursuit of greater efficiency, but the tensions and dilemmas of rapid and unpredictable change. The results are frequently high levels of stress and overload which tend to spill over into 'personal life'. At the same time, however, these managers have engaged with the challenge of building more responsive, flexible and user oriented public services. Many have welcomed the opportunities for innovation, or come to enjoy the challenge of competition. Some have sought to modernise what they see as outdated organisations and

institutions in the pursuit of a new sense of public purpose. Others have been more cautious, expressing concern about the impact of change on users and communities and doubtful about the future of "public service" values in a culture which they see as dominated by the values of the business world. (Clarke and Newman, 1997, p x)

Such processes of subversion and resistance might be decried by those of a public choice theory persuasion, who would read them as undermining the very reform processes which they believe make public sector more responsive to the public it exists to serve (see Hay, 2007). But those who are more supportive of the positive potential of professions (see, for example, Freidson, 2001) are likely to support the attempts of planners to apparently maintain some reference to notions of the collective good despite the reforms. Similarly, those drawing on Lipsky (1980) might suggest that retention of some kind of autonomy and discretion is the only way through which frontline planners can negotiate the web of tensions, of conflicting demands, in which they are caught.

Questions of space and time

The themes of space and time recur throughout the empirical chapters. Spatially, we can say that geography does matter. Interestingly, there was little evidence of post-devolutionary geography over matters such as participation or targets. Certainly, there was a much greater emphasis placed on performance targets in England than in Scotland or Wales, but development control processing time was measured and reported in all three countries. Similarly, agendas for both speeding up planning and making it more participatory appeared in all three territories. This may reflect the similar starting points, in terms of planning systems and practice, or that the reforms are responding to more globalised pressures (Allmendinger et al, 2005). Nevertheless, despite the commonalities, there were differences in emphases on some of these same policies. Therefore, the fact that responses showed common themes in all three (Chapters Five, Six and Seven) may have more to do with a strong, interconnected planning culture than down to the fact that place does not matter. Professionalism appears to transcend post-devolutionary boundaries within a continuing (but weakening) UK nation-state.

Chapter Four, however, did reveal some post-devolutionary difference, with quite different policy planning proposals for England, Scotland and Wales despite the commonality of ideas about local spatial planning. In this context, through the LDF, it is in England that reform has been implemented quickest and appears to have been the most wrenching. This was clearly shown by the contrast in the percentage of survey respondents thinking the reforms were, on balance, a good thing. In England, only 32.7 per cent agreed, compared to 60.4 per cent in Scotland. Planners there spoke, in interview, of the then Scottish Executive taking a more measured approach, being more consultative of frontline professionals. This may just be down to size of the country, of course: several planners pointed out that having only 30 LPAs meant that they could easily sit down together to discuss proposals, and many heads of planning seemed to know the Scottish Executive's chief planner personally, saying they would just telephone him directly if they had any concerns. There may also be a time factor here, with planners becoming more negative once they actually have to put the new local policy frameworks into practice in Scotland. In England, the view of central government appeared much more akin to Sullivan and Gillanders' (2005) finding that local government officers and civil servants conceive themselves as inhabiting different worlds.

Wales offers quite a different picture. Despite its small size, with only 25 LPAs, there was much less regard for planning reform here, with just 35.7 per cent thinking it was on balance a good thing. There also appeared to be a much worse image of the Welsh government. The key concern here, mentioned by every interviewee, was that they felt the government was implementing things too slowly compared to England. Unlike Scotland, there was a common legislative underpinning of the key changes (through PCPA 2004), and the slower approach to putting that into practice in Wales appeared a source of some confusion and resentment. There was also concern from one or two London local authority planners regarding the added complexity caused by the Mayor of London's agenda.

That identical national agendas are being implemented in different ways in different places highlights the fact that reform outcomes are context-dependent and frequently unpredictable (Clarke and Newman, 1997). Planning reform agendas must intersect not just with wider public sector modernisation policies, but also with existing structural arrangements, cultures and organisational factors in individual authorities. While the intersection of the planning reform agendas with a 'planning culture' nationally explains some of the resultant practice on the ground, so do far more local conditions of implementation, hence the much greater progress made with reforms in some LPAs than others. Place matters. As Lowndes (2001) suggests, local institutional constraints and 'implementation habits' can mean that some national policies are implemented in quite different ways in different places.

Alongside such spatial concerns, there is room for thought about time. There appeared an inherent 'future optimism' in the default assumption of many interviewees that the local spatial planning system would 'bed down' over time, but it is noticeable that more experienced planners were more opposed to those policy reforms (Chapter Four). The survey results point to the relationship but do not reveal the causality, and one can only speculate that older planners are either simply more used to previous ways of working or, as another interviewee suggested, they had all seen reform 'before' and were thus more cynical about change. That said, even older planners often conceded a need for reform in interview; there was little sense of planning being timeless, and some thought that there had been a need for change, for example, speeding up the production of plans and the processing of applications (Chapter Five). Wenger (1999) notes that identity has a temporal dimension and is continually negotiated over time, so that generational inheritance, combined with renegotiated identity, may help us understand older planners being both cynical about change but also seeing the need for it. Interestingly, despite the talk of a certain generation of planners having entered the profession when it was the 'bright young, evangelical bureaucracy' (Chapter Seven), few planners waxed nostalgically about a lost 'golden age' located sometime in the past. Instead, the public service ethos was seen as still existing in the present day. Perhaps the fact that so many planning achievements of the 1960s are now so widely discredited explains this apparent lack of the past as a reference point for planners in the face of modernisation.

Resourcing modernisation

A final broad strand related to reform emerging from the research concerns the 'nuts and bolts' of the reform process, and how important these are. Although often seemingly overlooked by central government and academics alike, issues surrounding resourcing the implementation of reforms appear to have a considerable bearing over the success of such reforms. These factors, while easier to raise than to solve, do appear to go a long way to explaining why 'there is still a concern that the new system is not speeding up the plan making process nor leading to earlier decision making' (Baker Associates et al, 2008, p 106). Similarly, the Egan review (2004) recognised that recruitment and retention of planners matter, and that failure to tackle these issues might threaten the then Sustainable Communities agenda. The current economic climate aside, these problems must remain a concern, particularly given the demographic profile of the profession. Although pay is apparently a factor in people leaving for the private sector, so are conditions: people tend to leave the public sector due to push factors such as paperwork and red tape rather than due to the pull of the private sector (Audit Commission, 2002). This suggests that there are alternatives to tackling recruitment and retention beyond simply offering more pay.

Poor quality and untimely guidance was raised as a particular issue with regard to implementing reforms (Chapter Four). Although it seemed the aims of the reforms were perceived to be generally well set out, precise technical guidance was seen as lacking, or late in coming. This was a particular problem in England with the introduction of the LDF system. For development management and culture change, concern was expressed about a lack of clarity from government about precisely what these meant in practice. Alongside this, there was a very strong concern about inadequate resources to support reform implementation: 86.0 per cent of English survey respondents agreed or strongly agreed that the resource implications of the reforms had been underestimated, compared to 84.8 per cent of Scottish survey respondents and 75.0 per cent of Welsh survey respondents. Although this reflects longstanding concerns about central government failing to support local government in implementing its agendas (Barrett and Fudge, 1981), it is nonetheless a serious issue. There is a limit to what efficiency savings can achieve, and in England PDG (before its abolition) tended to be focused more on development control than policy, and as a reward to support those who had done well rather than as an aid to those who were struggling. This can partly (but not fully) explain some of the slow progress with LDFs. Although sometimes overlooked, factors such as clarity of aims, timely production of guidance and sufficient resource support matter, and can threaten much larger agendas if not properly managed.

Planners and the roll-out of modernisation

Picturing planning

Throughout the chapters of this book, a picture emerges of what planners at the coalface seem to imagine the purpose of planning to be, and of the place of professional planners in it. The picture is not always coherent, nor are all aspects of the picture universally accepted, and nor is it static. The picture of planning emerging is not sufficiently captured by much of the existing literature. For example, much of the literature would imply planners largely had 'little regard' for public participation (see Chapters One and Six). In fact, there was strong support for the idea of participation. This was not just because of a narrow instrumental conception of it as somehow useful (although 63 per cent of respondents agreed it was useful), but because it was seen as 'morally right'. There was a strong framing in the interviews of planning as about communities and as a fundamentally democratic process, in which planners did not know everything, and local knowledge should be incorporated.

The purpose of planning very much appeared to be seen through appeals to the 'greater good', to Benthamite ideals of the greatest good for the greatest number. This was seen in Chapter Five, where there was talk of the unrepresentativeness of participation and the need to consider the 'silent majority'. Similarly, in Chapter Seven, there were strong appeals to planning serving the interests of the community and environment, which might be threatened by too narrow a conception of 'customers' as just applicants. Such appeals are longstanding in planning and probably reflect the fact that they justify the very need for an interventionist, state planning system.

Within these appeals to the needs of community and environment, there was a clear picturing of the role of the planner as balancing competing participants and competing customers, and indeed the competing needs of economy, society and environment. Planning was not seen as simply achieving harmonious consensus. Indeed there was some scepticism about the idea that frontloading (opening up more opportunities for early dialogue and collaboration between groups and agencies) would lead to greater consensus, although there was support for frontloading in practice. This support appeared to be because it offered the opportunity to be aware of, and attempt to manage, opposition earlier rather than being about achieving consensus (Chapter Four). Therefore, there was an active role for the planner in delivering developments that might benefit the local community despite NIMBY opposition (Chapter Six). Similarly the planner must ensure all 'customers' receive a fair service, even if the outcome is not what they would like (Chapter Six), must listen to objections so that people 'feel they have had their say', and must mediate within participation events (Chapter Six).

Ultimately, there is a strong discourse of the planner being there to try to represent the 'silent majority' and to meet the needs of the 'greater good'. Such ideals are easily criticised, and have been strongly questioned over the years. Gunder summarises such critique:

Planning is still socially predicated on its constituting fantasy of "truth" that its practitioners are unbiased, rational, scientific technical experts serving the public interest.... Unfortunately, this is perhaps the greatest fantasy and is seldom, if ever, the case....Yet even with decades of critical planning research demonstrating the inherent biases in planning practices and the multiplicity of public interests, the fantasy of unbiased experts seeking an idealized 'public good' – originally instrumental, now communicative – continues. (Gunder, 2003, p 288)

But despite such critique, there are still frequent appeals to the public good. Proudfoot and McCann have noticed this with SLBs elsewhere:

[Despite] the problematic and contestable nature of appeals to the "public good" in urban policymaking, the bureaucrats interviewed believe strongly that their everyday practice promotes a safer, fairer, more liveable, enjoyable, and efficiently run city that offered benefits to all its residents. We have no grounds upon which to question their good intentions, although it is important to note the existence of large structures that favor [sic] certain interests in society at the expense of others. (2008, pp 355-6)

In fact, we might term this idea 'the imagined space of the greater good' since it appears to be more about planners justifying their role than any innate ability to represent the greater good. That said, as Campbell comments, there is a need for thinking about the collective good, and planners can at least try to represent that, even if there is a need to recognise its inevitable partiality so as to try and avoid the 'worst traditions of bureaucratic elitism' (2002, p 284). She argues that place making cannot just be left down to narrow individualism and self-interest due to the 'wicked problems' it must overcome. For present purposes, we are less interested in assessing the actual ability of planners to represent the silent majority and more in the fact that this continues to be an organising frame for planners at the coalface. Likewise, environmental and societal needs are still placed highly despite the push to make planning more economically responsive as part of the reform agenda. This highlights the importance of identity in response to reform pressures, which we return to later in this chapter.

Much of the talk about the needs of the greater good responds to the wider culture of the profession. There was a clear 'public sector planning culture' evident, characterised by a sense of a reflexive, interconnected British local authority planning profession, with a certain 'planning ethos' and sense of vocation. The evidence for there being a particular culture for the profession comes from the similar attitudes and responses to the reform agendas across England, Scotland and Wales, particularly seen in Chapters Five and Six, despite some differences in the specific policies pursued by London, Edinburgh and Cardiff (differences which are probably accelerating with respect to England since the election of the Coalition government). In this sense, the profession has a particular culture framed by common ideals of professionalism and public service, and by the fact that practitioners share a common educational framework, professional organisation and professional newsletter across Britain. There is also considerable fluidity to the profession through the movement of staff between local authorities. These issues explain how planners are knowledgeable about reforms in each nation (many Scottish and Welsh planners interviewed were well aware of developments in England) and share similar reactions to audit and participation, for example. This culture is by no means fixed, although it probably only ever changes slowly. Certainly the profession is becoming increasingly female, which might lead to a very different planning profession in 20 years' time.

In the broader concept of the 'British planning profession', there do appear to be shared narratives, cultures and repertoires between planners across the nation, between those in Shetland and those in Cornwall. We can continue to understand planning through the concept of a profession with shared historical roots, discourses and enterprises which its members are engaged in. It certainly appears that despite its apparent status as a 'semi-profession', the professional model continues to offer a useful route to better understanding planners. There was some evidence of a reflexive profession, as those pushing collaborative planning (Forester, 1989; Healey, 2006) have called for. Planners certainly actively questioned their role and knowledge when considering public participation, for example (Chapter Six). Frequently, the opportunities and concerns raised by planners with regard to things such as targets or participation closely reflected academic commentary. This raises the question of the nature of the circulation of knowledge and whether planners are merely reflecting things they have read or been taught, or whether this is because academics so closely describe the realities of frontline experience.

There also appeared to be a certain 'local authority planner' ethos, which particularly came across in Chapter Seven. Fagermoen (1997) suggests identity is directly linked to everyday practice, for example, the conception of what it means to be and to act as a nurse represents that person's 'philosophy of nursing'. There was clearly a 'philosophy of local government planning'. This might be linked with the comparatively small movement from the private to the public sector. Many planners seemed to conceptualise their role as a distinctly public sector one, with talk of different ethical considerations in the public as opposed to the private sector. More broadly, there was a strong sense of a public service ideal, with reference back to the 'greater good' reflecting the resilience of the public realm (Clarke, 2004). Most planners seem to have entered the profession for environmental and public service reasons. Planners also tended to be proudest of technical achievements. This may help explain the somewhat sceptical approach to concepts such as the 'customer' ideal; in their minds, planners were making reference to achievements other than having processed a developer's application efficiently. Indeed, there was something of a sense of planning as a 'vocation' (cf Weber, 2004). Many planners strongly believed in the power of planning and genuinely seemed to believe in the idea of it as a public service. Whatever the accuracy of such ideals in practice, whatever the slipperiness of the 'public sector ethos', the fact that planners were making mental appeals to it is important. This is reason enough not to entirely dismiss the concept, as some scholars do (see Chapter Seven). If nothing else, the ideals of neoliberalism are partially rejected just through the fact that rather than internalising reform goals, planners made reference to much older ideas and alternative discourses (indeed, almost 'higher purposes') to legitimate their role.

This is especially important because new public management is essentially an 'identity project' (du Gay, 1996; Davies and Thomas, 2003). While Bolton questions whether 'the imposition of efficiency quotas and performance measurements, along with the enterprise discourse of "consumer as king", has meant that public service work no longer represents a liberation from the "commodity form"' (2002, p 131), the enactment of new public management is at best a 'contested terrain' of meaning where spaces are presented for alternative meanings and identities (Davies and Thomas, 2003). There is a tendency to draw on traditional discourses of the public sector ethos rather than those of new public management to assert legitimacy, just as noted by Thomas and Linstead (2002). The success of an identity project is thus questionable if people's identities do not appear to be undergoing major change.

Understanding the roll-out of modernisation

Through the evidence presented in the preceding chapters, we would argue strongly for a more implementation-focused research agenda to understand the true implications for reform. As Clarke highlights, we need to look 'for the grit ... recalcitrance, resistance, obstruction ... rather than throwing them in as gestural paragraph after the "big story" has been told' (2004, p 44). There is a tendency for all embracing accounts of deterministic new public management and neoliberalism across the social sciences. Within planning, the literature on new plan making arrangements, in particular, seems characterised by descriptive accounts of new structures, legislative arrangements and central government policy pronouncements; perhaps that is inevitable in the immediate aftermath of change and enactment. But reform does not just happen because central government says it will; policy involves ongoing implementation by frontline public sector actors. With four distinctive reform processes to planning in England at least since 1997, it is now time for the practical implications to be assessed. This book has shown that planning reform depends not just on planners putting the new policies into action, but also on how they manage conflicting demands on their time and other resources, and conflicting elements of the reform agenda. Indeed, embedded tensions in the elements of New Labour's modernisation agenda seemed to have opened up spaces for local discretion that mean practice cannot simply be 'read off' from government policy. The same is likely to be true of the post-2010 Coalition reforms. Change happens, but happens uniquely in different places, at different times, and creates its own new forms and practices that are often unexpected.

There are existing accounts that make this same argument. Clarke and Newman highlight the dangers of 'totalising' accounts of change, suggesting there is a need for a more nuanced understanding of the implementation of managerial governance because 'issues of consent, compromise and contradiction are important in theorising the process of change' (1997, p 95), so that processes of change are shaped by the interplay of power and interests rather than just the result of economic or political factors. Peck and Tickell (2002, quoted in Proudfoot and McCann, 2008, p 364) highlight the need to avoid both 'overgeneralized accounts of a monolithic and omnipresent neoliberalism' and also 'excessively concrete and contingent analyses of (local) neoliberal strategies'. Generally, as Davies and Thomas argue, the 'enactment of NPM at the localized level is far less deterministic and coherent than has been suggested in previous studies' because of 'contested meanings that are negotiated' in the enactment of reform (2003, p 697). One of the key reasons appears to be because of the ability of powerful local actors to adapt the 'rules of the game' in reaction to reforms (Lowndes, 2005). We further consider the appropriateness of an institutionalist framework for understanding this below.

A focus on the 'how of government', on the messiness of implementation (MacKinnon, 2000), is important for furthering our understanding of how the state works. The reaction of frontline planners to reform initiatives highlights the danger of simple dichotomies of 'the state' and 'the citizenry'. The state is not a unified whole, not just in terms of its increasingly fragmented governance, but also in the sense that its actions are driven through peopled practices. Indeed, planners seemed to conceive of themselves as somehow not part of government – for example, speaking of reforms as 'government' when referring to ministers or DCLG – but clearly remain essential to the implementation of reforms and are the window through which the public interact with the state.

Conceptualising the role of the planner

This raises the issue of how to conceptualise the role of the planner, overviewed in Chapter Three. What does not seem to fit here is the idea that planners are simply 'subjected' by the reforms. Actors do not appear to be shaped evenly by the large-scale trends, and it is therefore possible to be over-deterministic in assuming certain responses to policies driven by economic forces (Clarke and Newman, 1997). Durant argues that bureaucrats 'are not passive bystanders who are merely "acted upon" by reform processes', but instead 'act strategically to influence agency design and evolution' (2006, p 470) and thus play a vital strategic role in the realignment of governmental institutions. Elsewhere, Sturdy (1998) suggests that talk of subjectivity implies too much coherence to new public management, neglecting internal contradictions and resistance. Accounts drawing on governmentality do allow for resistance, for example, Bondi and Laurie argue that 'neoliberalisation incorporates, co-opts, constrains and depletes activism' so that the 'professional(ised) subject inhabit and sometimes subvert the opportunities neoliberalisation opens up' (2005, p 2). Davies and Thomas suggest that individuals can 'assert, accommodate, challenge or deny the various subject positions offered within the NPM discourse' (2003, p 689). Furthermore, the fact that targets seem to have so colonised the public domain that planners cannot imagine living without them would seem to fit within this framework, but overall we do not believe such an approach best explains the data here. Talk of 'subjectification' seems to deny the planners a certain important element of active agency in responding to the reforms.

In a study of sustainability indicators, Rydin (2007) argues that the indicators did not render the field a governable object but stood instead to highlight the extent of competition, contestation and constructivist agency:

> This suggests that any use of the governmentality framework needs to allow for greater agency and conflict in the construction of objects and subjects. (Rydin, 2007, p 621)

Agency can involve contestation and resistance (MacKinnon, 2000) or an 'active form of compliance' (Herbert-Cheshire, 2003, quoted in Rydin, 2007) so that actors do not necessarily react to 'governmental technologies' in expected ways. While the reforms may be about attempting to exert greater control over frontline planners, to make the domain more knowable, there is little evidence of planners becoming self-disciplining subjects. The reason appears to be partly because the agenda is not clear enough. There is no unified set of neoliberal or managerial discourses and practices. This opens up space for alternative positions to be adopted, for elements of the reform to be used in unintended ways, and for agency to be expressed.

An alternative approach introduced in Chapter Three that allowed for far greater agency was Lipsky's (1980) concept of the 'street-level bureaucrat'. The data throughout the chapters that followed can clearly be understood through the SLB lens. Taylor and Kelly (2006) argue that the SLB concept is out of date due to a lack of discretion by contemporary public sector professionals, a defining feature of SLBs. They are too hasty in their dismissal of the concept. Conflicting agendas, resource constraints and unclear goals, among other defining features set out by Lipsky, can clearly be applied to planning at the coalface in a time of concerted and contested reform. While some elements of the reform agenda, such as targets, certainly do reduce some kinds of discretion, they also open up new areas for it, such as the increase in delegation. Where loss of autonomy is threatened by reforms, as with participation and the customer ideal, planners can reinscribe it through creating new roles for themselves and by reasserting public service identities.[1] Discretion is not dead, but rather changed, and can act in subtle – even covert – ways.

Most importantly, Lipsky's work serves to highlight the reality of policy initiatives as the actions of frontline public servants with whom the public interact. This helps explain the paradox that despite globalising policy initiatives, implementation and outcomes remain stubbornly 'embedded' at the local level (Peck, 1999). It therefore becomes important to understand reform processes from the perspective of SLBs. This is not to say they should be given total control of reform policy. Indeed, it is unclear what planning reform agenda might result if it were just left to frontline planners.

At the same time as showing the continued relevance of the SLB concept, there are also some weaknesses with it. One area insufficiently captured by the SLB model is the difference between professional managers and their subordinates. We would conceive of all those planners surveyed and interviewed as SLBs, since even the senior planners get involved directly in more important planning work, and retain their professional status. Nevertheless, seniority seemed more important than job focus or geographical location in determining how planners might respond to reform agendas. Analysis of the survey results strongly suggests that planning managers were more supportive of targets (Chapter Five) and of the ideals of customer service (Chapter Six). This reflects some of the literature about managerialism, with Jones (2001) suggesting managers are more in favour of neoliberal-type reforms (see also Hebson et al, 2003; Cochrane, 2004;). Indeed, Taylor and Kelly argue that through reforms:

> Managers ... in effect become the direct agents of central government. It must be noted however, that many new service managers had also served their time as street-level bureaucrats ... reinforcing Flynn's [1997] observation that simple dichotomies of either professional autonomy or bureaucratic control are inadequate. (2006, p 633)

We would not quite agree with the idea of managers as direct agents of central government. We would suggest instead that planning managers are the ones who, for example, can make most strategic use of targets to further their own or their organisation's agendas, such as levering in greater resources, so this might explain their greater support for them. Certainly, target regimes work to make planning managers exert greater managerial control over their staff, but those same staff retain agency in other ways, while those same managers resist other reform elements. Clarke and Newman (1997) suggest it is public sector managers who are uniquely able to shape new institutional arrangements through the tensions between reform goals. But we can see this same process, albeit in more limited ways, being enacted by even less experienced planners, for example, using targets to control opposition to development proposals. Additionally, there continues to be a common planning ethos embracing senior and junior planners, and what unites them as SLBs is greater than what divides them.

A more striking difficulty is that the SLB concept has little to say explicitly about issues of identity. It became clear during the progress of the research that issues of identity appeared quite central in framing how planners perceived the reforms and reacted to them. This can be seen most explicitly when we consider how almost all local authority planners appeared to explicitly subscribe to an identity around public service and the unique attributes of public sector planning (Chapter Seven). For a certain generation of planners, this identity may have been strongly influenced in opposition to anti-planning discourses prevalent during the ascendancy of the New Right in the 1980s. As Wenger argues, we are social beings who participate in the practices of social communities and construct identities related to those communities, with identity closely linked to practice and acting as 'a pivot between the social and the individual' (1999, p 145). This certainly appears evident with regard to planners at the coalface, but SLB appears to offer comparatively little to help our understanding of the role of identity in reacting to reform, and therefore cannot offer a conceptual framework as a whole.

Supporting an institutionalist perspective

A more embracing framework is offered through the sociological institutionalist approach introduced in Chapter Three. Identity is seen by sociological institutionalists as of vital importance in terms of how actors respond to reform initiatives, both constraining actors but also being negotiated and recast in response to changing environments. In this perspective, identity is not fixed or static but the result of the interplay of multiple rule sets, for example, the managerial, professional, bureaucratic and constitutional. We can see that planners may be influenced by their identity as at one and the same time a planner, a local government officer, a public servant, a development control officer or policy planner or a middle or senior manager. The rule sets associated with each strand of this identity may change at different rates and even in different directions, leading to a more complex overall picture. Lowndes (2005) uses this to explain both inertia and innovation coexisting in local government modernisation. Furthermore, it is precisely because values and identities are at stake that institutional change can be so traumatic for individuals. The result is often that challenges to institutional settlements are likely to be met by resistance and by the ability of 'institutional entrepreneurs' to use reform as an opportunity to defend or further their status, as already discussed.

An example of this was given in Chapter Five, where there was evidence of planners finding opportunities in targets to promote their own agendas. Nevertheless, there was also strong evidence that Best Value targets were a powerful constraining rule set. Indeed, structure and agency are both at play here: at the most simplistic level, central government frames the context within which planners work by passing legislation and formulating reform policy (which can be understood as resulting from deeper structural forces, for example, neoliberalism), but planners can use these for their own ends. In that sense alone, the framework of sociological institutionalism introduced in Chapter Three seems helpful in trying to understand planning at the coalface. It is important to note that at the level of the individual, reaction to any one reform element can vary; for example, some planners were clearly more in favour of participation than others (Chapter Six). That said, there were commonalities in many responses and similar ways of framing things, hence talk of a 'planning culture' and references to 'planners' in discussing results. Institutionalism allows for this, since the individual may display agency and act in a new way, but change to structures only occurs if that new way of performing is more generally accepted. There is agency but it is clearly constrained, as Healey (2006) outlines.

The reaction to reform elements often appeared to come down to narrow sets of imagined possibilities, because the structures of the planning system, of local government and of the profession act to make only a limited number of responses appear plausible. Rather than 'autonomous agency', or simply being able to read off outcomes from deterministic economic or political structures, these imperatives have an 'inseparable and embedded connection to humanly made structures' (Wilson, 2004, p 780). Actors remember, borrow and share institutional repertoires so experience is transferred in structured networks (Lowndes, 2005). This helps explain how similar opinion trends could often be seen across Britain, for example, in response to targets (Chapter Five), since some institutions cross boundaries within the larger British nation-state. It can also help us understand how some experienced planners strongly supported local spatial planning since it appeared to resonate with an institutional memory of returning to an older vision and purpose of planning (Chapter Four).

When reforms are implemented, institutionalists suggest that old and new institutions often coexist (Lowndes and Wilson, 2003). This may help explain how some individuals were more supportive of some reforms than others (for example, participation, in Chapter Six). It may also help us understand some of the apparently contradictory positions held by many planners within themselves in their perception of reforms; for example, the interaction of a modern notion of customer service with an older public service identity meaning the idea of having 'customers' in planning is supported but the concept and the associated reform purpose is undermined by the subsequent definition of customers as 'everyone' (Chapter Six). This is less a conscious rendering than a result of the existing norms and routine practices of the profession creating path dependencies in the face of attempted reforms. Path dependency can also be seen in the response to participation initiatives (Chapter Six). That participation is seen as so important may reflect the strong public service identity that appeared to matter so much to many planners, but equally participation might threaten their privileged role and expert identity. The result of this interplay is a framing of participation as vital, but in need of managing by the professional planner, and further attempts to increase participation may simply result in further attempts to reinscribe professional autonomy.

A final key concept of institutionalism is the idea that while particular moments can generate relentless pressure for change, how much this activity sediments down to deeper levels and becomes institutionalised into future governance culture is hard to tell (Healey, 2007b). Only time will tell which elements of the planning and public sector reform discussed in this book is sediment in the longer term. Drawing on an example from Chapter Five, it might be that the fact some younger planners seemed to see their purpose as providing an efficient service means target culture is indeed altering their identity and practices of planners at the coalface. Equally, however, the majority of planners appeared to still maintain an ideal of planning as about creating and protecting quality environments (and not being about the efficient processing of applications), and this might prove the more resistant frame.

Some institutionalist scholars seek to normatively offer advice for good reform design, with emphasis placed on clear values and sufficient capacity being offered for learning and adaption, combing robust aims and enforcement of implementation with room for revisability through adaption to local context through practical experience (Lowndes and Wilson, 2003). We do not seek to offer such advice here, but instead to note the apparent suitability and strength of the sociological institutionalist framework for conceptualising planning reform and the role of planners at the coalface in it, helping us understand the constrained yet active agency apparent, and the importance of identity, local context and the interaction of different rule sets in guiding behaviour while being made and remade by actors. In this sense, responding to our original (provocative) question, planners are neither collaborators nor resisters in the process of the neoliberal remaking of the state, but are both. The structures and rule sets of being a professional planner, a local government officer, a public servant are all being remade through a concerted process of reform, and planners are helping to enact policies that are part of a broad neoliberalisation of our governance, but at the same time the tensions between reforms and the resilience of certain values and identities is creating a situation where policies on the ground cannot simply be 'read off' from reform intentions. Reform is implemented through actors changing their subject positions, adopting new tools and techniques of government, but this happens against a backdrop of people's sense of what it means to be a 'good planner' (Gunder and Hillier, 2007), which continues to place value on some rather traditional public service and welfare state ideals.

The future role of the planner?

We have shown clearly the importance of not seeing frontline professionals as mere passive recipients of modernisation agendas. Planning's front line is vitally important, it is a distinct space of meaning, and planning is more than just a structure, a collection of laws and procedures – it is a peopled process. Evidence from reaction to New Labour's reforms remains relevant today as different governments in the devolved UK pursue further planning and public sector reforms.

Nowhere does change currently feel more dramatic than in England, where the Coalition government is currently enacting large cuts to public spending. Taylor-Gooby and Stoker argue that:

> The Coalition programme is more than an immediate response to a large current account deficit. It involves a restricting of welfare benefits and public services that takes the country in a new direction, rolling back the state to a level of intervention below that in the United States – something which is unprecedented....The policies include substantial privatisation and a shift of responsibility from state to individual. (2011, p 14)

Similarly, Kerr et al suggest that the government is now pursuing a 'radical, aggressive and seemingly regressive onslaught on public sector provision, particularly in relation to those so-called "front-line" public services' (2011, p 196). This is creating a very different context for planning than existed under New Labour, and is having a dramatic effect on both local government and the planning service.

Anecdotal evidence suggests that although planning as a public service has not been particularly targeted by the spending regime, local authorities have been required to reduce their expenditure through non-replacement of retiring staff and their staffing costs. The result has been a heavy increase in workloads for those staff remaining in their posts. Senior staff have also taken early retirement or else been made redundant, and this has meant a vacuum being created of more experienced officers with middle managers and less experienced officers struggling with their workloads. At a time when the government is committed to development delivery, economic growth and infrastructure provision, the implications of the spending cuts for local planning authorities are hitting at exactly the wrong time. This demonstrates either a lack of joined-up thinking between different parts of government, or else a fundamental failure to recognise the importance of planning delivery in the wider objectives of government policy. The next few years are likely to be extremely difficult for planning compared to the preceding decade. Yet the response at the 'coalface' will, as this research has demonstrated, be more complex than the headlines suggest. It is likely some 'institutional entrepreneur' planners may find opportunities to further the interests of the planning professional, even in this extremely negative context. Professional planners will continue to both resist and mediate some aspects of reform through the opportunity spaces opened up by them and in the light of enduring professional identities, but the force of a dedicated neoliberal government will not leave planning unchanged.

More generally, one of the key messages emanating from this discussion is what positive role planners can play, especially for a more plural constituency. There is a desire evident in the profession to be more proactive, not reactive, even if the continual cycle of reform and the participatory and performance management pressures on planners occasionally conspire to dent spirits. Planners do think beyond the legal confines of statutory town and country planning with the intention to inspire, give confidence and provide understanding; they enable change to occur in the right locations. The key challenge rests on finding visionary aspects of planning and of making connections within increased complexity and increasing expectations on planning as a delivery vehicle. Planning, by its very nature, should promote innovation and experimentation, allow creativity, and create a sense of confidence. It should not be straightjacketed. More people are becoming involved within planning through consideration of places and how they might change in the future; participants will need to be encouraged, provided with knowledge, science and options and helped to develop their critical understanding of change. Planners will need to communicate a sense of realism: no one should suggest that new processes of planning will be easy or achieved quickly.

Planning will increasingly become an activity of many people, and it will no longer be 'owned' by planners but by those agencies and individuals who see a value for it. Planners both in the public and private sectors will be expected to deliver the locational aspects of a range of sectoral issues, and support businesses and communities in making sense of change. At the start of the 21st century, we have more expectations, we make more demands, we contest more and we are impatient. Planners' work will increase to make sense of these expectations. And so it is inevitable that planning changes periodically to respond to the challenges we face, but we need to continually question planning's value and purpose, and debate the changing role of planners, both within and external to the profession itself. Only then will planning demonstrate its important and vital, critical, scientific and reflective position in coordinating change.

Notes

Chapter One

[1] Planning in Northern Ireland has traditionally been operated by an agency of central government rather than by local government, and there is a very different political context in the province. Reform to decentralise planning here is also in the early stages.

[2] In talking about 'planning' we are referring to what was traditionally known as 'town and country planning' and is sometimes now also known as 'urban and environmental planning', as defined in the UK by statute. Since 2001, the planning system has also been labelled spatial planning, in part to reflect a post-reformed process. These labels remain contested (see Tewdwr-Jones, 2012).

[3] In a planning application, the developer is the 'first party' and the local authority the 'second party'. The 'third party' is anyone else with a view over the proposal. Currently the first party has a right of appeal if the second party refuses permission for a development it wants, but the third party has no right of appeal if the second party grants permission for a development they object to.

[4] Although there have been remarkably few public cases of corruption in the British planning system (given the sheer number of decisions made), there were a number of high profile cases in the early 1990s. This led to the Nolan Report of 1997 focusing on planning as one of the areas that 'seem to cause the most impropriety, or public suspicion of impropriety' (Nolan, 1997, quoted in Manns and Wood, 2001, p 245).

[5] Since this change was ongoing during the period of research analysis and book writing, many interviewees and respondents still used the term 'development control', clinging on to the historical term. We use the term 'development control' throughout this book. This does not imply any negative view of the idea of development management.

Chapter Two

[1] This has extended into sectoral spending departments' spatial and locational implications of key policy areas, such as education and health. But planning has even been promoted as a tool to help tackle terrorism (see West, 2008).

[2] Examples exist of planners being asked to enforce standards that might previously have been administered by Building Regulations inspectors, with the former remaining in the public sector and the latter now contracted out.

Chapter Five

[1] Those were:

- opinion on whether the targets had improved performance ($p \leq 0.001$, df = 12);

- opinion on whether targets had improved relations with the public ($p \leq 0.035$, df = 12);

- opinion on whether targets should be abolished ($p \leq 0.012$, df = 9); and,

- opinion on whether targets restricted discretion ($p \leq 0.018$, df = 12).

[2] Notoriously, Michael Heseltine, as the first Secretary of State for the Environment of the Thatcher government, complained that 'thousands of jobs every night are locked away in the filing trays of planning departments' (1979, quoted in Carmona and Sieh, 2004, p 118).

[3] Although in some authorities there were complaints that PDG went into the central finances of the council rather than being ring-fenced for planning, despite government figures suggesting 97 per cent of PDG directly benefits planning (ODPM, 2005e).

[4] Namely the Planning and Compulsory Purchase Act 2004, the Planning Act 2008 and the Local Democracy, Economic Development and Construction Act 2009.

[5] A relevant example here concerns the growing use of 'conditional cautions' in the criminal justice system. In an article in *The Times*, a practising solicitor highlighted how the cautions were being used in ways unintended by central government. The then Justice Minister Maria Eagle responded, 'this is not the case' (quoted in Ellis, 2009). Clearly the criminal justice system is simply what is set out in 'operational guidance' and the direct experience of those working in the system is irrelevant.

Chapter Six

[1] In recent years, the preferred term in England has been 'community involvement' and in Scotland 'community engagement'. Both these may seem to stem from the discourse of 'community' created by New Labour (see Imrie and Raco, 2003). We stick to the term 'public participation' throughout, both for consistency and since this is the term most commonly used by planners themselves.

[2] Kitchen lists the customer of planning as: applicants for planning permission, local residents affected by planning applications in an area, the wider general public in an area, the business community, interest or pressure groups in the community, other agencies whose actions impinge on the development

process, other departments of the local authority, the elected members of the council, the formal control mechanisms of central government and purchasers of planning services (Kitchen, 2006).

[3] Warren (2002) suggests that in some economically depressed areas of rural Scotland, there has been strong support for development proposals among the local population on economic grounds, but opposition from 'outsiders' on environmental grounds, and anecdotal evidence gained during my research visits suggests that, for example, in prosperous areas of South East England, planners are more likely to be mediating a string of applications for development against strong public opposition, whereas in less prosperous areas, planners see their role more as trying to encourage development (see also Clifford and Warren, 2005). Nevertheless, at the regional level, at least, there were planners who strongly agreed participation was NIMBY-dominated in every part of Britain.

Chapter Seven

[1] The other three reasons for entering were an existing interest in the built environment, perceiving planning a safe career choice and other construction and environmental professionals using planning as a way to expand their own professional knowledge.

Chapter Eight

[1] See also Fitzgerald and Ferlie (2000), who highlight how healthcare professionals retain autonomy despite quasi-market reforms.

References

Abbott, A. (1988) *The system of professions: An essay on the division of expert labour*, Chicago, IL: University of Chicago Press.

Albrechts, L. (2002) 'The planning community reflects on enhancing public involvement. Views from academics and reflective practitioners', *Planning Theory & Practice*, vol 3, no 3, pp 331-47.

Alexander, E.R. (2001) 'The planner-prince: Interdependence, rationalities and post-communicative practice', *Planning Theory & Practice*, vol 2, no 3, pp 311-24.

Alfasi, N. (2003) 'Is public participation making urban planning more democratic? The Israeli experience', *Planning Theory & Practice*, vol 4, no 2, pp 185-202.

Alford, J. (2002) 'Defining the client in the public sector: A social-exchange perspective', *Public Administration Review*, vol 62, no 3, pp 337-46.

Allen, C. (2001) 'They just don't live and breathe the policy like we do...: Policy intentions and practice dilemmas in modern social policy and implementation networks', *Policy Studies*, vol 22, pp 149-66.

Allmendinger, P. (1996) 'Development control and the legitimacy of planning decisions: a comment', *Town Planning Review*, vol 67, no 2, pp 229-33.

Allmendinger, P. (2001a) *Planning in postmodern times*, London: Routledge.

Allmendinger, P. (2001b) 'The head and the heart. National identity and urban planning in a devolved Scotland', *International Planning Studies*, vol 6, no 1, pp 33-54.

Allmendinger, P. (2001c) 'The future of planning under a Scottish Parliament', *Town Planning Review*, vol 72, no 2, pp 121-48.

Allmendinger, P. (2002a) *Planning theory*, Basingstoke: Palgrave Macmillan.

Allmendinger, P. (2002b) 'Prospects for a distinctly Scottish planning in a post-sovereign age', *European Planning Studies*, vol 10, no 3, pp 359-81.

Allmendinger, P. (2002c) 'Planning under a Scottish Parliament: A missed opportunity?', *European Planning Studies*, vol 10, no 6, pp 793-8.

Allmendinger, P. (2011) *New Labour and planning: From New Right to New Left*, Abingdon: Routledge.

Allmendinger, P. and Haughton, G. (2007) 'The fluid scales and scope of UK spatial planning', *Environment and Planning A*, vol 39, pp 1478-96.

Allmendinger, P. and Tewdwr-Jones, M. (1997) 'Mind the gap: planning theory – practice and the translation of knowledge into action; a comment on Alexander (1997)', *Environment and Planning B: Planning and Design*, vol 24, pp 802-6.

Allmendinger, P. and Tewdwr-Jones, M. (2000) 'New Labour, new planning? The trajectory of planning in Blair's Britain', *Urban Studies*, vol 37, no 8, pp 1379-402.

Allmendinger, P. and Tewdwr-Jones, M. (eds) (2002) *Planning futures: New directions in planning theory*, London: Routledge.

Allmendinger, P., Morphet J. and Tewdwr-Jones, M. (2005) 'Devolution and the modernization of local government: Prospects for spatial planning', *European Planning Studies*, vol 13, no 3, pp 349-70.

Allmendinger, P., Tewdwr-Jones, M. and Morphet, J. (2003a) 'New order – Planning and local government reforms', *Town & Country Planning*, October, pp 274-7.

Allmendinger, P., Tewdwr-Jones, M. and Morphet, J. (2003b) 'Public scrutiny, standards and the planning system: Assessing professional values within a modernized local government', *Public Administration*, vol 81, no 4, pp 761-80.

Andrews, R., Boyne, G.A., Law, J. and Walker, R.M. (2003) 'Myths, measures and modernisation: A comparison of local authority performance in England and Wales', *Local Government Studies*, vol 29, no 4, pp 54-75.

Archer, M.S. (1982) 'Morphogenesis versus structuration: On combining structure and action', *The British Journal of Sociology*, vol 33, no 4, pp 455-83.

Arnstein, S.R. (1969) 'A ladder of citizen participation', *Journal of the American Institute of planners*, vol 35, no 4, pp 216-24.

Audit Commission (2002) *Recruitment and retention: A public service workforce for the 21st century*, London: Audit Commission.

Audit Commission (2005a) *Planning services – Reinspection: Reigate and Banstead Borough Council*, London: Audit Commission.

Audit Commission (2005b) 'Audit Commission key lines of enquiry for service inspections: Environment: Planning' (www.audit-commission. gov.uk/kloe/downloads/KLOEEnvironmentPlanning.pdf).

Audit Commission (2006a) *The planning system: Matching expectations and capacity*, London: Audit Commission.

Audit Commission (2006b) *Planning services and the private sector – Myths explored*, London: Audit Commission.

Audit Scotland (2005) 'Statutory performance indicators – Summary information' (www.audit-scotland.gov.uk/performance/ documents/2005profiles/councilspdf/CPFf05.pdf).

Baker Associates, Terence O'Rourke, University of Liverpool, University of Manchester and University of the West of England (2008) *Spatial plans in practice: Supporting the reform of local planning – Final report*, London: Department for Communities and Local Government.

Baker, M., Coaffee, J. and Sherriff, G. (2007) 'Achieving successful participation in the new UK spatial planning system', *Planning, Practice & Research*, vol 22, no 1, pp 79-93.

Ball, A., Broadbent, J. and Moore, C. (2002) 'Best Value and the control of local government: Challenges and contradictions', *Public Money & Management*, April-June, pp 9-16.

Barker, K. (2004) *Review of housing supply: Final report – Recommendations*, London: The Stationery Office.

Barker, K. (2006) *Barker review of land use planning: Final report – Recommendations*, London: HM Treasury.

Barley, S.R. and Tolbert, P.S. (1997) 'Institutionalization and structuration: Studying the links between action and institution', *Organization Studies*, vol 18, no 10, pp 93-117.

Barnes, M., Newman, J. and Sullivan, H. (2007) *Power, participation and political renewal: Case studies in public participation*, Bristol: The Policy Press.

Barnes, M., Newman, J., Knops, A. and Sullivan, H. (2003) 'Constituting "the public" in public participation', *Public Administration*, vol 81, no 2, pp 379-99.

Barrett, S.M. (2004) 'Implementation studies: Time for a revival? Personal reflections on 20 years of implementation studies', *Public Administration*, vol 82, no 2, pp 249-62.

Barrett, S.M. and Fudge, C. (1981) *Policy and action: Essays on the implementation of public policy*, London: Methuen.

Barry, A., Osborne, T. and Rose, N. (1993) 'Liberalism, neo-liberalism and governmentality: An introduction', *Economy and Society*, vol 22, no 3, pp 265-6.

Beauregard, R. (1989) 'Between modernity and postmodernity: the ambiguous position of US planning', *Environment and Planning D*, vol 7, pp 381-95.

Beauregard, R. (1990) 'Bringing the city back in', *Journal of the American Planning Association*, vol 56, no 2, pp 210-14.

Becher, T. (1999) *Professional practices: Commitment and capability in a changing environment*, London: Transaction Publishers.

Beckford, J. (2002) *Quality*, London: Routledge.

Bedford, T., Clark, J. and Harrison, C. (2002) 'Limits to new public participation practices in local land use planning', *Town Planning Review*, vol 73, no 3, pp 311-31.

Berg, A.M. (2006) 'Transforming public services – Transforming the public servant?', *International Journal of Public Sector Management*, vol 19, no 6, pp 556-68.

Best Value Task Force (1999) *Best Value in local government: Long term arrangements*, Edinburgh: Scottish Executive.

Bickerstaff, K. and Walker, G. (2001) 'Participatory local governance and transport planning', *Environment and Planning A*, vol 33, pp 421-51.

BIS (Department for Business Innovation and Skills) (2012) 'Local Enterprise Partnerships' (www.bis.gov.uk/policies/economic-development/leps).

Bloggs, E.E., PC (2007) *Diary of an on-call girl: True stories from the front line*, Wolvey: Monday Books.

Bolton, S.C. (2002) 'Consumer as king in the NHS', *International Journal of Public Sector Management*, vol 15, no 2, pp 129-39.

Bondi, L. and Laurie, N. (2005) 'Introduction', in L. Bondi and N. Laurie (eds) *Working the spaces of neoliberalism*, Oxford: Blackwell, pp 1-8.

Bourdieu, P. (1990) *In other worlds: Essays towards a reflexive sociology*, Oxford: Polity Press.

Boyne, G., Martin, S.J. and Walker, R.M. (2001) *Best value, organizational change and performance improvement*, London: DTLR.

Boyne, G.A. and Chen, A.A. (2006) 'Performance targets and public service improvements', *Journal of Public Administration Research and Theory*, vol 17, pp 455-77.

Boyne, G.A., Gould-Williams, J., Law, J. and Walker, R. (2002a) 'Plans, performance information and accountability: The case of Best Value', *Public Administration*, vol 80, no 4, pp 691-710.

Boyne, G.A., Gould-Williams, J.S., Law, J. and Walker, R.M. (2002b) 'Best Value – Total Quality Management for local government?', *Public Money & Management*, July-September, pp 9-16.

Brenner, N. (1999) 'Globalisation as reterritorialisation: The re-scaling of urban governance in the European Union', *Urban Studies*, vol 36, no 3, pp 431-51.

Brenner, N. (2004) *New state spaces: Urban governance and the rescaling of statehood*, Oxford: Oxford University Press.

Brenner, N. and Theodore, N. (2002) 'Cities and the geographies of "actual existing neoliberalism"', *Antipode*, vol 34, no 3, pp 349-79.

Brereton, M. and Temple, M. (1999) 'The new public service ethos: An ethical environment for governance', *Public Administration*, vol 77, no 3, pp 455-74.

Brindle, D. (2004) 'Man with a plan', *The Guardian*, 23 June (www.guardian.co.uk/society/2004/jun/23/regeneration.communities).

Broadbent, J. and Laughlin, R. (1997) 'Evaluating the new public management reforms in the UK: A constitutional possibility?', *Public Administration*, vol 75, no 3, pp 487-507.

Broadbent, J., Dietrich, M. and Roberts, J. (2001) 'The end of professionals?', in J. Broadbent, M. Dietrich and J. Roberts (eds) *The end of professionals? The restructuring of professional work*, London: Routledge, pp 1-13.

Broadbent, T.A. (1977) *Planning and profit in the urban economy*, London: Methuen.

Brooks, J. (2000) 'Labour's modernization of local government', *Public Administration*, vol 78, no 3, pp 593-612.

Bruton, M.J. (ed) (1974) *The spirit and purpose of planning*, London: Hutchinson.

Bruton, M.J. (ed) (1984) *The spirit and purpose of planning* (2nd edn), London: Hutchinson.

Burns, W. (1967) *Newcastle: A study in replanning at Newcastle upon Tyne*, London: L. Hill.

Burrage, M. and Torstendahl, R. (1990) *Professions in theory and history: Rethinking the study of the professions*, London: Sage.

Cameron, D. (2011) 'Building a better future', speech to the Conservative Party Spring Forum Conference, Cardiff, 6 March (www.conservatives.com/News/Speeches/2011/03/David_Cameron_Building_a_better_future.aspx).

Cammack, P. (2007) 'Competitiveness, social justice and the third way', *Papers in the Politics of Global Competitiveness*, vol 6, pp 1-20.

Campbell, H. (2002) 'Planning: An idea of value', *Town Planning Review*, vol 73, no 3, pp 271-88.

Campbell, H. and Marshall, R. (1998) 'Acting on principle: Dilemmas in planning practice', *Planning Practice & Research*, vol 13, no 2, pp 117-28.

Campbell, H. and Marshall, R. (2000) 'Public involvement and planning: Looking beyond the one to the many', *International Planning Studies*, vol 5, no 3, pp 321-44.

Campbell, H. and Marshall, R. (2002) 'Utilitarianism's bad breath? A re-evaluation of the public interest justification for planning', *Planning Theory*, vol 1, no 2, pp 163-87.

Campbell, H. and Marshall, R. (2005) 'Professionalism and planning in Britain', *Town Planning Review*, vol 76, no 2, pp 191-214.

Carmona, M. (2007) 'Monitoring outcome quality in planning – Challenges and possibilities', Town and Country Planning Tomorrow Series Paper 8, *Town & Country Planning*, June/July, pp 2-12.

Carmona, M. and Sieh, L. (2004) *Measuring quality in planning: Managing the performance process*, Abingdon: Spon Press.

Carmona, M. and Sieh, L. (2005) 'Performance measurement innovation in English planning authorities', *Planning Theory & Practice*, vol 6, no 3, pp 303-33.

Carmona, M. and Sieh, L. (2008) 'Performance measurement in planning – Towards a holistic view', *Environment and Planning C*, vol 26, pp 428-54.

CBI (Confederation of British Industry) (2005) *Planning reform: Delivering for business?*, London: CBI.

Chettiparamb, A. (2007) 'Re-conceptualizing public participation in planning: A view through autopoiesis', *Planning Theory*, vol 6, no 3, pp 263-81.

City of Edinburgh (2005) *Planning audit review: Planning Committee Item Number 7, 26 May 2005*, Edinburgh: The City of Edinburgh Council.

Clarke, J. (2004) 'Dissolving the public realm? The logics and limits of neo-liberalism', *Journal of Social Policy*, vol 33, no 1, pp 27-48.

Clarke, J. (2005) 'New Labour's citizens: Activated, empowered, responsibilized, abandoned?', *Critical Social Policy*, vol 25, no 4, pp 447-63.

Clarke, J. and Newman, J. (1997) *The managerial state: Power, politics and ideology in the remaking of social welfare*, London: Sage Publications.

Clayton, D. (2000) 'Governmentality', in R.J. Johnston, D. Gregory, G. Pratt and M. Watts (eds) *The dictionary of human geography*, Oxford: Blackwell, pp 318-19.

Clemens, E.S. and Cook, J.M. (1999) 'Politics and institutionalism: Explaining durability and change', *Annual Review of Sociology*, vol 25, pp 441-66.

CLG (Department for Communities and Local Government) (2006) 'The Planning Delivery Grant Determination 2006 No 31/286', London: CLG.

CLG (2007a) *Planning for a sustainable future: White Paper – Summary*, London: CLG.

CLG (2007b) 'Statistics of planning applications' (www.communities. gov.uk/planningandbuilding/planningbuilding/planningstatistics/ statisticsplanning/).

CLG (2007c) 'The Planning Delivery (No 1) Grant Determination 2007 No 31/585', London: CLG.

CLG (2008a) *Local spatial planning*, Planning Policy Statement 12, London: CLG.

CLG (2008b) *Creating strong, safe and prosperous communities: Statutory guidance*, London: CLG.

CLG (2008c) 'National indicators for local authorities and local authority partnerships' (http://webarchive.nationalarchives.gov.uk/+/http:/www.communities.gov.uk/localgovernment/performance frameworkpartnerships/nationalindicators/).

CLG (2008d) *Housing and Planning Delivery Grant:Allocation mechanism and summary of consultation responses*, London: CLG.

Clifford, B.P. (2006) 'Only a town planner would run a toxic waste pipeline through a recreational area: Planning and planners in the British press', *Town Planning Review*, vol 77, no 4, pp 423-55.

Clifford, B.P. and Warren, C.R. (2005) 'Development and the environment: Perception and opinion in St Andrews, Scotland', *The Scottish Geographical Journal*, vol 121, no 4, pp 355-84.

Coaffee, J. and Healey, P. (2003) '"My voice: my place?" Tracking transformations in urban governance', *Urban Studies*, vol 40, no 10, pp 1979-99.

Coburn, J. (2003) 'Bring local knowledge into environmental decision making: Improving urban planning for communities at risk', *Journal of Planning Education and Research*, vol 22, pp 420-33.

Cochrane, A. (2004) 'Modernisation, managerialism and the culture wars: Reshaping the local welfare state in England', *Local Government Studies*, vol 30, no 4, pp 481-96.

Cooke, B. and Kothari, U. (eds) (2001) *Participation: The new tyranny*, London: Zed Books.

Cooke, P. (1983) *Theories of planning and spatial development*, London: Hutchinson.

Copperfield, D., PC (2006) *Wasting police time:The crazy world of the war on crime*, Wolvey: Monday Books.

Corby, S. (2000) 'Employee relations in the public services: a paradigm shift?', *Public Policy and Administration*, vol 15, no 3, pp 60-74.

Coulson, A. (2003) 'Land-use planning and community influence: A study of Selly Oak, Birmingham', *Planning Practice & Research*, vol 18, nos 2-3, pp 179-95.

Coulson, A. and Ferrario, C. (2007) 'Institutional thickness: Local governance and economic development in Birmingham, England', *International Journal of Urban and Regional Research*, vol 31, no 3, pp 591-615.

Counsell, D., Haughton, G., Allmendinger, P. and Vigar, G. (2003) 'New directions in UK strategic planning – From land use plans to spatial development strategies', *Town & Country Planning*, January, pp 15-18.

Cowan, R. (2004) 'Planning matters', *Planning*, 13 February, p 11.

Cowan, R. (2007a) 'Planning matters', *Planning*, 14 September, p 12.

Cowan, R. (2007b) 'Planning matters', *Planning*, 18 May, p 12.

Cowan, R. (2008) 'Planning matters', *Planning*, 26 September, p 12.

Cowell, R. and Martin, S. (2003) 'The joy of joining up: Modes of integrating the local government modernisation agenda', *Environment and Planning C*, vol 21, no 2, pp 159-80.

Craig, D. (2006) *Plundering the public sector*, London: Constable.

Cutler, T. and Waine, B. (2000) 'Managerialism reformed? New Labour and public sector management', *Social Policy & Administration*, vol 34, no 3, pp 318-32.

Davies, A.R. (2001) 'Hidden or hiding? Public perceptions of participation in the planning system', *Town Planning Review*, vol 72, no 2, pp 193-216.

Davies, A.R. and Thomas, R. (2003) 'Talking cop: Discourses of change and policing identities', *Public Administration*, vol 81, no 4, pp 681-99.

Davies, C. (1983) 'Professionals in bureaucracies: The conflict thesis revisited', in R. Dingwall and P. Lewis (eds) *The sociology of the professions: Lawyers, doctors and others*, Basingstoke: Macmillan, pp 177-94.

Davies, H.W.E. (1998) 'Continuity and change: The evolution of the British planning system, 1947-97', *Town Planning Review*, vol 69, no 2, pp 135-52.

Davies, J. (1970) 'Planning participation in public decision making', *Long Range Planning*, vol 2, no 4, pp 23-7.

Davies, J. (1972) *The evangelistic bureaucrat: A study of a planning exercise in Newcastle-upon-Tyne*, London: Tavistock Publications.

Davies, S. (2008) 'Contracting out employment services to the third and private sectors: A critique', *Critical Social Policy*, vol 28, no 2, pp 136-64.

Davis, H. and Geddes, M. (2000) 'Deepening democracy or elite governance? New political management arrangements in local government', *Public Money & Management*, April-June, pp 15-20.

Davis, H. and Martin, S. (2002) 'Evaluating the Best Value pilot programme: Measuring "success" and "improvement"', *Local Government Studies*, vol 28, no 2, pp 55-68.

Davoudi, S. and Strange, I. (eds) (2009) *Conceptions of place and space in strategic spatial planning*, London: Routledge.

DCLG (Department for Communities and Local Government) (2010) 'Eric Pickles puts stop to flawed regional strategies today' (https://www.gov.uk/government/news/eric-pickles-puts-stop-to-flawed-regional-strategies-today).

DCLG (2011a) 'Single data list' (www.communities.gov.uk/localgovernment/decentralisation/tacklingburdens/singledatalist/).

DCLG (2011b) 'An introduction to neighbourhood planning' (www. communities.gov.uk/documents/planningandbuilding/pdf/1985896. pdf).

DCLG (2012a) *National planning policy framework*, London: DCLG.

DCLG (2012b) 'Neighbourhood planning' (www. communities.gov.uk/planningandbuilding/planningsystem/ neighbourhoodplanningvanguards/).

Dean, M. (1999) *Governmentality: Power and rule in modern society*, London: Sage Publications.

Deegan, J. (2002) 'Sub-regional planning case remains overwhelming', *Town & Country Planning*, March, pp 86-7.

Del Casino, V.J., Grimes, A.J., Hanna, S.P. and Jones, J.P. (2000) 'Methodological frameworks for the geography of organizations', *Geoforum*, vol 31, pp 523-38.

Denhart, R.B. and Denhart, J.V. (2000) 'The new public service: Serving rather than steering', *Public Administration Review*, vol 60, no 6, pp 549-59.

DETR (Department for the Environment, Transport and the Regions) (1998a) *Modernising planning: A White Paper*, London: DETR.

DETR (1998b) *Modern local government: In touch with the people*, London: DETR.

Dietrich, M. and Roberts, J. (2001) 'Beyond the economics of professionalism', in J. Broadbent, M. Dietrich and J. Roberts (eds) *The end of professionals? The restructuring of professional work*, London: Routledge, pp 14-33.

DiMaggio, P. (1988) 'Interest and agency in institutional theory' in L. Zucker (ed) *Institutional patterns and organizations: Culture and environment*, Cambridge, MA: Ballinger, pp 3-22.

DiMaggio, P. (1991) 'Constructing an organizational field as a professional project: U.S. art museums, 1920-1940' in W. Powell and P. DiMaggio (eds) *The new institutionalism in organizational analysis*, Chicago: University of Chicago Press, pp 267-92.

DoE (Department of the Environment) (1980) *Circular 22/80: Development control – Policy and practice*, London: DoE.

DoE (1985a) *Lifting the burden*, London: HMSO.

DoE (1986b) *Circular 14/85: Development and environment*, London: DoE.

Donnelly, M. (2011a) 'Planners defend system after coalition attack', *Planning*, issue 1904, 11 March, pp 6-7.

Donnelly, M. (2011b) 'Builder allowed to appeal regional plan ruling', *Planning*, issue 1903, 25 February, p 6.

Dorfman, J., Shames, V.A. and Kihlstrom, J.F. (1996) 'Intuition, incubation, and insight: Implicit cognition in problem solving', in G. Underwood (ed) *Implicit cognition*, Oxford: Oxford University Press, pp 257-96.

Downe, J., Grace, C., Martin, S. and Nutley, S. (2008) 'Best Value audits in Scotland: Winning without scoring?', *Public Money & Management*, April, pp 77-84.

Driver, S. and Martell, L. (2000) 'Left, Right and the Third Way', *Policy & Politics*, vol 28, no 2, pp 146-61.

DTI (Department for Trade and Industry) (1998) *Our competitive future*, White Paper, London: DTI.

DTLR (Department for Transport, Local Government and the Regions) (2001a) *Planning: Delivering a fundamental change*, Green Paper, London: DTLR.

DTLR (2001b) *Stronger leadership – Quality public service: A White Paper*, London: DTLR.

du Gay, P. (1996) *Consumption and identity at work*, London: Sage Publications.

du Gay, P. (2000) *In praise of bureaucracy*, London: Sage Publications.

du Gay, P. and Salaman, G. (1992) 'The cult[ure] of the customer', *Journal of Management Studies*, vol 29, no 5, pp 615-33.

Durant, R. (2006) 'Agency evolution, new institutionalism and "hybrid" policy domains: Lessons from the "greening" of the US military', *Policy Studies Journal*, vol 22, pp 469-90.

Durkheim, E. (1992) *Professional ethics and civic morals*, London: Routledge.

Durning, B. and Glasson, J. (2006) 'Delivering the planning system in England: Skills' capacity constraints', *Town Planning Review*, vol 77, no 4, pp 457-84.

Durning, B., Carpenter, J., Glasson, J. and Watson, G.B. (2010) 'The spiral of knowledge development: Professional knowledge development in planning', *Planning, Practice & Research*, vol 25, no 4, pp 497-516.

Eddington, R. (2006) *The Eddington transport study*, London: HM Treasury.

Egan, J. (2004) *The Egan Review: Skills for sustainable communities*, London: Office of the Deputy Prime Minister.

Ehrenberg, J. (1999) *Civil society: A critical history of an idea*, New York: New York University Press.

Ellis, G. (2002) 'Party rights of appeal in planning: Reflecting on the experience of the Republic of Ireland', *Town Planning Review*, vol 73, no 4, pp 437-66.

Ellis, G. (2004) 'Discourses of objection: Towards an understanding of third-party rights in planning', *Environment and Planning A*, vol 36, pp 1549-70.

Ellis, H. (2000) 'Planning and public empowerment: Third party rights in development control', *Planning Theory & Practice*, vol 1, no 2, pp 203-17.

Ellis, K. (2011) '"Street-level bureaucracy" revisited: The changing face of frontline discretion in adult social care in England', *Social Policy & Administration*, vol 45, no 3, pp 221-44.

Ellis, R. (2009) 'The quick decision that could become a miscarriage of justice', *The Times*, 5 February (http://business.timesonline.co.uk/tol/business/law/article5661673.ece).

European Commission (1999) *European spatial development perspective: Towards balanced and sustainable development of the territory of the European Union*, Brussels: European Commission.

Eversley, D. (1973) *The planner in society: The changing role of a profession*, London: Faber & Faber.

Exworthy, M. and Powell, M. (2004) 'Big windows and little windows: Implementation in the "congested state"', *Public Administration*, vol 82, no 2, pp 263-81.

Fagermoen, M.S. (1997) 'Professional identity: Values embedded in meaningful nursing practice', *Journal of Advanced Nursing*, vol 25, pp 434-41.

Fainstein, S.S. and Fainstein, N. (1979) 'New debates in urban planning: The impact of Marxist theory within the United States', *International Journal of Urban and Regional Research*, 3, pp 381-403.

Faludi, A. (1973) *Planning theory*, Oxford: Pergamon.

Faludi, A. (1987) *A decision-centred view of environmental planning*, Oxford: Pergamon Press.

Faludi, A. and Waterhout, B. (2002) *The making of the European spatial development perspective*, London: Routledge.

Ferlie, E., Ashburner, L., Fitzgerald, L. and Pettigrew, A. (1996) *The new public management in action*, Oxford: Oxford University Press.

Finlayson, A. (2009) 'Planning people: The ideology and rationality of New Labour', *Planning, Practice & Research*, vol 24, no 1, pp 11-22.

Fitzgerald, L. and Ferlie, E. (2000) 'Professionals: Back to the future?', *Human Relations*, vol 53, no 5, pp 713-39.

Flyvbjerg, B. (1998) *Rationality and power*, Chicago, IL: Chicago University Press.

Forester, J. (1989) *Planning in the face of power*, Berkeley, CA: University of California Press.

Forester, J. (1993) *Critical theory, public policy and planning practice. Toward a critical pragmatism*, Albany, NY: State University of New York Press.

Forester, J. (1999a) *The deliberative practitioner: Encouraging participatory planning processes*, Cambridge, MA: The MIT Press.

Forester, J. (1999b) 'Dealing with deep value differences: how can consensus building make a difference?', in L. Susskind, S. McKearnon and J. Thomas-Larmer (eds) *Consensus-building handbook*, Thousand Oaks, CA: Sage Publications, pp 463-93.

Forester, J. (1999c) 'Reflections on the future understanding of planning practice', *International Planning Studies*, vol 4, no 2, pp 175-94.

Foster, D. and Hoggett, P. (1999) 'Change in the Benefits Agency: Empowering the exhausted worker?', *Work, Employment & Society*, vol 13, no 1, pp 19-39.

Freeden, M. (1998) 'The ideology of New Labour', *Political Quarterly*, vol 70, no 1, pp 52–61.

Freeden, M. (1999) 'The ideology of New Labour', *The Political Quarterly*, pp 42-51.

Friedmann, J. (1973) *Retracking America: A theory of transactive planning*, Garden City, NY: Double Day Anchor.

Friedmann, J. (1987) *Planning in the public domain*, Princeton, NJ: Princeton University Press.

Freidson, E. (1983) 'The theory of professions: The state of the art', in R. Dingwall and P. Lewis (eds) *The sociology of the professions: Lawyers, doctors and others*, Basingstoke: Macmillan, pp 19-37.

Freidson, E. (1992) 'Professionalism as model and ideology', in R.L. Nelson, D.M. Trubek and R.L. Solomon (eds), *Lawyers' ideals / lawyers' practice: Transformations in the American legal profession*, Ithaca, NY: Cornell University Press, pp 215-29.

Freidson, E. (2001) *Professionalism, the third logic: On the practice of knowledge*, Chicago, IL: University of Chicago Press.

Fudge, C. and Barrett, S. (1981) 'Restructuring the field of analysis', in S. Barrett and C. Fudge (eds) *Policy and action: Essays on the implementation of public policy*, London: Methuen, pp 249-78.

Gallent, N. and Robinson, S. (2012) *Neighbourhood planning: Communities, network and governance*, Bristol: The Policy Press.

Gallent, N., Morphet, J. and Tewdwr-Jones, M. (2008) 'Parish plans and the spatial planning approach in England', *Town Planning Review*, vol 79, no 1, pp 1-29.

Gaster, L. and Rutqvist, H. (2000) 'Changing the "front line" to meet citizen needs', *Local Government Studies*, vol 26, no 2, pp 53-70.

Giddens, A. (1976) *New rules of sociological method*, London: Hutchinson.

Giddens, A. (1979) *Central problems in social theory: Action, structure and contradictions in social analysis*, London: Macmillan.

Giddens, A. (1984) *The constitution of society: Outline of the theory of structuration*, Cambridge: Polity Press.

Giddens, A. (1998) *The Third Way: The renewal of social democracy*, Cambridge: Polity Press.

Giddings, B. and Hopwood, B. (2006) 'From Evangelistic bureaucrat to visionary developer: The changing character of the master plan in Britain', *Planning, Practice & Research*, vol 21, no 3, pp 337-48.

Gillman, S. (2008) 'Professional promotion', *Planning*, 4 July, p 10.

Glasson, J. and Marshall, T. (2007) *Regional planning*, London: Routledge.

Glazer, N. (1974) 'The schools of the minor professions', *Minerva*, vol 12, no 3, pp 346-64.

Goffman, E. (1959) *The presentation of self in everyday society*, Edinburgh: Anchor Books.

Goldsmith, M.J. and Page, E.C. (1997) 'Farewell to the British state', in J.E. Lane (ed) *Public sector reform: Rationale, trends and problems*, London: Sage Publications, pp 147-67.

Gonzalez, S. and Healey, P. (2005) 'A sociological institutionalist approach to the study of innovation in governance capacity', *Urban Studies*, vol 42, no 11, pp 2055-69.

Goodwin, M. and Painter, J. (1996) 'Local governance, the crises of Fordism and the changing geographies of regulation', *Transactions of the Institute of British Geographers*, NS 21, no 4, pp 635-48.

Government Office for Science (2010) *Foresight land use futures: Final project report*, London: Government Office for Science.

Grace, C. (2005) 'Change and improvement in audit and inspection: A strategic approach for the twenty-first century', *Local Government Studies*, vol 31, no 5, pp 575-96.

Grant, M. (1999) 'Planning as a learned profession', *Plans and Planners*, vol 1, pp 21-6.

Green, R. (2003) 'Top-up, bottom-down – A defining moment in English planning', *Town & Country Planning*, August, pp 211-12.

Gunder, M. (2003) 'Planning policy formulation from a Lacanian perspective', *International Planning Studies*, vol 8, no 4, pp 279-94.

Gunder, M. and Hillier, J. (2007) 'Problematising responsibility in planning theory and practice: On seeing the middle of the string?', *Progress in Planning*, vol 68, pp 57-96.

Gwilliam, M. (2002) 'The planning Green Paper – A curate's egg', *Town Planning Review*, vol 73, no 2, pp iii-vii.

Hall, P.A. and Taylor, R.C.R. (1996) *Political science and the three new institutionalisms*, MPIFG Discussion Paper 96/6, Cologne: MPIFG.

Hall, P.A. and Tewdwr-Jones, M. (2011) *Urban and regional planning* (5th edn), London: Routledge.

Hansen, K. (2001) 'Local councillors: Between local "government" and local governance', *Public Administration*, vol 79, no 1, pp 105-23.

Haralambos, M. and Holborn, M. (2000) *Sociology: Themes and perspectives*, London: HarperCollins.

Harris, N. and Hooper, A. (2004) 'Rediscovering the "spatial" in public policy and planning: An examination of the spatial content of sectoral policy documents', *Planning Theory & Practice*, vol 5, no 2, pp 147-69.

Harrison, C.M., Munton, R.J.C. and Collins, K. (2004) 'Experimental discursive spaces: Policy processes, public participation and the Greater London Authority', *Urban Studies*, vol 41, no 4, pp 903-17.

Harvey, D. (1974) 'What kind of geography for what kind of public policy?', *Transactions of the Institute of British Geographers*, vol 63, pp 18-24.

Harvey, D. (1978) 'On planning the ideology of planning' in R. Burchell, and G. Sternlieb (eds) *Planning theory in the 1980s: A search for future directions*, New Brunswick, NJ: Center for Urban Policy Research, Rutgers University, pp 213-34.

Harvey, D. (2005) *A brief history of neoliberalism*, Oxford: Oxford University Press.

Harvey, D. (2007) 'Neoliberalism as creative destruction', *The Annals of the American Academy of Political and Social Science*, vol 610, no 1, pp 21-44.

Haughton, G., Allmendinger, P., Counsell, D. and Vigar, G. (2010) *The new spatial planning: Territorial management with soft spaces and fuzzy boundaries*, London: Routledge.

Haughton, G. and Counsell, D. (2002) 'Going through the motions? Transparency and participation in English regional planning', *Town & Country Planning*, April, pp 120-3.

Hay, C. (1995) 'Re-stating the problem of regulation and re-regulating the local state', *Economy and Society*, vol 24, no 3, pp 387-407.

Hay, C. (2007) *Why we hate politics*, Cambridge: Polity Press.

Hay, C. and Jessop, B. (1995) 'Introduction: Local political economy: Regulation and governance', *Economy and Society*, vol 24, no 3, pp 303-6.

Hayton, K. (1994) 'Planning and Scottish local government reform', *Planning Practice and Research*, vol 9, no 1, pp 55-62.

Hayton, K. (2002) 'Scottish development planning: On the brink of change?', *Planning Practice and Research*, vol 17, no 3, pp 317-30.

Healey, P. (1985) 'The professionalisation of planning in Britain: Its form and consequences', *Town Planning Review*, vol 56, pp 429-507.

Healey, P. (1997) *Collaborative planning: Shaping places in fragmented societies*, London: Macmillan.

Healey, P. (1999) 'Institutionalist analysis, communicative planning, and shaping places', *Journal of Planning Education and Research*, vol 19, pp 111-21.

Healey, P. (2003) 'Collaborative planning in perspective', *Planning Theory*, vol 2, no 2, pp 101-23.

Healey, P. (2006) *Collaborative planning: Shaping places in fragmented societies* (2nd edn), Basingstoke: Macmillan.

Healey, P. (2007a) *Urban complexity and spatial strategies*, London: Routledge.

Healey, P. (2007b) 'The new institutionalism and the transformative goals of planning', in N. Verma (ed) *Institutions and planning*, Bingley: Emerald Group Publishing Ltd., pp 61-87.

Healey, P. (2010) *Making better places: The planning project in the 21st century*, Basingstoke: Palgrave Macmillan.

Healey, P. and Underwood, J. (1978) 'Professional ideals and planning practice: A report on research into planner's ideas in practice in London borough planning departments', *Progress in Planning*, vol 9, pp 73-127.

Hebson, G., Grimshaw, D. and Marchington, M. (2003) 'PPPs and the changing public sector ethos: Case-study evidence from the health and local authority sectors', *Work, Employment & Society*, vol 17, no 3, pp 481-501.

Held, D. (1995) *Democracy and the global order: From the modern state to cosmopolitan governance*, Cambridge: Polity Press.

Hickson, K. (2011) 'The political ideology of the Cameron-Clegg Coalition government' (www.psa.ac.uk/journals/pdf/5/2011/869_401.pdf).

Higgins, P., James, P. and Roper, I. (2004) 'Best Value: Is it delivering?', *Public Money & Management*, August, pp 251-8.

Hill, M. (1981) 'The policy-implementation distinction', in S. Barrett and C. Fudge (eds) *Policy and action*, London: Methuen, pp 207-24.

Hill, M. (2004) *The public policy process*, Harlow: Longman.

Hill, M. and Hupe, P.L. (2002) *Implementing public policy: Governance in theory and in practice*, London: Sage Publications.

Hillier, J. (1993) 'To boldly go where no planers have ever…', *Environment and Planning D: Society and Space*, vol 11, no 1, pp 89-113.

Hillier, J. (2000) 'Going round the back? Complex networks and informal action in local planning processes', *Environment and Planning A*, vol 32, no 1, pp 33-54.

Hillier, J. (2003) 'Agonizing over consensus: Why Habermasian ideals cannot be real', *Planning Theory*, vol 2, no 1, pp 37-59.

Hirst, P. (2000) 'Democracy and governance', in J. Pierre (ed) *Debating governance: Authority, steering and democracy*, Oxford: Oxford University Press, pp 13-35.

HMSO (Her Majesty's Stationery Office) (2004a) *Planning and Compulsory Purchase Act 2004 (c. 5)*, London: HMSO.

HMSO (2004b) 'Statutory Instrument 2004 No 2204: The Town and Country Planning (Local Development) (England) Regulations 2004' (www.opsi.gov.uk/si/si2004/20042204.htm).

HMSO (2008) 'The Town and Country Planning (Local Development) (England) (Amendment) Regulations 2008' (www.opsi.gov.uk/si/si2008/uksi_20081371_en_1).

HM Treasury (2011) *Budget 2011*, London: The Stationery Office.

Hoch, C. (1994) *What planners do*, Chicago, IL: Planners Press.

Hoggett, P. (1996) 'New modes of control in the public service', *Public Administration*, vol 74, pp 9-32.

Holman, N. and Rydin, Y. (forthcoming) 'What can social capital tell us about planning under localism?', *Local Government Studies*.

Hood, C. (1991) 'A public management for all seasons?', *Public Administration*, vol 69, no 1, pp 3-19.

Hood, C. (1995) 'The "new public management" in the 1980s: Variations on a theme', *Accounting, Organizations and Society*, vol 20, nos 2-3, pp 93-109.

Hood, C. (2007) 'Public service management by numbers: Why does it vary? Where has it come from? What are the gaps and the puzzles?', *Public Money & Management*, April, pp 95-102.

Horton, S. (2006) 'New public management: Its impact on public servants' identity', *International Journal of Public Sector Management*, vol 19, no 6, pp 533-42.

Houghton, M. (1997) 'Performance indicators in town planning: Much ado about nothing?', *Local Government Studies*, vol 23, no 2, pp 1-13.

Hugman, R. (2003) 'Professional values and ethics in social work: Reconsidering postmodernism?', *British Journal of Social Work*, vol 33, pp 1023-41.

Hull, A. (2000) 'Modernizing democracy: Constructing a radical reform of the planning system?', *European Planning Studies*, vol 8, no 6, pp 767-82.

Hunt, J. and Shackley, S. (1999) 'Reconceiving science and policy: Academic, fiducial and bureaucratic knowledge', *Minerva*, vol 37, pp 141–64.

Huxley, M. (1999) 'If planning is anything, maybe it's geography', *Australian Planner*, vol 36, no 3, pp 128-33.

Hwang, S.W. (1996) 'The implications of the nonlinear paradigm for integrated environmental design and management', *Journal of Planning Literature*, vol 11, pp 167-87.

Idox Group (2007) *Delivering inspiring places: The role and status of planning*, Idox PLC report to the National Planning Forum, London: Idox.

Imrie, R. and Raco, M. (1999) 'How new is the new local governance?', *Transactions of the Institute of British Geographers*, NS, 24, pp 45-64.

Imrie, R. and Raco, M. (eds) (2003) *Urban renaissance? New Labour, community and urban policy*, Bristol: The Policy Press.

Imrie, R., Lees, L. and Raco, M. (2009) *Regenerating London*, London: Routledge.

Inch, A. (2010) 'Culture change as identity regulation: The micro-politics of producing spatial planners in England', *Planning Theory & Practice*, vol 11, no 3, pp 359-74.

Innes, J.E. (1995) 'Planning theory's emerging paradigm: Communicative action and interactive practice', *Journal of Planning Education and Research*, vol 14, pp 183-398.

Innes, J.E. and Booher, D.E. (2004) 'Reframing public participation: Strategies for the 21st century', *Planning Theory & Practice*, vol 5, no 4, pp 419-36.

Inspector Gadget (2008) 'Police inspector blog' (http://inspectorgadget.wordpress.com/).

Jackson, P.M. (2001) 'Public sector added value: Can bureaucracy deliver?', *Public Administration*, vol 79, no 1, pp 5-28.

Jeffrey, C. (2004) 'Devolution: What difference has it made? Interim findings from the ESRC Research Programme on Devolution and Constitutional Change' (www.devolution.ac.uk/Interim_Findings_04.pdf).

Jessop, B. (1998) 'The rise of governance and the risks of failure: The case of economic development', *International Social Science Journal*, vol 155, pp 29-45.

Jessop, B. (2000) 'Globalization and the national state' (www.lancs.ac.uk/fass/sociology/papers/jessop-globalization-and-the-national-state.pdf).

Jessop, B. (2001) 'Institutional re(turns) and the strategic-relational approach', *Environment and Planning A*, vol 33, pp 1213-35.

Jessop, B. (2002) 'Liberalism, neoliberalism and urban governance: A state-theoretical perspective', *Antipode*, vol 34, no 3, pp 452-72.

Johnson, T. (1993) 'Expertise and the state', in M. Gane, and T. Johnson (eds) *Foucault's new domain*, London: Routledge, pp 139-52.

Johnson, T.J. (1972) *Professions and power*, Basingstoke: Macmillan.

Johnston, B. (2011) 'Slow road to nirvana', *Planning*, issue 1900, 14 January, pp 20-1.

Jones, C. (2001) 'Voices from the front line: State social workers and New Labour', *British Journal of Social Work*, vol 31, pp 547-62.

Jones, R. (2002) 'With a little help from my friends: Managing public participation in local government', *Public Money & Management*, April-June, pp 31-6.

Jordan, A (1995) *Implementation failure or policy making? How do we theorise the implementation of European Union (EU) environmental legislation*, CSERGE Working Paper GEC 95-18, London: University College London (www.uea.ac.uk/env/cserge/pub/wp/gec/gec_1995_18. pdf).

Kaufman, J. and Escuin, M. (1996) 'A comparative study of Dutch, Spanish and American planner attitudes', Paper presented to ASP/AESOP Joint Congress, Toronto.

Kearl, J.R. (1983) 'Rules, rule intermediaries and the complexity and stability of regulation', *Journal of Public Economics*, vol 22, no 2, pp 215-26.

Kelly, B. (1991) 'The professional values of English nursing undergraduates', *Journal of Advanced Nursing*, vol 16, pp 867-72.

Kelly, J. (2006) 'Central regulation of English local authorities: An example of meta-governance?', *Public Administration*, vol 84, no 3, pp 603-21.

Kerr, P., Byrne, C. and Foster, E. (2011) 'Theorising Cameronism', *Political Studies Review*, vol 9, pp 193-207.

Killian, J. and Pretty, D. (2008a) *Planning applications: A faster and more responsive system – A call for solutions*, London: Department for Communities and Local Government.

Killian, J. and Pretty, D. (2008b) *Planning applications: A faster and more responsive system – Final report*, London: Department for Communities and Local Government.

Killian, J. and Pretty, D. (2008c) *A call for solutions: Appendix 3: Statistical analysis*, London: CLG.

Kirkpatrick, I. and Ackroyd, S. (2003) 'Archetype theory and the changing professional organization: A critique and an alternative', *Organization*, vol 10, no 4, pp 731-50.

Kirkup, J. (2012) 'David Cameron in new assault on green belt planning rules', *Daily Telegraph*, 2 September (www.telegraph.co.uk/earth/greenpolitics/planning/9516335/David-Cameron-in-new-assault-on-green-belt-planning-rules.html).

Kitchen, T. (1997) *People, politics, policies and plans: The city planning process in contemporary Britain*, London: Paul Chapman Publishing.

Kitchen, T. (1999) 'The structure and organisation of the planning service in English local government', *Planning Practice and Research*, vol 14, no 3, pp 313-27.

Kitchen, T. (2006) *Skills for planning practice*, Basingstoke: Palgrave Macmillan.

Kitchen, T. and Whitney, D. (2004) 'Achieving more effective public engagement with the English planning system', *Planning, Practice & Research*, vol 19, no 4, pp 393-413.

Kitchener, M., Kirkpatrick, I. and Whipp, R. (2000) 'Supervising professionals under new public management: Evidence from an "invisible trade"', *British Journal of Management*, vol 11, pp 213-26.

Korczynski, M. and Ott, U. (2004) 'When production and consumption meet: Cultural contradictions and the enchanting myth of customer sovereignty', *Journal of Management Studies*, vol 41, no 4, pp 575-99.

Lane, J.E. (ed) (1997) *Public sector reform: Rationale, trends and problems*, London: Sage Publications.

Lane, M.B. and Corbett, T. (2005) 'The tyranny of localism: Indigenous participation in community-based environmental management', *Journal of Environmental Policy & Planning*, vol 7, no 2, pp 141-59.

Larner, W. (2000) 'Neo-liberalism: Policy, ideology, governmentality', *Studies in Political Economy*, vol 63, pp 5-25.

Larner, W. (2003) 'Guest editorial: Neoliberalism?', *Environment and Planning D*, vol 21, pp 509-12.

Larner, W. and Le Heron, R. (2002) 'The spaces and subjects of a globalising economy: a situated exploration of method', *Environment and Planning D*, vol 20, pp 753-74.

Larner, W. and Le Heron, R. (2005) 'Neo-liberalizing spaces and subjectivities: Reinventing New Zealand universities', *Organization*, vol 12, no 6, pp 843-62.

Latour, B. (1987) *Science in action*, Cambridge, MA: Harvard University Press.

Le Grand, J. (1998) 'The Third Way begins with CORA', *New Statesman*, 6 March, pp 26-7.

Lindblom, C.E. (1959) 'The science of "muddling through"', *Public Administration Review*, vol 19, no 2, pp 79-88.

Lipsky, M. (1980) *Street-level bureaucracy: Dilemmas of the individual in public services*, New York: Russell Sage Foundation.

Lloyd, M.G. and Illsley, B.M. (2001) 'A community leadership initiative for Scotland?', *Politics*, vol 21, no 2, pp 124-9.

Lloyd, M.G. and Peel, D. (2005) 'Tracing a spatial turn in planning practice in England', *Planning, Practice & Research*, vol 20, no 3, pp 313-25.

Lloyd, M.G. and Peel, D. (2007) 'Strategic planning in Scotland: Nurturing a complex idea with modest optimism', *Town Planning Review*, vol 78, no 3, pp i-vi.

Lord, A. (2012) *The planning game*, London: Routledge.

Lowndes, V. (2001) 'Rescuing Aunt Sally: Taking institutional theory seriously in urban politics', *Urban Studies*, vol 38, no 11, pp 1953-71.

Lowndes, V. (2005) 'Something old, something new, something borrowed...: How institutions change (and stay the same) in local governance', *Policy Studies*, vol 24, nos 3/4, pp 291-309.

Lowndes, V. and Pratchett, L. (2012) 'Local governance under the Coalition government: Austerity, localism and the "Big Society"', *Local Government Studies*, vol 38, no 1, pp 21-40.

Lowndes, V. and Wilson, D. (2003) 'Balancing revisability and robustness? A new institutionalist perspective on local government modernization', *Public Administration*, vol 81, no 2, pp 275-98.

Lowndes, V., Pratchett, L. and Stoker, G. (2001a) 'Trends in public participation: Part 1 – Local government perspectives', *Public Administration*, vol 79, no 1, pp 205-22.

Lowndes, V., Pratchett, L. and Stoker, G. (2001b) 'Trends in public participation: Part 2 – Citizens' perspectives', *Public Administration*, vol 79, no 2, pp 445-55.

Lyons, M. (2007) *The Lyons Inquiry into local government: Final report*, London: The Stationery Office.

MacDonald, K. (2007) 'The Planning Reform Agenda: The 2007 White Paper', *Town Planning Review*, vol 78, no 4, pp x-xiii.

MacKinnon, D. (2000) 'Managerialism, governmentality and the state: A neo-Foucauldian approach to local economic governance', *Political Geography*, vol 19, pp 293-314.

MacKinnon, D. (2001) 'Regulating regional spaces: State agencies and the production of governance in the Scottish Highlands', *Environment and Planning A*, vol 33, pp 823-44.

MacLeod, G. and Goodwin, M. (1999) 'Space, scale and state strategy: Rethinking urban and regional governance', *Progress in Human Geography*, vol 23, no 4, pp 503-27.

McConnell, P. (1981) *Theories or planning*, London: David and Charles.

McDonough, P. (2006) 'Habitus and the practice of public service', *Work, Employment & Society*, vol 20, no 4, pp 629-47.

McHugh, M., O'Brien, G. and Ramondt, J. (2001) 'Finding an alternative to bureaucratic models of organization in the public sector', *Public Money & Management*, January-March, pp 35-42.

McLean, I., Haubrich, D. and Guiterres-Romero, R. (2007) 'The perils and pitfalls of performance measurement: The CPA regime for local authorities in England', *Public Money & Management*, April, pp 111-18.

Maesschalck, J. (2004) 'The impact of new public management reforms on public servants' ethics: Towards a theory', *Public Administration*, vol 82, no 2, pp 465-89.

Majone, G. (1989) *Evidence, argument and persuasion in the policy process*, New Haven, CT: Yale University Press.

Manns, S. and Wood, C. (2001) 'The power of public speaking', *Town & Country Planning*, September, pp 245-9.

March, J.G. and Olsen, J.P. (1984) 'The new institutionalism: Organizational factors in political life', *The American Political Science Review*, pp 734-49.

Marinetto, M. (2001) 'The settlement and process of devolution: Territorial politics and governance under the Welsh Assembly', *Political Studies*, vol 49, pp 306-22.

Marquand, D. (2001) 'Professionalism and politics', in J. Broadbent, M. Dietrich and J. and Roberts (eds) *The end of professionals? The restructuring of professional work*, London: Routledge, pp 140-7.

Marshall, T. (2004) 'Regional planning in England: Progress and pressures since 1997', *Town Planning Review*, vol 75, no 4, pp 447-72.

Marshall, P. and Laws, D. (eds) (2004) *The Orange Book: Reclaiming liberalism*, London: Profile Books.

Middlehurst, R. and Kennie, T. (2001) *Insight into HESDA's top management programme for higher education (UK)*, HESDA Briefing Paper 95, Sheffield: Higher Education Staff Development Agency.

Millar, S. (2012) 'Pickles agrees to CALA homes rethink', *Planning*, issue 1928, 24 February, pp 8-9.

Morphet, J. (2005) 'Viewpoint: A meta-narrative of planning reform', *The Town Planning Review*, vol 76, no 4, pp iv-ix.

Morphet, J. (2011) *Effective spatial planning in practice*, London: Routledge.

Morphet, J., Gallent, N., Tewdwr-Jones, M., Hall, B., Spry, M. and Howard, R. (2007) *Shaping and delivering tomorrow's places: Effective practice in spatial planning*, London: Royal Town Planning Institute.

Morris, H. (2007) 'Marathon man moves on', *Planning*, 23 November, p 15.

Myers, G. and Macnaghten, P. (1998) 'Rhetorics of environmental sustainability: Commonplaces and places', *Environment and Planning A*, vol 30, pp 333-53.

Nadin, V. (2007) 'The emergence of the spatial planning approach in England', *Planning, Practice & Research*, vol 22, no 1, pp 43-62.

Newman, J. (2001) 'What counts is what works? Constructing evaluations of market mechanisms', *Public Administration*, vol 79, no 1, pp 89-103.

Newman, J. (2005) *Modernising governance: New Labour, policy and society*, London: Sage Publications.

Newman, J., Raine, J. and Skelcher, C. (2001) 'Transforming local government: Innovation and modernization', *Public Money & Management*, April-June, pp 61-8.

Nicholson, D. (1991) 'Planners' skills in planning practice', in H. Thomas and P. Healey (eds) *Dilemmas of planning practice*, Aldershot: Avebury, pp 53-62.

ODPM (Office of the Deputy Prime Minister) (2002) *Sustainable communities: Delivering through planning*, London: ODPM.

ODPM (2004a) *Community involvement in planning: The government's objectives*, London: ODPM.

ODPM (2004b) 'Planning Delivery Grant 2004-2005', London: ODPM.

ODPM (2005a) *Delivering sustainable development*, Planning Policy Statement 1, London: The Stationery Office.

ODPM (2005b) *Best Value performance indicators 2005/06*, London: ODPM.

ODPM (2005c) *Local spatial planning*, Planning Policy Statement 12, London: ODPM.

ODPM (2005d) 'The Planning Delivery Grant (No 2) Determination 2005 No 31/159', London: ODPM.

ODPM (2005e) *Evaluation of Planning Delivery Grant 2004/05*, London: ODPM.

ODPM (2006) 'Planning Delivery Grant 2006-2007 allocation criteria' (www.odpm.gov.uk/index.asp?id=1147819).

OPSI (Office of Public Sector Information) (2006) 'Planning etc (Scotland) Act 2006' (www.opsi.gov.uk/legislation/scotland/acts2006/pdf/asp_20060017_en.pdf).

Osborne, G. (2011) '2011 Budget statement by the Chancellor of the Exchequer, the Rt Hon George Osborne MP' (www.hm-treasury.gov.uk/2011budget_speech.htm).

Osborne, D. and Gaebler, T. (1992) *Reinventing government: The political theory of reinvention*, Reading, MA: Addison-Wesley.

O'Toole, L.J. (2000) 'Research on policy implementation: Assessment and prospects', *Journal of Public Administration Research and Theory*, vol 10, no 2, pp 263-88.

O'Toole, L. (2004) 'The theory-practice issue in policy implementation research', *Public Administration*, vol 82, no 2, pp 309-29.

Painter, C. (2005) 'Managing criminal justice: Public service reform writ small?', *Public Money & Management*, October, pp 307-14.

Painter, J. (2000) 'Governance', in R.J. Johnston, D. Gregory, G. Pratt and M.Watts (eds) *The dictionary of human geography*, Oxford: Blackwell.

Painter, M. (2004) 'The politics of administrative reform in East and Southeast Asia: From gridlock to continuous self-improvement?', *Governance*, vol 17, no 3, pp 361-86.

Painter, J. and Goodwin, M. (1995) 'Local governance and concrete research: Investigating the uneven development of regulation', *Economy and Society*, vol 24, pp 334-56.

Parker, J. (2000) *Structuration*, Buckingham: Open University Press.

PAS (Planning Advisory Service) (2008) 'Plan making manual' (www.pas.gov.uk/pas/core/page.do?pageId=51391).

Peccei, R. and Rosenthal, P. (2001) 'Delivering customer-oriented behaviour through empowerment: An empirical test of HRM assumptions', *Journal of Management Studies*, vol 38, no 6, pp 831-57.

Peck, J. (2004) 'Geography and public policy: Constructions of neoliberalism', *Progress in Human Geography*, vol 28, no 3, pp 392-405.

Peck, J. and Tickell, A. (2002) 'Neoliberalizing space', *Antipode, vol 34*, no 3, pp 380-404.

Peters, B.G. (1999) *Institutional theory in political science: The 'new institutionalism'*, London: Pinter.

Petts, J. and Brooks, C. (2006) 'Expert conceptualisations of the role of lay knowledge in environmental decisionmaking: Challenges for deliberative democracy', *Environment and Planning A*, vol 38, pp 1045-59.

Phelps, N. and Tewdwr-Jones, M. (2008) 'If geography is anything, maybe it's planning alter ego? Reflections on policy relevance in two disciplines concerned with place and space', *Transactions of the Institute of British Geographers*, vol 33, no 4, pp 566-84.

Pierre, J. (1999) 'Models of urban governance: The institutional dimension of urban politics', *Urban Affairs Review*, vol 34, pp 372-96.

PINS (Planning Inspectorate) (2011) *The Planning Inspectorate: Annual report and accounts*, London: The Stationery Office.

Pløger, J. (2001) 'Public participation and the art of governance', *Environment and Planning B: Planning and Design*, vol 28, pp 219-41.

Pollitt, C. (1993) *Managerialism and the public services: Cuts or cultural change in the 1990s?*, Oxford: Blackwell.

Portney, K.E. (2003) *Taking sustainable cities seriously*, Cambridge, MA: The MIT Press.

Poulton, M.C. (1991) 'The case for a positive theory of planning: part I, what is wrong with planning theory?', *Environment and Planning B: Planning and Design*, vol 18, pp 263-75.

Power, M. (1999) *The audit society: Rituals of verification*, Oxford: Oxford University Press.

Power, M. (2002) *The audit society: Rituals of verification* (2nd edn), Oxford: Oxford University Press.

Pratchett, L. (2004) 'Local autonomy, local democracy and the "new localism"', *Political Studies*, vol 52, no 2, pp 358-75.

Pratchett, L. and Wingfield, M. (1996) 'Petty bureaucracy and woollyminded liberalism? The changing ethos of local government officers', *Public Administration*, vol 74, no 4, pp 639-56.

Prescott, J. (2004) 'Speech to LGA General Assembly', 15 December (http://archive.cabinetoffice.gov.uk/dpm/speeches/041215_local_government_association_general_assembly.html).

Prescott, J. (2006) 'Foreword', in 'Planning renaissance: Delivering and implementing planning reform', Supplement to *Planning*, March.

Pressman, J.L. and Wildavsky, A. (1979) *Implementation: How great expectations in Washington are dashed in Oakland*, Berkeley, CA: University of California Press.

Preston, P. (2006) 'A little local difficulty', *The Guardian*, 23 January (www.guardian.co.uk/Columnists/Column/0,,1692603,00.html).

Prior, A. (2005) 'UK planning reform: A regulationist interpretation', *Planning Theory & Practice*, vol 6, no 4, pp 465-84.

Proudfoot, J. and McCann, E.J. (2008) 'At street level: Bureaucratic practice in the management of neighbourhood change', *Urban Geography*, vol 29, no 4, pp 348-70.

Raco, M. (2000) 'Assessing community participation in local economic development – Lessons for the new urban policy', *Political Geography*, vol 19, pp 573-99.

Raco, M. (2005) 'Sustainable development, rolled-out neoliberalism and sustainable communities', *Antipode*, vol 37, pp 324-46.

Raco, M. (2007) 'Securing sustainable communities: Citizenship, safety and sustainability in the new urban planning', *European Urban and Regional Studies*, vol 14, no 4, pp 305-20.

Raco, M. and Flint, J. (2001) 'Communities, places and institutional relations: Assessing the role of area-based community representation in local governance', *Political Geography*, vol 20, no 5, pp 585-612.

Rashman, L. and Radnor, Z. (2005) 'Learning to improve: Approaches to improving local government services', *Public Money & Management*, January, pp 19-26.

Reade, E. (1983) 'If planning is anything, maybe it can be identified', *Urban Studies*, vol 20, pp 159-71.

Reade, E. (1987) *British town and country planning*, Milton Keynes: Open University Press.

Regan, D.E. (1978) 'The pathology of British land use planning', *Local Government Studies*, vol 4, pp 3-23.

Rein, M. and Schön, D. (1993) 'Reframing policy discourse', in F. Fischer and J. Forester (eds) *The argumentative turn in policy analysis and planning*, Durham, NC: Duke University Press, pp 145-66.

Rhodes, R. (1997) *Understanding governance*, Buckingham: Open University Press.

Rhodes, R. (1999) *Control and power in central-local government relations*, Aldershot: Ashgate.

Richardson, T. (1996) 'Foucauldian discourse: Power and truth in urban and regional policy making', *European Planning Studies*, vol 4, no 3, pp 279-92.

Roper, I., James, P. and Higgins, P. (2005) 'Workplace partnership and public service provision: The case of the "Best Value" performance regime in British local government', *Work, Employment & Society*, vol 19, no 3, pp 639-49.

Rose, N. (1999) *Powers of freedom*, Cambridge: Cambridge University Press.

Rose, N. and Miller, P. (1992) 'Political power beyond the state: Problematics of government', *British Journal of Sociology*, vol 43, no 2, pp 172-205.

Rosenthal, P. (2004) 'Management control as an employee resource: The case of front-line service workers', *Journal of Management Studies*, vol 41, no 4, pp 601-22.

Rosenthal, P. and Peccei, R. (2006a) 'Consuming work: Front-line workers and their customers in Jobcentre Plus', *International Journal of Public Sector Management*, vol 19, no 7, pp 659-72.

Rosenthal, P. and Peccei, R. (2006b) 'The customer concept in welfare administration: Front-line views in Jobcentre Plus', *International Journal of Public Sector Management*, vol 19, no 1, pp 67-78.

Rosenthal, P. and Peccei, R. (2006c) 'The social construction of clients by service agents in reformed welfare administration', *Human Relations*, vol 59, no 12, pp 1633-58.

Rosenthal, P. and Peccei, R. (2007) '"The work you want, the help you need": Constructing the customer in Jobcentre Plus', *Organization*, vol 14, no 2, pp 201-23.

Rowan-Robinson, J. (1997) 'The organisation and effectiveness of the Scottish planning system', in R. MacDonald and H. Thomas (eds) *Nationality and planning in Scotland and Wales*, Cardiff: University of Cardiff Press, pp 56-74.

Rueschemeyer, D. (1983) 'Professional autonomy and the social control of expertise', in R. Dingwall and P. Lewis (eds) *The sociology of the professions: Lawyers, doctors and others*, Basingstoke: Macmillan, pp 38-58.

Rydin, Y. (2003) *Urban and environmental planning in the UK*, Basingstoke: Palgrave Macmillan.

Rydin, Y. (2006) 'Reassessing the role of planning in delivering sustainable development', SDRN/RICS Lecture: 'Sustainability and the Built Environment' (www.rics.org/NR/rdonlyres/8422B461-32E6-4618-9032-B3DCDD5EF164/0/policybrief_lecture_sustainabledevelopment.pdf).

Rydin, Y. (2007) 'Indicators and a governmental technology? The lessons of community-based sustainability indicator projects', *Environment and Planning D: Society and Space*, vol 25, pp 610-24.

Rydin, Y. (2010) *Governing for sustainable urban development*, London: Earthscan.

Rydin, Y. and Pennington, M. (2000) 'Public participation and local environmental planning: The collective action problem and the potential of social capital', *Local Environment*, vol 5, no 2, pp 153-69.

Rydin, Y., Thornley, A., Scanlon, K. and West, K. (2004) 'The Greater London Authority – A case of conflict of cultures? Evidence from the planning and environmental policy domains', *Environment and Planning C*, vol 22, pp 55-76.

Rydin, Y., Amjad, U. and Whitaker, M. (2007) 'Environmentally sustainable construction: Knowledge and learning in London planning departments', *Planning Theory & Practice*, vol 8, no 3, pp 363-80.

Sager, J.K. (1994) 'A structural model depicting salespeople's job stress', *Journal of the Academy of Marketing Science*, vol 22, pp 74-84.

Samuels, A. (1993) *The political psyche*, London: Routledge.

Sanderson, I. (2001) 'Performance management, evaluation and learning in "modern" local government', *Public Administration*, vol 79, no 2, pp 291-313.

Schofield, J. (2004) 'A model of learned implementation', *Public Administration*, vol 82, no 2, pp 283-308.

Schofield, J. and Sausman, C. (2004) 'Symposium on implementing public policy: Learning from theory and practice. Introduction', *Public Administration*, vol 82, no 2, pp 235-48.

Schön, D. (1983) *The reflective practitioner: How professionals think in action*, London: Temple Smith.

Schön, D. and Rein, M. (1994) *Frame reflection: Towards the resolution of intractable policy controversies*, New York: Basic Books.

Scott, P. (1997) 'Dispersion versus decentralization: British location of industry policies and regional development 1945-60', *Economy and Society*, vol 26, no 4, pp 579-98.

Scottish Executive (2001) *Review of strategic planning*, Edinburgh: Scottish Executive.

Scottish Executive (2002) *Scottish Planning Policy 1*, Edinburgh: Scottish Executive.

Scottish Executive (2004a) *National planning framework for Scotland*, Edinburgh: Scottish Executive.

Scottish Executive (2004b) *Rights of appeal in planning: Analysis of consultation responses*, Edinburgh: Scottish Executive.

Scottish Executive (2004c) 'What is Best Value?' (www.scotland.gov. uk/about/FCSD/LG-PERF4/00014838/Home.aspx).

Scottish Executive (2005) *Modernising the planning system*, Edinburgh: Scottish Executive.

Scottish Executive (2007) *Community engagement: Planning with people*, Edinburgh: Scottish Executive Development Department, Edinburgh.

SEDD (Scottish Executive Development Department) (2005) *Seventh annual report of the Planning Audit Unit*, Edinburgh: SEDD.

Scottish Government (2008a) 'Progress and implementation of the modernising agenda', Edinburgh: Scottish Government.

Scottish Government (2008b) *National planning framework for Scotland 2: Discussion draft*, Edinburgh: Scottish Government.

Scottish Government (2011) 'Planning authority performance statistics' (www.scotland.gov.uk/Topics/Statistics/Browse/Planning/Publications).

Scottish Office (1999) *Land use planning under a Scottish Parliament*, Edinburgh: Scottish Office.

Shaw, D. and Lord, A. (2007) 'The cultural turn? Culture change and what it means for spatial planning in England', *Planning Practice and Research*, vol 22, no 1, pp 63-78.

Shotter, J. (1993) *Conversational realities: Constructing life through language*, Thousand Oaks, CA: Sage Publications.

Skeffington, A.M. (1969) *People and planning: Report of the Committee on Public Participation in Planning*, London: HMSO.

Smulian, M. (2011a) 'Cut choices', *Planning*, issue 1901, 28 January, pp 21-3.

Smulian, M. (2011b) 'DCLG plans penalty for tardy decisions', *Planning*, issue 1915, 12 August, pp 4-5.

Smulian, M. (2012) 'DCLG warned on costs of neighbourhood planning', *Planning*, issue 1925, 13 January, pp 8-9.

Stern, N. (2006) *Stern review: The economics of climate change*, London: HM Treasury.

Stewart, H. (2012) 'Osborne's austerity drive cut 270,000 public sector jobs last year', *The Guardian*, 14 March (www.guardian.co.uk/business/2012/mar/14/osborne-austerity-270000-public-sector-jobs?INTCMP=SRCH).

Stoker, G. (1997) 'Local government in Britain after Thatcher', in J.E. Lane (ed) *Public sector reform: Rationale, trends and problems*, London: Sage Publications, pp 225-34.

Stoker, G. (1998) 'Governance as theory: Five propositions', *International Social Science Journal*, vol 155, pp 17-28.

Stoker, G. (2004) 'New localism, progressive politics and democracy', *The Political Quarterly*, vol 75, pp 117-29.

Sturdy, A. (1998) 'Customer care in a consumer society: Smiling and sometimes meaning it?', *Organization*, vol 5, no 1, pp 27-53.

Sullivan, H. and Gillanders, G. (2005) 'Stretched to the limit? The impacts of local Public Service Agreements on service improvement and central-local relations', *Local Government Studies*, vol 31, no 5, pp 555-74.

Sutcliffe, A. (1981) 'Introduction: British town planning and the historian', in A. Sutcliffe (ed) *British town planning: The formative years*, Leicester: Leicester University Press, pp 2-14.

Swain, C. and Tait, M. (2007) 'The crisis of trust and planning', *Planning Theory & Practice*, vol 8, no 2, pp 229-47.

Tait, M. and Campbell, H. (2000) 'The politics of communication between planning officers and politicians', *Environment and Planning A*, vol 32, pp 489-506.

Taylor, I. and Kelly, J. (2006) 'Professionals, discretion and public sector reform in the UK: Re-visiting Lipsky', *International Journal of Public Sector Management*, vol 19, no 7, pp 629-42.

Taylor, M. (2007) 'Community participation in the real world: Opportunities and pitfalls in new governance spaces', *Urban Studies*, vol 44, no 2, pp 297-317.

Taylor-Gooby, P. and Stoker, G. (2011) 'The Coalition programme: A new vision for Britain or politics as usual?', *The Political Quarterly*, vol 82, no 1, pp 4-15.

Tewdwr-Jones, M. (1995) 'Development control and the legitimacy of planning decisions', *Town Planning Review*, vol 66, pp 163-81.

Tewdwr-Jones, M. (1996) 'Reflective planning theorising and professional protectionism', *Town Planning Review*, vol 67, no 2, pp 235-47.

Tewdwr-Jones, M. (1999) 'Reconciling competing voices: Institutional roles and political expectations in the new governance of planning', *Town Planning Review*, vol 70, no 4, pp 417-23.

Tewdwr-Jones, M. (2001) 'Planning and the National Assembly for Wales: Generating distinctiveness and inclusiveness in a new political context', *European Planning Studies*, vol 9, no 4, pp 553-62.

Tewdwr-Jones, M. (2002) *The planning polity: Planning, government and the policy process*, London: Routledge.

Tewdwr-Jones, M. (2011) 'A delicate balance', *Town & Country Planning*, January, pp 29-32.

Tewdwr-Jones, M. (2012) *Spatial planning and governance: Understanding UK planning*, Basingstoke: Palgrave Macmillan.

Tewdwr-Jones, M. and Allmendinger, P. (1998) 'Deconstructing communicative rationality: A critique of Habermasian collaborative planning', *Environment and Planning A*, vol 30, no 11, pp 1975-89.

Tewdwr-Jones, M. and Allmendinger, P. (eds) (2006) *Territory, identity and spatial planning: Spatial governance in a fragmented nation*, London: Routledge.

Tewdwr-Jones, M. and Thomas, H. (1998) 'Collaborative action in local plan-making: Planners' perceptions of "planning through debate"', *Environment and Planning B*, vol 25, pp 127-44.

Tewdwr-Jones, M. and Williams, R.H. (2001) *The European dimension of British planning*, London: Routledge.

Tewdwr-Jones, M., Bishop, K. and Wilkinson, D. (2000) 'Euroscepticism, political agendas and spatial planning: British national and regional planning policy in uncertain times', *European Planning Studies*, vol 8, no 3, pp 651-68.

Tewdwr-Jones, M., Morphet, M. and Allmendinger, P. (2006) 'The contested strategies of local governance: Community strategies, development plans, and local government modernisation', *Environment and Planning A*, vol 38, pp 533-51.

The Conservative Party (2010) *Open source planning: Green Paper*, London: Conservative Party.

Thomas, H. (1996) 'Public participation in planning', in M. Tewdwr-Jones, *British planning policy in transition*, London: UCL Press, pp 168-88.

Thomas, H. and Lo Piccolo, F. (2000) 'Best Value, planning and race equality', *Planning Practice & Research*, vol 15, nos 1/2, pp 79-94.

Thomas, R. and Linstead, A. (2002) 'Losing the plot? Middle managers and identity', *Organization*, vol 9, no 1, pp 71-93.

Thornley, A. (1991) *Urban planning under Thatcherism*, London: Routledge.

Townsend, A. (2002) 'Public speaking rights, members and officers in a planning committee', *Planning Practice & Research*, vol 17, no 1, pp 59-68.

Townsend, S. (2011) 'Coalition names initial 11 new enterprise zones', *Planning*, issue 1905, 29 March, pp 6-7.

Townsend, S. (2011) 'Just two partnerships to have economic planning role', *Planning*, issue 1903, 25 February, pp 6-7.

Underwood, G. (ed) (1996) *Implicit cognition*, Oxford: Oxford University Press.

Underwood, G. and Bright, J.E.H. (1996) 'Cognition with and without awareness', in G. Underwood (ed) *Implicit cognition*, Oxford: Oxford University Press, pp 1-40.

Underwood, J. (1980) *Town planners in search of a role*, Occasional Paper No 6, Bristol: School for Advanced Urban Studies, University of Bristol.

Underwood, J. (1981) 'Development control: A case study of discretion in action', in S. Barrett and C. Fudge (eds) *Policy and action: Essays on the implementation of public policy*, London: Methuen, pp 143-61.

Vigar, G. (2009) 'Towards an integrated spatial planning?', *European Planning Studies*, vol 17, no 11, pp 1571-90.

von Bockel, J. and Noordegraaf, M. (2006) 'Identifying identities: Performance-drive, but professional public managers', *International Journal of Public Sector Management*, vol 19, no 6, pp 585-97.

Wadley, D. and Smith, P. (1998) 'If planning is about anything, what is it about?', *International Journal of Social Economics*, vol 25, pp 1005-29.

WAG (Welsh Assembly Government) (2002a) *Planning policy Wales*, Cardiff: WAG.

WAG (2002b) *Planning: Delivering for Wales (Consultation Paper)*, Cardiff: WAG.

WAG (2004) *People, places, futures: The Wales spatial plan*, Cardiff: WAG.

WAG (2005a) *Planning: Delivering for Wales Newsletter*, vol 3, February.

WAG (2005b) 'Wales improvement plan: Guidance for local authorities' (www.wales.gov.uk/subilocalgov/content/consultation/walesprogramme-improvement-e.pdf).

WAG (2008a) 'Progress on adopting development plans in Wales, Position at 30 September 2007' (http://wales.gov.uk/topics/planning/policy/developplans/dppos/?lang=en).

WAG (2008b) *People, places, futures: The Wales spatial plan 2008 update*, Cardiff: WAG.

Warburton, D. (2002) 'Participation – Delivering a fundamental challenge', *Town & Country Planning*, March, pp 82-4.

Warren, C.R. (2002) *Managing Scotland's environment*, Edinburgh: Edinburgh University Press.

Weber, M. (2004) *The vocation lectures* (translated by R. Livingstone), Indianapolis, IN: Hackett Publishing Company.

Welsh Government (2011) 'Development control quarterly survey' (http://wales.gov.uk/topics/planning/planningstats/devcontrolquarterlysurvey/?lang=en).

Welsh Office (1998) *Modernising local government in Wales: Improving local services through Best Value*, Cardiff: Welsh Office.

Wenger, E.C. (1999) *Communities of practice: Learning, meaning, and identity*, Cambridge: Cambridge University Press.

West, Lord (2008) 'Training to tackle terror', *Planning*, 7 February, p 10.

Wildavsky, A. (1972) 'If planning is everything, maybe it's nothing', *Policy Sciences*, vol 4, pp 127-53.

Wilson, D. (2004) 'Toward a contingent urban neoliberalism', *Urban Geography*, vol 25, no 8, pp 771-83.

Wilson, T.D. and Stone, J.I. (1985) 'Limitations of self-knowledge: More on telling more than we can know', in P. Shaver (ed) *Review of Personality and Social Psychology, Vol 6*, Beverly Hills, CA: Sage, pp 167–83.

Winkley, R. (2004) 'Universal challenge', *Planning*, 9 January, p 10.

Wintour, P. (2012) 'Eric Pickles threatens to strip councils of planning powers', *The Guardian*, 6 September (www.guardian.co.uk/politics/2012/sep/06/eric-pickles-councils-planning-powers).

Wong, C. (2002) 'Is there a need for a fully integrated spatial planning framework for the United Kingdom?', *Planning Theory & Practice*, vol 3, no 3, pp 277-300.

Yates, J. (1997) 'Using Giddens' structuration theory to inform business history', *Business and Economic History*, vol 26, no 1, pp 159-83.

Young, I.M. (1990) *Justice and the politics of difference*, Princeton, NJ: Princeton University Press.

Index

Lightning Source UK Ltd.
Milton Keynes UK
UKHW020751120223
416801UK00007B/237